Mark Campbell is a theatre critic and writer on crime fiction; he has written books on Sherlock Holmes, Agatha Christie and the Carry On films. He lives in London.

Recent titles from the series

Temples, Tombs and Hieroglyphs, A Brief History of Ancient Egypt
Barbara Mertz

A Brief Guide to Classical Civilization
Stephen Kershaw

A Brief Guide to Cloud Computing
Christopher Barnatt

A Brief History of Hitmen and Assassinations
Richard Belfield

A Brief History of the Holy Grail
Giles Morgan

A Brief History of How the Industrial Revolution Changed the World
Thomas Crump

A Brief History of Khubilai Khan
Jonathan Clements

A Brief History of King Arthur
Mike Ashley

A Brief History of the Middle East
Christopher Catherwood

A Brief History of Robin Hood
Nigel Cawthorne

A Brief History of the Samurai
Jonathan Clements

A Brief History of Vampires
MJ Trow

A Brief Guide to William Shakespeare
Peter Ackroyd

His Finest Hour: A Brief Life of Winston Churchill
Christopher Catherwood

A Brief History of Witchcraft
Lois Martin

DOCTOR WHO

The Complete Guide

MARK CAMPBELL

ROBINSON

RUNNING PRESS
PHILADELPHIA · LONDON

For Emily and Ben, my favourite critics.

ROBINSON

First published in Great Britain by Robinson in 2010
This edition published by Robinson in 2013

Copyright © Mark Campbell 2010

The moral right of the author has been asserted.

A CIP catalogue record for this book
is available from the British Library.

UK ISBN: 978-1-47211-038-1

Printed and bound in Great Britain by CPI Group (UK) Ltd., Croydon, CR0 4YY

Robinson
is an imprint of
Constable & Robinson Ltd
100 Victoria Embankment
London EC4Y 0DY

An Hachette UK Company
www.hachette.co.uk

www.littlebrown.co.uk

3 5 7 9 10 8 6 4 2

First published in the United States by Running Press Book Publishers in 2013
All rights reserved under the Pan-American and International Copyright Conventions

Books published by Running Press are available at special discounts for bulk
purchases in the United States by corporations, institutions and other organizations.
For more information, please contact the Special Markets Department at the
Perseus Books Group, 2300 Chestnut Street, Suite 200, Philadelphia, PA 19103,
or call (800) 810-4145, ext. 5000, or email special.markets@perseusbooks.com.

US ISBN 978-0-7624-5240-8
US Library of Congress Control Number 2013937988

10 9 8 7 6 5 4 3
Digit on the right indicates the number of this printing

Running Press Book Publishers
2300 Chestnut Street
Philadelphia, PA 19103-4371

Visit us on the web!

www.runningpress.com

ACKNOWLEDGEMENTS

As ever, many thanks to Ion Mills and Claire Watts for all their hard work, and for Him Upstairs for keeping me grounded.

CONTENTS

FOREWORD

by Kim Newman

So, still here then?

There used to be people walking around who had lived through World War I and then, a generation or so later, went through it all again with World War II. When it comes to *Doctor Who*, I feel like that. I remember vividly the way *Doctor Who* – and, almost more than Doctor Who, the Daleks! – was a Beatlemania-type phenomenon in the early 1960s. I saw *The Curse of the Daleks* at the theatre, I owned a plastic Mechonoid, I had a battered paperback (it fell to pieces and was replaced) of *The Dalek Pocketbook and Space Travellers Guide*, I saw the two Peter Cushing films the week they opened, and I was watching television when – with no advance notice! – William Hartnell fell down and got up again as Patrick Troughton.

At some point, soon after, it became just another television programme: part of the schedule and important to watch – like, say, *Dad's Army* or *Monty Python* – but not quite as huge as it had been. *Thunderbirds* and *Batman* came and went too, with much more merchandising, and even *The Avengers* didn't stay on the schedules quite as long as *Doctor Who*, which, as a children's programme, was less liable to summary cancellation. Besides, the genius stroke of incorporating a changeover of leading actor into the premise meant it could theoretically go on forever. But it didn't. I stopped regularly watching the series just about the time K-9 showed up, but came back to it intermittently for the rest of its original run – most of Peter Davison's first two seasons – and, when the old stuff started being recycled on video or cable, I filled in the gaps I'd missed, though without much enthusiasm. Seriously, John Nathan-Turner, *what were you thinking . . . ?*

When the axe fell in 1989, it was long past due. *Doctor Who* began, and caught on, as a show which appealed to a wide audience – it died when it appealed only to *Doctor Who* fans and even they scorned most of it. When it came back in 2005, it was like the 1960s all over again. It became the favourite programme of children of the new millennium, just as it had been my favourite programme when I was a child. The merchandising began, in a regimented way that made all those Dalek toys of the 1960s seem half-hearted. This *Who* has had spin-off shows! We await the 'I'm Gonna Spend My Christmas With a Dalek' remix, though. The new *Doctor Who* has had highs and lows and troughs the way the old show did, and at the time of writing it may just about be reaching its K-9 point. Or it may regenerate, again.

Whatever, as the Time Lords know, this is unlikely to be the final end . . . and this is equally unlikely to be the last edition of this useful little book.

Kim Newman is a contributing editor to *Sight & Sound* and *Empire* magazines. His fiction includes the novels *Anno Dracula* and *Life's Lottery* and the novella *Doctor Who: Time and Relative*.

INTRODUCTION

DOCTOR WHO: SELLING THE MYTH

Has *Doctor Who* ever been more popular?

In the last eight years we've been treated to more than seventy-five new episodes of this once-defunct series. We've gone through three new Doctors and a cornucopia of old baddies: Daleks, Cybermen, The Master, Davros, Sontarans, Silurians and . . . erm . . . the Macra. Alongside that we've had a surfeit of spin-off shows and specials: *Totally Doctor Who*, *Torchwood*, *The Sarah Jane Adventures*, *Time Crash*, *The Infinite Quest*, *Doctor Who Live* and . . . erm . . . *K-9*.

Back in the day, the idea of *any* TV spin-off of *Doctor Who* was a pretty wild notion. Remember how fandom gave a collective swoon at that lone pilot episode, *K-9 and Company*, in 1981? Who would have thought that, a quarter of a century on, it would have led to a hugely popular children's series? Even at the height of the Daleks' popularity in the late 1960s, they never had their own show, despite creator Terry Nation's canny wooing of the American market.

Doctor Who's current popularity may seem entirely positive. However, whilst it undoubtedly makes oodles of money for the cash-strapped BBC and its licensees, it also pushes our favourite programme into previously uncharted waters. Alongside *Toy Story* or *Wallace and Gromit, Doctor Who* is now perceived by anyone with any kind of business sense as a very fat cash cow. Dare I say with pendulous milk-filled udders? I dare.

Books, CDS, comics, magazines, annuals, toys, ties, socks, voice-changer helmets . . . is there nothing that hasn't had the garish new *Doctor Who* logos plastered across it? Not a lot. Some of the merchandise is good, intelligent stuff. A lot of it isn't. The kids may beg for a *Doctor Who* pencil case, but it'll be the Bank of Mum and Dad who has the final say-so. (That's a 'yes' then – for the moment.)

There's nothing wrong with pushing a successful brand, but this uniquely eccentric little show of ours is in danger of being watered-down so much that its famously 'indefinable magic' may one day just wink out of existence.

The 2009 'gap year' received a mixed response, as has the recent policy of splitting seasons in two. Matt Smith's first season offered up much that was good, but compared with recent years it all seemed rather prosaic. His second was mired in a convoluted and uninteresting story arc, but his third, finally, is showing definite signs of promise. Great news as we head towards the fiftieth anniversary and a marketing meltdown not seen since the last Star Wars trilogy.

I love *Doctor Who*. I'll always love *Doctor Who*. Matt Smith may be the best Doctor yet.

But if the BBC continues with its emphasis on populism over quality in its 'core business model' (i.e. the programme itself), then things will go pear-shaped pretty quickly and it won't be long before you see those horrible new Dalek toys lining the shelves of Poundland . . .

Actually, even if *Doctor Who* does go from strength to strength, it won't be long before you see those horrible new Dalek toys lining the shelves of Poundland . . .

Mark Campbell
Plumstead, London November 2010
(Updated March 2013)

TELEVISION

Notes on the format:

Cast: Principal artistes only.
Crew: If 'Music' is unlisted, no specially composed music was used.
Broadcast: Original UK transmission dates, followed by average rating in millions, with Novelisation (N), DVD, soundtrack CD and Audiobook (A) dates where relevant.
Précis: The set-up in a nutshell.
Observations: Technical notes, locations and miscellaneous trivia.
Verdict: Is it any good?

Episodes are approximately twenty-five minutes in duration unless otherwise specified. All existent episodes up to *Doctor Who* (156) released on BBC Video between 1983–2003.

SEASON 1

Producer: Verity Lambert
Story Editor: David Whitaker
First Doctor: William Hartnell
Companions: Carole Ann Ford (*Susan Foreman*), William Russell (*Ian Chesterton*) & Jacqueline Hill (*Barbara Wright*)

1. AN UNEARTHLY CHILD (four episodes)
1: AN UNEARTHLY CHILD, 2: THE CAVE OF SKULLS, 3: THE FOREST OF FEAR, 4: THE FIREMAKER

Cast: Reg Cranfield (*Policeman*), Derek Newark (*Za*), Jeremy Young (*Kal*), Alethea Charlton (*Hur*), Eileen Way (*Old Mother*), Howard Lang (*Horg*) | **Crew:** Director: Waris Hussein; Writer: Anthony Coburn; Music: Norman Kay | **Broadcast:** 23 November–14 December 1963, 5.9m (N, 1981; DVD, 2006)

Précis: Schoolteachers Ian and Barbara follow their pupil Susan to a junkyard where they meet her grandfather, the Doctor, and are taken back to the Stone Age in his time/space machine . . .

Observations: Bernard Lodge and Joe Starie designed *Doctor Who*'s innovative title sequence with specially shot electronic 'howlround' (a video camera capturing its own output from a monitor screen, akin to audio feedback), mixed with surreal footage from Gian Carlo Menotti's television nativity opera *Amahl and the Night Visitors*. Ron Grainer composed the theme tune, which was arranged by Delia Derbyshire of the BBC Radiophonic Workshop. An unbroadcast pilot of the first episode was recorded, with minor changes. Peter Brachacki designed the Tardis interior for the pilot, replicated by Barry Newbery for the transmitted version. A widespread power cut prevented many from seeing the first episode and so it was hastily repeated the following Saturday before episode two.

Verdict: The first episode's collision of mundane reality and science fantasy is audacious. The following cavemen adventure is gritty and violent, and no other story comes close to capturing the discomfort of being uprooted from familiar surroundings and having to survive in a strange, hostile world. 10/10

2. THE DALEKS (seven episodes)
1: THE DEAD PLANET, 2: THE SURVIVORS, 3: THE ESCAPE, 4: THE AMBUSH, 5: THE EXPEDITION, 6: THE ORDEAL, 7: THE RESCUE

Cast: Philip Bond (*Ganatus*), John Lee (*Alydon*), Virginia Wetherell (*Dyoni*), Alan Wheatley (*Temmosus*), Gerald Curtis (*Elyon*), Jonathan Crane (*Kristas*), Marcus Hammond (*Antodus*), Peter Hawkins, David Graham (*Dalek voices*), Robert Jewell, Kevin Manser, Peter Murphy, Michael Summerton, Gerald Taylor (*Daleks*) | **Crew:** Directors: Christopher Barry (1–2, 4–5) & Richard Martin (3, 6–7); Writer: Terry Nation; Music: Tristram Cary | **Broadcast:** 21 December 1963–1 February 1964, 9m (N, 1964; DVD, 2006; A, 2005)

Précis: The Tardis lands on Skaro, home to the beautiful Thals and the mutated, metallic Daleks . . .

Observations: The Daleks were designed by Raymond Cusick, based on a description by Terry Nation. Four fibreglass and plywood props were constructed by Shawcraft Models and, as with most 1960s Dalek stories, life-size cardboard cut-outs were used to swell their ranks. Dalek actors' voices were passed through a ring modulator (an electronic device used in early synthesisers) to give them their unique sound. *The Dead Planet* was remounted because of an audio feedback problem.

Verdict: Memorable moments abound, particularly episode one's cliffhanger, but the simplistic morality fable sags in the middle and virtually comes to a halt halfway through the last episode. But the conviction of the cast just about carries it off. 7/10

3. THE EDGE OF DESTRUCTION (two episodes)
1: THE EDGE OF DESTRUCTION, 2: THE BRINK OF DISASTER

Crew: Directors: Richard Martin (1) & Frank Cox (2); Writer: David Whitaker; Special Sound: Brian Hodgson | **Broadcast:** 8–15 February 1964, 10.2m (N, 1988; DVD, 2006; A, 2011)

Précis: The Tardis appears to be under alien control . . .

Observations: This unusual two-parter, featuring only the four regular cast members and the Tardis interior, was written to offset overspends on the previous stories, to introduce a 'sideways' narrative (instead of 'past' or 'future'), and to complete the series' probationary run of thirteen episodes.

Verdict: Strong imagery, weak plot – it's sometimes painfully slow, although there are some exquisite moments of psychological horror. 6/10

4. MARCO POLO (seven episodes)
1: THE ROOF OF THE WORLD, 2: THE SINGING SANDS, 3: FIVE HUNDRED EYES, 4: THE WALL OF LIES, 5: RIDER FROM SHANG-TU, 6: MIGHTY KUBLAI KAHN, 7: ASSASSIN AT PEKING

Cast: Mark Eden (*Marco Polo*), Zienia Merton (*Ping-Cho*), Derren Nesbitt (*Tegana*), Jimmy Gardner (*Chenchu*), Charles Wade (*Malik*), Philip Voss (*Acomat*), Gabor Baraker (*Wang-Lo*), Paul Carson (*Ling-Tau*), Tutte Lemkow (*Kuiju*), Peter Lawrence (*Vizier*), Martin Miller

(*Kublai Khan*), Claire Davenport (*Empress*) | **Crew:** Directors: Waris Hussein (1–3, 5–7) & John Crockett (4); Writer: John Lucarotti; Music: Tristram Cary | **Broadcast:** 22 February–4 April 1964, 9.5m (N, 1984; DVD, 2006 [abridged reconstruction]; CD, 2003)

Précis: The Doctor and his companions accompany Marco Polo on his journey to Kublai Khan's court in Peking ...

Observations: Lucarotti had previously written a Canadian radio serial on the same subject. Filmed inserts punctuated the narrative, showing Marco Polo writing his diary and a map of the route thus far. This was the first *Doctor Who* story to feature on the cover of the *Radio Times*.

Verdict: It's a major feat to produce a serial as ambitious as this in Lime Grove's tiny Studio D, and the attention to detail in the script and settings is impressive. The narrative takes place over a period of several months, adding a welcome note of reality to proceedings. 9/10

5. THE KEYS OF MARINUS (six episodes)
1: THE SEA OF DEATH, 2: THE VELVET WEB, 3: THE SCREAMING JUNGLE, 4: THE SNOWS OF TERROR, 5: SENTENCE OF DEATH, 6: THE KEYS OF MARINUS

Cast: George Coulouris (*Arbitan*), Robin Phillips (*Altos*), Katharine Schofield (*Sabetha*), Heron Carvic (*Morpho voice*), Edmund Warwick (*Darrius*), Francis de Wolff (*Vasor*), Dougie Dean (*Eprin*), Henley Thomas (*Tarron*), Michael Allaby (*Larn*), Fiona Walker (*Kala*), Martin Cort (*Aydan*), Donald Pickering (*Eyesen*) | **Crew:** Director: John Gorrie; Writer: Terry Nation; Music: Norman Kay | **Broadcast:** 11 April–16 May 1964, 9m (N, 1980; DVD, 2009)

Précis: On Marinus, the Tardis crew hunt for four keys to a strange machine that will overcome the hideous Voords ...

Observations: The Tardis was seen materialising for the first time, albeit as a silent model shot. Hartnell was on holiday for episodes three and four.

Verdict: The series' first turkey, this is a badly written, badly realised homage to old film serials with very shoddy production values. There *are* effective moments, but not many. 3/10

6. THE AZTECS (four episodes)
1: THE TEMPLE OF EVIL, 2: THE WARRIORS OF DEATH, 3: THE BRIDE OF SACRIFICE, 4: THE DAY OF DARKNESS

Cast: John Ringham (*Tlotoxl*), Keith Pyott (*Autloc*), Ian Cullen (*Ixta*), Margot Van Der Burgh (*Cameca*), Tom Booth (*First Victim*), David Anderson (*Aztec Captain*), Walter Randall (*Tonila*), Andre Boulay (*Perfect Victim*) | **Crew:** Director: John Crockett; Writer: John Lucarotti; Music: Richard Rodney Bennett | **Broadcast:** 23 May–13 June 1964, 7.5m (N, 1984; DVD, 2002)

Précis: Barbara is mistaken for an Aztec god in fifteenth-century Mexico . . .

Observations: The Doctor's flirtation with Cameca was his only obvious romantic liaison until the 1996 *Doctor Who* TV movie (156). The story was the first to have episodes videoed at the BBC Television Centre, which opened in 1960. Carole Ann Ford was absent from studio recording for the middle two episodes.

Verdict: John Ringham's hammy Richard III impersonation spoils the seriousness of the story, but the production is strong and there are some well-crafted scenes. 7/10

7. THE SENSORITES (six episodes)
1: STRANGERS IN SPACE, 2: THE UNWILLING WARRIORS, 3: HIDDEN DANGER, 4: A RACE AGAINST DEATH, 5: KIDNAP, 6: A DESPERATE VENTURE

Cast: Ilona Rodgers (*Carol*), Stephen Dartnell (*John*), Lorne Cossette (*Maitland*), Ken Tyllsen (*First Sensorite/First Scientist*), Joe Greig (*Second Sensorite/Second Scientist*), Peter Glaze (*Third Sensorite*), Arthur Newall (*Fourth Sensorite*), Eric Francis (*First Elder*), Bartlett Mullins (*Second Elder*), John Bailey (*Commander*), Martyn Huntley (*First Human*),

Giles Phibbs (*Second Human*) | **Crew:** Directors: Mervyn Pinfield (1–4) & Frank Cox (5–6); Writer: Peter R Newman; Music: Norman Kay | **Broadcast:** 20 June–1 August 1964, 6.9m (N, 1987; CD, 2008)

Précis: Telepathic balloon-headed aliens terrorise a twenty-eighth century spaceship crew . . .

Observations: Peter Glaze was better known for his appearances on the BBC children's show *Crackerjack* ('Crackerjack!') from 1960–79. *Hidden Danger* was delayed for a week by an extended edition of *Grandstand*. Jacqueline Hill took time off from episodes four and five.

Verdict: A spooky first episode gives way to a humdrum story set against the bland environs of the Sense-Sphere. The Sensorites, although initially impressive, end up looking rather silly. 3/10

8. THE REIGN OF TERROR (six episodes)

1: A LAND OF FEAR, 2: GUESTS OF MADAME GUILLOTINE,
3: A CHANGE OF IDENTITY, 4: THE TYRANT OF FRANCE, 5: A
BARGAIN OF NECESSITY, 6: PRISONERS OF CONCIERGERIE

Cast: James Cairncross (*Lemaître*), Jack Cunningham (*Jailer*), Donald Morley (*Jules Renan*), Peter Walker (*Jean-Pierre*), Laidlaw Dalling (*Rouvray*), Neville Smith (*D'Argenson*), Howard Charlton (*Judge*), Jeffry Wickham (*Webster*), Dallas Cavell (*Road Works Overseer*), Roy Herrick (*Jean*), John Barrard (*Shopkeeper*), Caroline Hunt (*Danielle*), Edward Brayshaw (*Leon Colbert*), Keith Anderson (*Robespierre*), Ronald Pickup (*Physician*), John Law (*Paul Barrass*), Tony Wall (*Napoleon*) | **Crew:** Director: Henric Hirsch (1–2, 4–6) & John Gorrie (3); Writer: Dennis Spooner; Music: Stanley Myers | **Broadcast:** 8 August–12 September 1964, 6.7m (N, 1987; CD, 2006)

Précis: The Tardis lands in Paris during Robespierre's infamous Reign of Terror . . .

Observations: This story featured the first location filming for the series – Tilehouse Lane, Denham, Bucks, represented a poplar-lined French lane (with Brian Proudfoot doubling for Hartnell), while other brief inserts were filmed in the Gerrards Cross area. William Russell was absent from studio recording for episodes two and three.

Verdict: With a little more humour than on previous occasions, this is a well-observed, albeit slow, historical story in which the Doctor exhibits a suprisingly violent streak. 6/10

SEASON 2

Producer: Verity Lambert
Story Editors: David Whitaker (9–10), Dennis Spooner
(11–16) & Donald Tosh (17)
First Doctor: William Hartnell
Companions: William Russell (*Ian Chesterton,* 9–16),
Jacqueline Hill (*Barbara Wright,* 9–16), Carole Ann Ford
(*Susan Foreman,* 9–10), Maureen O'Brien (*Vicki,* 11–17) &
Peter Purves (*Steven Taylor,* 16–17)

9. PLANET OF GIANTS (three episodes)
1: PLANET OF GIANTS, 2: DANGEROUS JOURNEY, 3: CRISIS

Cast: Frank Crawshaw (*Farrow*), Alan Tilvern (*Forester*), Reginald
Barratt (*Smithers*), Rosemary Johnson (*Hilda Rowse*), Fred Ferris
(*Bert Rowse*) | **Crew:** Directors: Mervyn Pinfield (1–3) & Douglas
Camfield (3); Writer: Louis Marks; Music: Dudley Simpson | **Broadcast:**
31 October–14 November 1964, 8.5m (N, 1990)

Précis: A miniaturised Tardis crew try to prevent the manu-
facture of a lethal insecticide . . .
Observations: Appropriately reduced from four episodes to
three shortly before transmission (the fourth was originally

entitled *The Urge to Live*), this story featured many large props built by Raymond Cusick. This was the first serial for composer Dudley Simpson and director Douglas Camfield, who would both go on to be prolific contributors to the programme.

Verdict: The fantastic props never fail to impress and the adherence to realism is commendable, but the story drags a little even in its truncated form. 7/10

10. THE DALEK INVASION OF EARTH
(six episodes)
1: WORLD'S END, 2: THE DALEKS, 3: DAY OF RECKONING, 4: THE END OF TOMORROW, 5: THE WAKING ALLY, 6: FLASHPOINT

Cast: Peter Fraser (*David Campbell*), Bernard Kay (*Tyler*), Alan Judd (*Dortmun*), Ann Davies (*Jenny*), Michael Goldie (*Craddock*), Richard McNeff (*Baker*), Graham Rigby (*Larry Madison*), Nicholas Smith (*Wells*), Patrick O'Connell (*Ashton*), Jean Conroy, Meriel Hobson (*Women in Wood*), Peter Hawkins, David Graham (*Dalek voices*), Robert Jewell, Gerald Taylor, Kevin Manser, Peter Murphy, Ken Tyllsen, Nick Evans (*Daleks*) | **Crew:** Director: Richard Martin; Writer: Terry Nation; Music: Francis Chagrin | **Broadcast:** 21 November–26 December 1964, 11.9m (N, 1977; DVD, 2003; A, 2009)

Précis: On a devastated twenty-second-century Earth the Daleks have subjugated the population with brainwashed Robomen . . .

Observations: London locations included Westminster and Hammersmith Bridges, Trafalgar Square, the South Bank, the Albert Memorial and Whitehall. The six Daleks were given 'solar energy receptors' on their backs and larger 'bumpers' to navigate exterior terrain. Hartnell was written out of episode four after sustaining an injury during camera rehearsals for *Day of Reckoning*. The serial saw the programme's second *Radio Times* cover.

Verdict: Clumsy direction and dire modelwork are symptomatic of this wildly overambitious tale that seems predicated to fail. The moody build-up in the first episode and Susan's farewell scene in the last are nicely done, but in every other way the 1965 big-screen version is superior. 4/10

11. THE RESCUE (two episodes)
1: THE POWERFUL ENEMY, 2: DESPERATE MEASURES

Cast: Ray Barrett (*Bennett/Koquillion*), John Stuart, Colin Hughes (*Didonians*), Tom Sheridan (*Space Captain Voice/Sand Monster*) | **Crew:** Director: Christopher Barry; Writer: David Whitaker; Music: Tristram Cary | **Broadcast:** 2–9 January 1965, 12.5m (N, 1987; DVD, 2009)

Précis: On Dido, two survivors of a crashed spaceship are living in fear of a hideous alien . . .
Observations: Koquillion was credited as 'Sydney Wilson' for episode one – a pseudonym based on *Doctor Who* creators Sydney Newman and Donald Wilson – to maintain the secret of his identity. Vicki's character was originally called Lukki.
Verdict: A nice character study with good production values and an effective climax – although why Bennett didn't just kill Vicki is never explained. 7/10

12. THE ROMANS (four episodes)
1: THE SLAVE TRADERS, 2: ALL ROADS LEAD TO ROME,
3: CONSPIRACY, 4: INFERNO

Cast: Nicholas Evans (*Didius*), Derek Sydney (*Sevcheria*), Derek Francis (*Nero*), Bart Allison (*Maximus Pettulian*), Barry Jackson (*Ascaris*), Peter Diamond (*Delos*), Michael Peake (*Tavius*), Dorothy-Rose Gribble (*Woman Slave*), Gertan Klauber (*Galley Master*), Brian Proudfoot (*Tigilinus*), Kay Patrick (*Poppaea*), Ann Tirard (*Locusta*) | **Crew:** Director: Christopher Barry; Writer: Dennis Spooner; Music: Raymond Jones | **Broadcast:** 16 January–6 February 1965, 11.6m (N, 1987; DVD, 2009)

Précis: In first-century Italy, Ian and Barbara are captured by slave traders and the Doctor falls in with Nero . . .

Observations: Inspired by a visit to the *Carry On Cleo* film set at Pinewood, Dennis Spooner penned the series' first deliberately humorous *Doctor Who* story.

Verdict: Confidently played by all concerned, this sparkling comedy has many fine jokes and a particularly charming performance by Hartnell, clearly revelling in the slapstick. 8/10

13. THE WEB PLANET (six episodes)
1: THE WEB PLANET, 2: THE ZARBI, 3: ESCAPE TO DANGER,
4: CRATER OF NEEDLES, 5: INVASION, 6: THE CENTRE

Cast: Roslyn de Winter (*Vrestin*), Arne Gordon (*Hrostar*), Martin Jarvis (*Hilio*), Arthur Blake (*Hrhoonda*), Jolyon Booth (*Prapillus*), Jocelyn Birdsall (*Hlynia*), Ian Thompson (*Hetra*), Barbara Joss (*Nemini*), Catherine Fleming (*Animus voice*), Robert Jewell, Jack Pitt, Gerald Taylor, Kevin Manser, John Scott Martin (*Zarbi*), Hugh Lund (*Larvae Gun*) | **Crew:** Director: Richard Martin; Writer: Bill Strutton | **Broadcast:** 13 February–20 March 1965, 12.6m (N, 1965; DVD, 2005; A, 2005)

Précis: On Vortis, the winged Menoptra are at war with the ant-like Zarbi, slaves of the Animus . . .

Observations: The only *Doctor Who* story not to feature humanoid characters other than the regular cast, director Richard Martin employed Vaseline-smeared lenses to create an alien feel to the planet Vortis. Jacqueline Hill was absent for episode three. The story featured on a third *Radio Times* cover.

Verdict: In 1965 it may have been a laudable attempt to create an alien world, but nowadays a huge suspension of disbelief is required. Nonetheless, there is some striking imagery. 5/10

14. THE CRUSADE (four episodes)
1: THE LION, 2: THE KNIGHT OF JAFFA, 3: THE WHEEL OF FORTUNE, 4: THE WARLORDS

Cast: Julian Glover (*Richard*), Jean Marsh (*Joanna*), John Flint (*William des Preaux*), Walter Randall (*El Akir*), Bruce Wightman (*William de*

Tornebu), David Anderson (*Reynier de Marun*), Reg Pritchard (*Ben Daheer*), Tony Caunter (*Thatcher*), Roger Avon (*Saphadin*), Bernard Kay (*Saladin*), Robert Lankesheer (*Chamberlain*), George Little (*Haroun*), Zohra Segal (*Sheyrah*), Gabor Baraker (*Luigi*), Petra Markham (*Safiya*), John Bay (*Earl of Leicester*), Tutte Lemkow (*Ibrahim*) | **Crew:** Director: Douglas Camfield; Writer: David Whitaker; Music: Dudley Simpson | **Broadcast:** 27 March–17 April 1965, 9.4m (N, 1966; DVD, 2004 [episodes 1 & 3]; CD, 2005; A, 2005)

Précis: The Tardis occupants are caught in a Holy War between Richard the Lionheart and the Saracen ruler Saladin . . .

Observations: Dialogue concerning Richard's incestuous relationship with his sister Joanna was cut prior to recording. William Russell refused to do a scene with real ants crawling along his arm, so production assistant Viktors Ritelis doubled for him. Russell took a week's holiday during studio production on part three.

Verdict: Intelligent costume drama, if a little mannered. 7/10

15. THE SPACE MUSEUM (four episodes)
1: THE SPACE MUSEUM, 2: THE DIMENSIONS OF TIME,
3: THE SEARCH, 4: THE FINAL PHASE

Cast: Peter Craze (*Dako*), Richard Shaw (*Lobos*), Peter Sanders (*Sita*), Jeremy Bulloch (*Tor*), Ivor Salter (*Commander*), Peter Hawkins (*Dalek voice*), Murphy Grumbar (*Dalek*) | **Crew:** Director: Mervyn Pinfield; Writer: Glyn Jones | **Broadcast:** 24 April–15 May 1965, 9.2m (N, 1987; DVD, 2010; CD, 2009)

Précis: The Tardis jumps a time-track and arrives on Xeros in its own future . . .

Observations: Episode one is virtually a story on its own, the only speaking roles being those of the regular cast. Writer Glyn Jones would later play Krans in *The Sontaran Experiment* (77).

Verdict: Stunning first episode aside, this is a very dull 'rebels vs dictators' runaround. 2/10

16. THE CHASE (six episodes)
1: THE EXECUTIONERS, 2: THE DEATH OF TIME, 3: FLIGHT
THROUGH ETERNITY, 4: JOURNEY INTO TERROR, 5: THE DEATH
OF DOCTOR WHO, 6: THE PLANET OF DECISION

Cast: Robert Marsden (*Abraham Lincoln*), Hugh Walters
(*Shakespeare*), Roger Hammond (*Francis Bacon*), Vivienne Bennett
(*Queen Elizabeth*), Ian Thompson (*Malsan*), Hywel Bennett
(*Rynian*), Al Raymond (*Prondyn*), Arne Gordon (*Guide*), Peter
Purves (*Morton Dill*), Dennis Chinnery (*Richardson*), David Blake
Kelly (*Briggs*), Patrick Carter (*Bosun*), Douglas Ditta (*Willoughby*),
John Maxim (*Frankenstein's Monster*), Malcolm Rogers (*Dracula*),
Roslyn de Winter (*Grey Lady*), Edmund Warwick (*Robot Doctor*),
David Graham (*Dalek voices/Mechonoid voices*), Murphy Grumbar,
Jack Pitt (*Mechonoids*), Peter Hawkins (*Dalek voices*), Robert
Jewell, Kevin Manser, Gerald Taylor (*Daleks*), John Scott Martin
(*Mechonoid/Dalek*) | **Crew:** Director: Richard Martin; Writer: Terry
Nation; Music: Dudley Simpson | **Broadcast:** 22 May–26 June 1965,
9.4m (N, 1989; DVD, 2010)

Précis: The Daleks chase the Tardis crew though space and
time . . .

Observations: Very brief location filming was conducted at
Camber Sands, East Sussex, and White City Underground
Station, London. Unusually, new companion Peter Purves
played another role in the same story – hillbilly Morton
Dill atop the Empire State Building. *The Chase* was the
first story showing the Daleks (two of which were modified
movie versions) with vertical slats on their midriffs. Three
Mechonoids with fully operating flamethrowers were built
by Raymond Cusick.

Verdict: Neither witty enough to be amusing nor fast
enough to be exciting, *The Chase* ends up looking cheap
and tired. The Mechonoids impress, but they're only in it
for half an episode. 3/10

17. THE TIME MEDDLER (four episodes)
1: THE WATCHER, 2: THE MEDDLING MONK, 3: A BATTLE OF WITS, 4: CHECKMATE

Cast: Peter Butterworth (*Monk*), Alethea Charlton (*Edith*), Peter Russell (*Eldred*), Michael Miller (*Wulnoth*), Norman Hartley (*Ulf*), David Anderson (*Sven*), Geoffrey Cheshire (*Viking Leader*), Ronald Rich (*Gunnar*), Michael Guest (*Saxon Hunter*) | **Crew:** Director: Douglas Camfield; Writer: Dennis Spooner | **Broadcast:** 3–24 July 1965, 8.4m (N, 1987; DVD, 2008)

Précis: In 1066, a shady monk wants to reverse the outcome of the Battle of Hastings . . .

Observations: *The Time Meddler* saw several debuts – the first appearance of another member of the Doctor's own race, the first appearance of another Tardis and the first blending of science fiction and history. William Hartnell was on holiday for the second episode.

Verdict: This story marks a change in the programme's philosophy – history *can* be altered – but Peter Butterworth aside, it's a pity the whole thing's so dull. 6/10

SEASON 3

Producers: Verity Lambert (18–19), John Wiles (20–23) & Innes Lloyd (24–27)
Story Editors: Donald Tosh (18–22) & Gerry Davis (23–27)
First Doctor: William Hartnell (18, 20–27)
Companions: Maureen O'Brien (*Vicki* 18, 20), Peter Purves (*Steven Taylor*, 18, 20–26), Adrienne Hill (*Katarina*, 20–21), Jean Marsh (*Sara Kingdom*, 21), Jackie Lane (*Dodo Chaplet*, 22–27), Michael Craze (*Ben Jackson*, 27) & Anneke Wills (*Polly*, 27)

18. GALAXY 4 (four episodes)
1: FOUR HUNDRED DAWNS, 2: TRAP OF STEEL, 3: AIR LOCK, 4: THE EXPLODING PLANET

Cast: Stephanie Bidmead (*Maaga*), Marina Martin (*Drahvin One*), Susanna Carroll (*Drahvin Two*), Lyn Ashley (*Drahvin Three*), Robert Cartland (*Rill voice*), Barry Jackson (*Garvey*) | **Crew:** Director: Derek Martinus; Writer: William Emms | **Broadcast:** 11 September–2 October 1965, 9.9m (N, 1985; CD, 2000)

Précis: On a disintegrating planet, female Drahvins are at war with the Rills and their robot pets . . .

Observations: The Drahvins were originally intended to be male. Richard Hunt designed four fibreglass Chumblies operated by midget actors.

Verdict: A confidently produced, if somewhat clichéd, morality tale. 6/10

19. MISSION TO THE UNKNOWN (one episode)

Cast: Barry Jackson (*Garvey*), Edward de Souza (*Cory*), Robert Cartland (*Malpha*), Jeremy Young (*Lowery*), Ronald Rich (*Trantis*), Sam Mansary (*Sentreal*), Johnny Clayton (*Beaus*), Pat Gorman (*Gearon*), Len Russell (*Warrien*), David Graham, Peter Hawkins (*Dalek voices*), Gerald Taylor, John Scott Martin, Kevin Manser, Robert Jewell (*Daleks*) | **Crew:** Director: Derek Martinus; Writer: Terry Nation | **Broadcast:** 9 October 1965, 8.3m (N, 1989; CD, 2001; A, 2010)

Précis: On Kembel, secret agent Marc Cory finds the Daleks massing to attack the solar system . . .

Observations: This prelude to *The Daleks' Master Plan* (21) was an extra episode slotted in to make up for the shortened *Planet of Giants* (9) and contained none of the regular cast.

Verdict: This odd little segment makes an asset of its small cast and sports some ingenious aliens. 7/10

20. THE MYTH MAKERS (four episodes)
1: TEMPLE OF SECRETS, 2: SMALL PROPHET, QUICK RETURN, 3: DEATH OF A SPY, 4: HORSE OF DESTRUCTION

Cast: Francis de Wolff (*Agamemnon*), Max Adrian (*Priam*), Barrie Ingham (*Paris*), Ivor Salter (*Odysseus*), Cavan Kendall (*Achilles*), Jack Melford (*Menelaus*), Tutte Lemkow (*Cyclops*), Frances White (*Cassandra*), James Lynn (*Troilus*), Alan Haywood (*Hector*) | **Crew:** Director: Michael Leeston-Smith; Writer: Donald Cotton; Music: Humphrey Searle | **Broadcast:** 16 October–6 November 1965, 8.3m (N, 1985; CD, 2001; A, 2008)

Précis: The Tardis lands in Ancient Greece during the Trojan War . . .

Observations: Frensham Ponds, Surrey, stood in for Greece. Location filming saw the programme's first use of a glass shot, representing Troy.

Verdict: A witty script from Donald Cotton that blends farce and violence to intriguing effect. 7/10

21. THE DALEKS' MASTER PLAN (twelve episodes)
1: THE NIGHTMARE BEGINS, 2: DAY OF ARMAGEDDON, 3: DEVIL'S PLANET, 4: THE TRAITORS, 5: COUNTER PLOT, 6: CORONAS OF THE SUN, 7: THE FEAST OF STEVEN, 8: VOLCANO, 9: GOLDEN DEATH, 10: ESCAPE SWITCH, 11: THE ABANDONED PLANET, 12: DESTRUCTION OF TIME

Cast: Kevin Stoney (*Mavic Chen*), Peter Butterworth (*Monk*), Brian Cant (*Kert Gantry*), Nicholas Courtney (*Bret Vyon*), Julian Sherrier (*Zephon*), Roy Evans (*Trantis*), Douglas Sheldon (*Kirksen*), Geoff Cheshire (*Garge*), Dallas Cavell (*Bors*), Maurice Browning (*Karlton*), Jack Pitt (*Gearon/Dalek*), Roger Avon (*Daxter*), James Hall (*Borkar*), Bill Meilen (*Froyn*), John Herrington (*Rhynmal*), Terence Woodfield, Ian East (*Celation*), Jeffrey Isaac (*Khepren*), Derek Ware (*Tuthmos*), Walter Randall (*Hyksos*), Bryan Mosley, Brian Edwards (*Malpha*), Gerry Videl (*Beaus*), Peter Hawkins, David Graham (*Dalek voices*), John Scott Martin, Kevin Manser, Gerald Taylor, Robert Jewell (*Daleks*) **| Crew:** Director: Douglas Camfield; Writers: Terry Nation (1–5, 7) & Dennis Spooner (6, 8–12); Music: Tristram Cary **| Broadcast:** 13 November 1965–29 January 1966, 9.4m (N, 1989; DVD, 2004 [episodes 2, 5 & 10]; CD, 2001; A, 2010)

Précis: The Doctor joins forces with secret agents Bret Vyon and Sara Kingdom to stop Mavic Chen and the Daleks from constructing the Time Destructor . . .

Observations: Two companions were killed during this story – Katarina in the fourth episode and Sara Kingdom in the twelfth. Episode seven fell on Christmas Day 1965 and was played as a comedy, with the Doctor wishing the viewers a Merry Christmas.

Verdict: A well-structured epic that sees the shocking death of two companions, the Daleks at their most manipulative and an arch-villain played to perfection by the great Kevin Stoney. *The Feast of Steven* is unexpectedly charming and the production values throughout appear excellent. 10/10

22. THE MASSACRE OF ST BARTHOLOMEW'S EVE (four episodes)
1: WAR OF GOD, 2: THE SEA BEGGAR, 3: PRIEST OF DEATH, 4: BELL OF DOOM

Cast: William Hartnell (*Abbot of Amboise*), Andre Morell (*Tavannes*), Leonard Sachs (*de Coligny*), David Weston (*Nicholas*), Annette Robinson (*Anne Chaplet*), John Tillinger (*Simon*), Eric Thompson (*Gaston*), Edwin Finn (*Landlord*), Eric Chitty (*Preslin*), Christopher Tranchell (*Roger*), Barry Justice (*Charles IX*), Joan Young (*Catherine de Medici*), Michael Bilton (*Teligny*), Norman Claridge (*Priest*) | **Crew:** Director: Paddy Russell; Writers: John Lucarotti & Donald Tosh | **Broadcast:** 5–26 February 1966, 6.4m (N, 1987; DVD, 2001; CD, 1999)

Précis: Paris, 1572, and on the eve of a Catholic plan to murder all French Protestants, Steven is shocked to discover that the Abbot of Amboise is the spitting image of the Doctor . . .

Observations: The massacre was represented by authentic line drawings overlaid with appropriate sound effects. The Doctor and the Abbot, both played by William Hartnell, never appeared on screen together. Brief filming was conducted on Wimbledon Common, London.

Verdict: A complex and engagingly downbeat historical, with Steven allowed to dominate proceedings for once. 9/10

23. THE ARK (four episodes)
1: THE STEEL SKY, 2: THE PLAGUE, 3: THE RETURN, 4: THE BOMB

Cast: Inigo Jackson (*Zentos*), Eric Elliott (*Commander*), Roy Spencer (*Manyak*), Kate Newman (*Mellium*), Michael Sheard (*Rhos*), Ian Frost (*Baccu*), Terence Woodfield (*Maharis*), Terence Bayler (*Yendom*), Brian Wright (*Dassuk*), Eileen Helsby (*Venussa*), Roy Skelton, John Halstead

(*Monoid voices*), Richard Beale (*Refusian voice*) | **Crew:** Director: Michael Imison; Writer: Paul Erickson; Music: Tristram Cary | **Broadcast:** 5–26 March 1966, 6.8m (N, 1986; DVD, 2011; CD, 2006)

Précis: Dodo's cold nearly kills the humans aboard a huge space ark, but arriving 700 years later the Tardis crew find their one-eyed slaves have taken over . . .

Observations: The Monoids' single eyes were actually painted ping-pong balls held in the actors' mouths. Various zoo animals were supplied for the Ealing film shoot in episode one.

Verdict: The two-part narrative is a clever idea. The invisible Refusians are silly, but the Ark itself has a certain grandeur. 6/10

24. THE CELESTIAL TOYMAKER (four episodes)
1: THE CELESTIAL TOYROOM, 2: THE HALL OF DOLLS,
3: THE DANCING FLOOR, 4: THE FINAL TEST

Cast: Michael Gough (*Toymaker*), Carmen Silvera (*Clara/Queen of Hearts/Mrs Wiggs*), Campbell Singer (*Joey/King of Hearts/Sgt Rugg*), Peter Stephens (*Knave of Hearts/Kitchen Boy/Cyril*), Reg Lever (*Joker*), Delia Lindon, Ann Harrison, Beryl Braham (*Ballerina Dolls*) | **Crew:** Director: Bill Sellars; Writer: Brian Hayles; Music: Dudley Simpson | **Broadcast:** 2–23 April 1966, 8.3m (N, 1986; DVD, 2004 [episode 4]; CD, 2001)

Précis: The Tardis lands in the fantasy domain of the malevolent Toymaker . . .

Observations: Originally based on Gerald Savory's 1937 play *George and Margaret*, the story was rewritten by Gerry Davis when the playwright objected to the use of his characters' names. Hartnell was absent for the middle two episodes.

Verdict: A weird, and at times plodding, excursion into pure fantasy (some might say whimsy). Not as interesting as its reputation might suggest. 4/10

25. THE GUNFIGHTERS (four episodes)
1: A HOLIDAY FOR THE DOCTOR, 2: DON'T SHOOT THE PIANIST,
3: JOHNNY RINGO, 4: THE O.K. CORRAL

Cast: John Alderson (*Wyatt Earp*), Anthony Jacobs (*Doc Holliday*), William Hurndell (*Ike Clanton*), Laurence Payne (*Johnny Ringo*), Maurice Good (*Phineas Clanton*), David Cole (*Billy Clanton*), Sheena Marshe (*Kate*), Shane Rimmer (*Seth Harper*), David Graham (*Charlie*), Richard Beale (*Bat Masterson*), Reed de Rouen (*Pa Clanton*), Martyn Huntley (*Warren Earp*), Victor Carin (*Virgil Earp*), Lynda Baron (*Ballad singer*) | **Crew:** Director: Rex Tucker; Writer: Donald Cotton; Music: Tristram Cary | **Broadcast:** 30 April–21 May 1966, 6.3m (N, 1985; CD, 2007)

Précis: Arriving in Tombstone, Arizona, in 1881, the Doctor and his friends are soon caught up in the infamous gunfight at the OK Corral . . .
Observations: Rex Tucker was originally to have directed the show's first story. For the twenty-five-verse 'Ballad of the Last Chance Saloon', Tristram Cary set Rex Tucker and Donald Cotton's lyrics to music. John Alderson had appeared in the American TV series *Bonanza*.
Verdict: A charming Wild West pastiche with Hartnell clearly loving every minute of it. The unusual framing device of the ballad is an effective counterpoint to the action, some of which is surprisingly brutal. Much underrated. 9/10

26. THE SAVAGES (four episodes)

Cast: Frederick Jaeger (*Jano*), Ewen Solon (*Chal*), Patrick Godfrey (*Tor*), Geoffrey Frederick (*Exorse*), Robert Sidaway (*Avon*), Peter Thomas (*Edal*), Kay Patrick (*Flower*), Norman Henry (*Senta*), Clare Jenkins (*Nanina*), Edward Caddick (*Wylda*) | **Crew:** Director: Christopher Barry; Writer: Ian Stuart Black; Music: Raymond Jones | **Broadcast:** 28 May–18 June 1966, 4.9m (N, 1986; CD, 2002)

Précis: A ruthless elite is sucking the life force from its innocent workers . . .

Observations: Location filming was conducted at a Surrey sandpit and a Bucks quarry. This was the first *Doctor Who* story to carry an overall story title.

Verdict: The story's moralistic overtones may be obvious, but the existing soundtrack indicates this is a well-made story full of dramatic moments. 8/10

27. THE WAR MACHINES (four episodes)

Cast: William Mervyn (*Charles Summer*), John Harvey (*Brett*), John Cater (*Krimpton*), Alan Curtis (*Major Green*), Sandra Bryant (*Kitty*), John Rolfe (*Captain*), John Boyd-Brent (*Sergeant*), Kenneth Kendall (*Himself*), WOTAN (*Itself*), Gerald Taylor (*WOTAN voice*) | **Crew:** Director: Michael Ferguson; Writer: Ian Stuart Black | **Broadcast:** 25 June–16 July 1966, 5.2m (N, 1989; CD, 2007)

Précis: At the top of the Post Office Tower, super-computer WOTAN is brainwashing humans to build terrifying War Machines . . .

Observations: The first story set entirely on contemporary Earth; extensive London filming included Bedford Square, Covent Garden Market and Cornwall Gardens, as well as shots of the newly opened Post Office Tower. A single War Machine was built, with changeable numbers to represent different machines.

Verdict: This pre-Internet scare story has some convincing action scenes and an impressive War Machine, but Hartnell's performance is best described as erratic. 7/10

SEASON 4

Producer: Innes Lloyd
Story Editors: Gerry Davis & Peter Bryant (36)
First Doctor: William Hartnell (28–29)
Second Doctor: Patrick Troughton (29–36)
Companions: Michael Craze (*Ben Jackson*, 28–35), Anneke
Wills (*Polly*, 28–35), Frazer Hines (*Jamie McCrimmon*,
31–36) & Deborah Watling (*Victoria Waterfield*, 36)

28. THE SMUGGLERS (four episodes)

Cast: George A Cooper (*Cherub*), Terence de Marney (*Churchwarden*),
David Blake Kelly (*Jacob Kewper*), Mike Lucas (*Tom*), Paul Whitsun-
Jones (*Squire*), Michael Godfrey (*Pike*), Elroy Josephs (*Jamaica*), John
Ringham (*Blake*), Jack Bligh (*Gaptooth*) | **Crew:** Director: Julia Smith;
Writer: Brian Hayles | **Broadcast:** 10 September–1 October 1966, 4.8m
(N, 1988; CD, 2002)

Précis: The Doctor is caught up in a seventeeth-century
treasure hunt . . .
Observations: A week's location filming in Cornwall – the
most extensive yet for the programme – took in Nanjizal
Bay, Church Cove and Bosistow Cliffs. The fishing boat

Bonny Mary stood in for the piratical *Black Albatross* and the story saw the first use of the HAVOC stunt team.
Verdict: A swashbuckling adventure full of ripe characterisation and OTT dialogue. 8/10

29. THE TENTH PLANET (four episodes)

Cast: Robert Beatty (*General Cutler*), Earl Cameron (*Williams*), David Dodimead (*Barclay*), Dudley Jones (*Dyson*), Alan White (*Schultz*), Steve Plytas (*Wigner*), Christopher Matthews (*Radar Technician*), Ellen Cullen (*Geneva Technician*), Christopher Dunham (*R/T Technician*), Callen Angelo (*Terry Cutler*), Peter Hawkins, Roy Skelton (*Cybermen voices*), Reg Whitehead (*Krail/Jarl*), Harry Brooks (*Talon/Krang*), Gregg Palmer (*Shav/Gern*) | **Crew:** Director: Derek Martinus; Writers: Kit Pedler & Gerry Davis | **Broadcast:** 8–29 October 1966, 6.8m (N, 1976; CD, 2004)

Précis: Cybermen – humanoids augmented with machine parts – land at a South Pole tracking station and drain the Earth's energy . . .
Observations: Costume designer Sandra Reid created the look of the seven Cybermen by dressing actors in cloth body stockings overlaid with transparent polythene suits. They wore jersey masks with truck headlamps on their heads; bare hands suggested their human roots, as did their individual names. The programme's first regeneration sequence made use of a faulty mixing desk that created a flaring, overexposed picture.
Verdict: Poor modelwork aside, this is a gripping production. The subhuman Cybermen with their meandering voices are chilling creations and the Doctor's transformation is particularly effective. 9/10

30. THE POWER OF THE DALEKS (six episodes)

Cast: Bernard Archard (*Bragen*), Robert James (*Lesterson*), Nicholas Hawtrey (*Quinn*), Pamela Ann Davy (*Janley*), Peter Bathurst (*Hensell*), Richard Kane (*Valmar*), Steven Scott (*Kebble*), Martin King

(*Examiner*), Peter Hawkins (*Dalek voices*), Gerald Taylor, Kevin Manser, Robert Jewell, John Scott Martin, Alan Whibley (*Daleks*) | **Crew:** Director: Christopher Barry; Writer: David Whitaker; Music: Tristram Cary | **Broadcast:** 5 November–10 December 1966, 7.8m (N, 1993; CD, 2003)

Précis: The Daleks infiltrate an Earth colony on the planet Vulcan in the twenty-first century . . .

Observations: This was the first Dalek story not to be penned by their creator, Terry Nation. The Doctor's clothes changed with his new body (as with his boots in *Castrovalva*, 116). Various new costume ideas were mooted, such as a Victorian sea captain or a blacked-up *Arabian Nights* figure, but in the end a scruffier version of Hartnell's attire was chosen (with a 'Harpo Marx' wig rejected as too comical). The *Radio Times* promoted the story with a Daleks cover.

Verdict: An average story improved by Patrick Troughton's invigorating portrayal of the central character and the impressively staged Dalek production line. 7/10

31. THE HIGHLANDERS (four episodes)

Cast: Donald Bisset (*Laird*), William Dysart (*Alexander*), Hannah Gordon (*Kirsty*), Michael Elwyn (*Lt Algernon ffinch*), Peter Welch (*Sergeant*), David Garth (*Grey*), Sydney Arnold (*Perkins*), Dallas Cavell (*Trask*), Barbara Bruce (*Mollie*), Andrew Downie (*Mackay*), Guy Middleton (*Attwood*) | **Crew:** Director: Hugh David; Writers: Gerry Davis & Elwyn Jones | **Broadcast:** 17 December 1966–7 January 1967, 7m (N, 1984; CD, 2000)

Précis: The Tardis crew meet some Scottish Highlanders after the Battle of Culloden in 1746 . . .

Observations: Frensham Ponds, Surrey, previously seen in *The Myth Makers* (20), represented the Scottish Highlands. A water tank at Ealing Studios was used for Inverness Harbour.

Verdict: A charming adventure story, in the style of *The Smugglers* (28), with some particularly funny moments for Patrick Troughton in disguise as 'Dr von Wer' (German for 'Doctor Who'). 8/10

32. THE UNDERWATER MENACE (four episodes)

Cast: Joseph Furst (*Zaroff*), Catherine Howe (*Ara*), Tom Watson (*Ramo*), Colin Jeavons (*Damon*), Peter Stephens (*Lolem*), Graham Ashley (*Overseer*), Paul Anil (*Jacko*), PG Stephens (*Sean*), Noel Johnson (*Thous*), Roma Woodnutt (*Nola*) | **Crew:** Director: Julia Smith; Writer: Geoffrey Orme; Music: Dudley Simpson | **Broadcast:** 14 January–4 February 1967, 7.5m (N, 1988; DVD, 2004 [episode 3]; CD, 2005)

Précis: In Atlantis, a mad professor plans to drain the world's oceans into the Earth's core . . .
Observations: The gateway to Atlantis was actually a cave mouth at Winspit Quarry in Dorset. Complaints were received from a children's charity about Polly's injection with a hypodermic syringe in episode one.
Verdict: A wonderfully bad story featuring a tongue-in-cheek script, tacky 'fish people' and, in Professor Zaroff (hammed up madly by Joseph Furst), easily the most ridiculous *Doctor Who* villain ever. 7/10

33. THE MOONBASE (four episodes)

Cast: André Maranne (*Benoit*), Patrick Barr (*Hobson*), John Rolfe (*Sam*), Michael Wolf (*Nils*), Mark Heath (*Ralph*), Alan Rowe (*Evans*), Victor Pemberton (*Jules*), Ron Pinnell (*Jim*), Edward Phillips (*Bob*), Peter Hawkins (*Cybermen voices*), Ronald Lee, Barry Noble, John Levene, Derek Schafer, Declan Cuffe, Terry Wallis, Bernard Reid, Reg Whitehead, Keith Goodman, Peter Greene, John Wills, Sonnie Willis (*Cybermen*) | **Crew:** Director: Morris Barry; Writer: Kit Pedler | **Broadcast:** 11 February–4 March 1967, 8.3m (N, 1975; DVD, 2004 [episodes 2 & 4]; CD, 2001; A, 2009)

Précis: Cybermen invade a lunar base in order to disrupt the Earth's weather . . .

Observations: Sandra Reid designed eleven new Cybermen costumes, consisting mainly of silver vinyl jumpsuits. Episode four's laser beam was the first use of a filmed optical effect. Victor Pemberton was script editor for *The Tomb of the Cybermen* (37) and wrote *Fury from the Deep* (42).

Verdict: An unimaginative, albeit at times scary, remake of *The Tenth Planet* (29), with many plot holes. 6/10

34. THE MACRA TERROR (four episodes)

Cast: Peter Jeffrey (*Pilot*), Graham Armitage (*Barney*), Ian Fairbairn (*Questa*), Jane Enshawe (*Sunnaa*), Sandra Bryant, Karol Keyes (*Chicki*), Terence Lodge (*Medok*), Gertan Klauber (*Ola*), Graham Leaman (*Controller*), Denis Goacher (*Control voice*), Richard Beale (*Broadcast voice*) | **Crew:** Director: John Davies; Writer: Ian Stuart Black; Music: Dudley Simpson | **Broadcast:** 11 March–1 April 1967, 8.2m (N, 1987; CD, 2000)

Précis: Huge crab-like Macra have infiltrated a human colony run like a holiday camp . . .

Observations: The single Macra prop was 10ft high and had to be transported to the studio on the back of a lorry. Very brief location filming was conducted in a cement quarry in Dunstable, Beds. A new howlround title sequence debuted with episode one, again designed by Bernard Lodge, and now featuring Patrick Troughton's face.

Verdict: Setting an alien menace in a bright, cheerful holiday camp, complete with muzak and jingles, is a brilliant idea. The first glimpse of the Macra is chilling. 8/10

35. THE FACELESS ONES (six episodes)

Cast: Wanda Ventham (*Jean Rock*), Colin Gordon (*Commandant*), Bernard Kay (*Crossland*), Donald Pickering (*Blade*), Pauline Collins

(*Samantha Briggs*), George Selway (*Meadows*), Victor Winding (*Spencer*), Christopher Tranchell (*Jenkins*), Madalena Nicol (*Nurse Pinto*), Gilly Fraser (*Ann Davidson*), Barry Wilshire (*Heslington*), Peter Whitaker (*Gascoigne*) | **Crew:** Director: Gerry Mill; Writers: David Ellis & Malcolm Hulke | **Broadcast:** 8 April–13 May 1967, 7.4m (N, 1986; DVD, 2004 [episodes 1 & 3]; CD, 2002)

Précis: Hideous aliens lure youngsters to their orbiting satellite in order to possess them . . .

Observations: Much location filming was done at Gatwick Airport, London. Actress Pauline Collins was invited to play a companion, but she declined. Following on from the new title sequence, Delia Derbyshire and the BBC Radiophonic Workshop provided a modified arrangement of the opening theme music from episode two onwards.

Verdict: Preposterous plot notwithstanding, the Chameleons are frighteningly soulless creatures (at least on audio) and there is much psychological horror involving identity loss. 8/10

36. THE EVIL OF THE DALEKS (seven episodes)

Cast: John Bailey (*Edward Waterfield*), Marius Goring (*Theodore Maxtible*), Windsor Davies (*Toby*), Alec Ross (*Bob Hall*), Griffith Davies (*Kennedy*), Geoffrey Colville (*Perry*), Jo Rowbottom (*Mollie*), Brigit Forsyth (*Ruth Maxtible*), Gary Watson (*Arthur Terrall*), Sonny Caldinez (*Kemel*), Roy Skelton, Peter Hawkins (*Dalek voices*), John Scott Martin, Robert Jewell, Gerald Taylor, Murphy Grumbar, Ken Tyllsen (*Daleks*) | **Crew:** Director: Derek Martinus; Writer: David Whitaker; Music: Dudley Simpson | **Broadcast:** 20 May–1 July 1967 (N, 1993; DVD, 2004 [episode 2]; CD, 2003)

Précis: The Doctor and Jamie are taken to Victorian England where the Daleks are experimenting with the 'Human Factor' in a bid to turn them into super-beings . . .

Observations: Grim's Dyke House, Harrow Weald, Middx, was the location for Maxtible's home. London locations included Kendal Avenue, W3 and Warehouse Lane,

W12. Louis Marx toy Daleks featured in climactic model scenes filmed at Ealing Film Studios.

Verdict: Despite its enormous reputation, this is a deeply implausible story that hinges on several improbable concepts. It only gets going – too late in the day – when the action shifts to Skaro in the last two episodes. 4/10

SEASON 5

Producers: Peter Bryant (37, 41–43) & Innes Lloyd (38–40)
Story Editors: Victor Pemberton (37), Peter Bryant
(38–40) & Derrick Sherwin (41–43)
Second Doctor: Patrick Troughton
Companions: Frazer Hines (*Jamie McCrimmon*), Deborah
Watling (*Victoria Waterfield*, 37–42) & Wendy Padbury
(*Zoe Heriot*, 43)

37. THE TOMB OF THE CYBERMEN (four episodes)

Cast: Aubrey Richards (*Parry*), George Pastell (*Klieg*), Cyril Shaps
(*Viner*), Roy Stewart (*Toberman*), Clive Merrison (*Callum*), Shirley
Cooklin (*Kaftan*), George Roubicek (*Hopper*), Alan Johns (*Rogers*),
Bernard Holley (*Haydon*), Peter Hawkins (*Cybermen voices*), Reg
Whitehead, Hans de Vries, Tony Harwood, John Hogan, Richard
Kerley, Ronald Lee, Charles Pemberton, Kenneth Seeger (*Cybermen*),
Michael Kilgarriff (*Cyberman Controller*) | **Crew:** Director: Morris
Barry; Writers: Kit Pedler & Gerry Davis | **Broadcast:** 2–23 September
1967, 6.7m (N, 1978; DVD, 2002; CD, 2006)

Précis: On Telos, an archaeological team penetrates the
long-lost tomb of the Cybermen . . .

Observations: A quarry in Gerrards Cross, Bucks, was the chosen venue for Telos. The murine Cybermats, designed by Michaeljohn Harris, made their first appearance. A new costume was designed for the Controller, with a larger cranium and no chest unit. Violent scenes were discussed on the BBC programme *Talkback*, while a *Radio Times* cover displayed a Cybermen montage.

Verdict: A generally polished production, featuring an uncharacteristically manipulative Second Doctor and an impressive set of Cybermen. On the downside, the direction is at times rather flat. 8/10

38. THE ABOMINABLE SNOWMEN (six episodes)

Cast: Jack Watling (*Professor Travers*), David Spenser (*Thonmi*), Wolfe Morris (*Padmasambhava*), Norman Jones (*Khrisong*), David Grey (*Rinchen*), Raymond Llewellyn (*Sapan*), Charles Morgan (*Songsten*), David Baron (*Ralpachan*), Reg Whitehead, Tony Harwood, Richard Kerley, John Hogan (*Yeti*) | **Crew:** Director: Gerald Blake; Writers: Mervyn Haisman & Henry Lincoln | **Broadcast:** 30 September–4 November 1967, 6.8m (N, 1974; DVD, 2004 [episode 2]; CD, 2001; A, 2009)

Précis: In 1930s Tibet, the Great Intelligence is attempting to take solid form using an army of robotic Yeti . . .

Observations: Welsh location filming was conducted at the breathtaking Nant Ffrancon Pass in Gwynedd. Four Yeti costumes were made, each one comprising fur skins over a bamboo frame.

Verdict: A ponderous, slow-moving tale, heavy on echoey Tibetan ritual. The role of the abominable snowmen is unclear and their appearance is more likely to provoke smiles than screams. 4/10

39. THE ICE WARRIORS (six episodes)

Cast: Peter Barkworth (*Clent*), Wendy Gifford (*Miss Garrett*), George Waring (*Arden*), Angus Lennie (*Storr*), Peter Sallis (*Penley*), Bernard Bresslaw (*Varga*), Roger Jones (*Zondal*), Sonny Caldinez (*Turoc*), Tony Harwood (*Rintan*), Michael Attwell (*Isbur*), Roy Skelton (*Computer voice*) | **Crew:** Director: Derek Martinus; Writer: Brian Hayles; Music: Dudley Simpson | **Broadcast:** 11 November–16 December 1967, 7.3m (N, 1976; CD, 2005; A, 2010)

Précis: It is AD 3000, and in the grip of a second Ice Age the crew of a scientific base defrost a Martian . . .
Observations: Martin Baugh designed four fibreglass Ice Warrior costumes. Glacier scenes were filmed at the BBC Film Studios in Ealing with jabolite (polystyrene) standing in for snow. The Tardis exterior prop, which materialised on its back, was refurbished prior to filming. A specially shot trailer for this story was shown after *The Abominable Snowmen* (38).
Verdict: Endless discussions about computer intelligence and the importance of individuality – worthy stuff, but dull. The Ice Warriors are impressive, until they start to move. 4/10

40. THE ENEMY OF THE WORLD (six episodes)

Cast: Patrick Troughton (*Salamander*), Bill Kerr (*Giles Kent*), Colin Douglas (*Donald Bruce*), Mary Peach (*Astrid*), Milton Johns (*Benik*), George Pravda (*Denes*), David Nettheim (*Fedorin*), Carmen Munroe (*Fariah*), Reg Lye (*Griffin*), Christopher Burgess (*Swann*), Adam Verney (*Colin*), Margaret Hickey (*Mary*) | **Crew:** Director: Barry Letts; Writer: David Whitaker | **Broadcast:** 23 December 1967–27 January 1968, 7.4m (N, 1981; DVD, 2004 [episode 3]; CD, 2002)

Précis: Australia in the near future and the dictator Salamander – the spitting image of the Doctor – has an insane plan to rule the world . . .
Observations: Climping Beach, Littlehampton, West Sussex, stood in for Australia, with use made of a hovercraft and

helicopter. Episode three was the first to be recorded on 625-line videotape (broadcast since 1964), as opposed to the old 405-line system. Frazer Hines and Deborah Watling were absent for episode four. A *Radio Times* cover accompanied the transmission of episode five.

Verdict: A well-crafted political thriller done on the cheap. The Australasian setting is a nice gimmick, although we only get to see the same old corridors. Troughton's Mexican accent should have had its own spin-off series. 6/10

41. THE WEB OF FEAR (six episodes)

Cast: Jack Watling (*Professor Travers*), Tina Packer (*Anne Travers*), Nicholas Courtney (*Colonel Lethbridge-Stewart*), Jack Woolgar (*Arnold*), Frederick Schrecker (*Silverstein*), Rod Beacham (*Lane*), Richardson Morgan (*Blake*), Ralph Watson (*Knight*), Jon Rollason (*Chorley*), Derek Pollitt (*Evans*), Stephen Whittaker (*Weams*), John Levene, Gordon Stothard, Colin Warman, John Lord, Jeremy King, Roger Jacombs (*Yeti*) | **Crew:** Director: Douglas Camfield; Writers: Mervyn Haisman & Henry Lincoln | **Broadcast:** 3 February–9 March 1968, 7.6m (N, 1976; DVD, 2004 [episode 1]; CD, 2000)

Précis: Reactivated by the Great Intelligence, the Yeti are at large in the London Underground . . .

Observations: London filming took place in Covent Garden. Four new Yeti costumes were made, with larger claws and glowing eyes. Patrick Troughton, on holiday during episode two, recorded a special trailer that was shown after the final part of the previous story.

Verdict: Archetypal *Who*: a small group of people fighting for their lives in claustrophobic (and eerily familiar) surroundings against fearsome alien invaders. We'd seen it done before, and we'd see it done again, but never quite as slickly as this. 9/10

42. FURY FROM THE DEEP (six episodes)

Cast: John Abineri (*Van Lutyens*), Victor Maddern (*Robson*), Roy Spencer (*Frank Harris*), June Murphy (*Maggie Harris*), Graham Leaman (*Price*), John Garvin (*Carney*), Hubert Rees (*Chief Engineer*), Richard Mayes (*Baxter*), John Gill (*Oak*), Bill Burridge (*Quill*), Margaret John (*Megan*), Brian Cullingford (*Perkins*), Peter Day (*Weed Monster*) | **Crew:** Director: Hugh David; Writer: Victor Pemberton; Music: Dudley Simpson | **Broadcast:** 16 March–20 April 1968, 7.2m (N, 1986; CD, 2004)

Précis: On a North Sea gas refinery, a parasitic seaweed creature is on the move . . .

Observations: This story borrows heavily from the writer's 1966 radio serial, *The Slide*. Botany Bay, near Margate in Kent, saw filmwork involving a helicopter and a model Tardis 'landing' on the sea. The Red Sand offshore platform in the Thames Estuary – built in 1943 to repel German attack – represented the refinery. Episode one sees the Doctor using his sonic screwdriver for the first time.

Verdict: Scary to listen to, with chilling sound effects, nicely judged performances and a largely unseen monster. The surviving clip shows Oak and Quill as bed-wettingly terrifying. 10/10

43. THE WHEEL IN SPACE (six episodes)

Cast: Eric Flynn (*Ryan*), Michael Turner (*Bennett*), Anne Ridler (*Corwyn*), Clare Jenkins (*Lernov*), Donald Sumpter (*Casali*), Michael Goldie (*Laleham*), Kenneth Watson (*Duggan*), Derrick Gilbert (*Vallance*), Kevork Malikyan (*Rudkin*), Peter Laird (*Chang*), James Mellor (*Flannigan*), Peter Hawkins, Roy Skelton (*Cybermen voices*), Jerry Holmes, Gordon Stothard, Tony Harwood (*Cybermen*) | **Crew:** Director: Tristan de Vere Cole; Writer: David Whitaker (from an idea by Kit Pedler); Music: Brian Hodgson | **Broadcast:** 27 April–1 June 1968, 7.3m (N, 1988; DVD, 2005 [episodes 3 & 6]; CD, 2004)

Précis: Cybermats infiltrate a space station and are soon followed by the Cybermen . . .

Observations: Two new Cybermen costumes were built by Martin Baugh, adding the distinctive 'tear ducts' under the eyes. In the final episode, the Doctor shows new companion Zoe one of his past adventures, neatly segueing into a rerun of *The Evil of the Daleks* (36), the programme's first scheduled repeat, which bridged the gap between Seasons 5 and 6.

Verdict: Utter tedium. 2/10

SEASON 6

Producers: Peter Bryant (44–49) & Derrick Sherwin (50)
Story Editors: Derrick Sherwin (44–45, 49) & Terrance Dicks (46–48, 50)
Second Doctor: Patrick Troughton
Companions: Frazer Hines (*Jamie McCrimmon*) & Wendy Padbury (*Zoe Heriot*)

44. THE DOMINATORS (five episodes)

Cast: Ronald Allen (*Rago*), Kenneth Ives (*Toba*), Walter Fitzgerald (*Senex*), Arthur Cox (*Cully*), Johnson Bayly (*Balan*), Felicity Gibson (*Kando*), Giles Block (*Teel*), Alan Gerrard (*Bovem*), Brian Cant (*Tensa*), Philip Voss (*Wahed*), Malcolm Terris (*Etnin*), Nicolette Pendrell (*Tolata*), Sheila Grant (*Quark voices*), John Hicks, Gary Smith, Freddie Wilson (*Quarks*) | **Crew:** Director: Morris Barry; Writer: Norman Ashby (pseudonym for Mervyn Haisman & Henry Lincoln) | **Broadcast:** 10 August–7 September 1968, 6.2m (N, 1984; DVD, 2010; CD, 2007)

Précis: Sadistic Dominators and their robot Quarks threaten the pacifist planet of Dulkis . . .
Observations: The much-used gravel pit in Gerrards Cross, Bucks, represented Dulkis. Three Quarks were built

by John and Jack Lovell and operated by drama-school students. The story was originally six episodes long, but was shortened by producer Peter Bryant.

Verdict: The Dominators argue, the Dulcians are timid and nothing ever really happens. 4/10

45. THE MIND ROBBER (five episodes)

Cast: Bernard Horsfall (*Gulliver*), Emrys Jones (*Master*), Hamish Wilson (*Jamie*), Christine Pirie (*Rapunzel*), Sue Pulford (*Medusa*), Christopher Robbie (*Karkus*), David Cannon (*Cyrano de Bergerac*), John Greenwood (*D'Artagnan/Sir Lancelot*), Gerry Wain (*Blackbeard*), John Atterbury, Ralph Carrigan, Bill Wiesener, Terry Wright (*White Robots*) | **Crew:** Director: David Maloney; Writers: Peter Ling & Derrick Sherwin | **Broadcast:** 14 September–12 October 1968, 6.7m (N, 1986; DVD, 2005; A, 2009)

Précis: The Tardis explodes, propelling its crew into a strange world peopled by fictional characters . . .

Observations: Derrick Sherwin wrote an extra episode appended to the beginning to make up for the previous story's diminished length. Brief location filming was conducted at Harrison's Rocks, Kent, and Kenley Aerodrome, Croydon. Hamish Wilson replaced Frazer Hines for episode two when the latter contracted chicken pox, while Gulliver (Bernard Horsfall) spoke only those lines that Jonathan Swift had written for him in *Gulliver's Travels*.

Verdict: Written with great intelligence and humour, this deeply satisfying slice of weirdness is as fresh, funny and scary today as it was all those years ago. 10/10

46. THE INVASION (eight episodes)

Cast: Nicholas Courtney (*Brigadier*), Kevin Stoney (*Vaughn*), Peter Halliday (*Packer/Cyberplanner voice/Cybermen voices*), Sally Faulkner (*Isobel*), John Levene (*Benton*), Geoffrey Cheshire (*Tracy*), Ian Fairbairn

(*Gregory*), James Thornhill (*Walters*), Robert Sidaway (*Turner*), Edward Burnham (*Watkins*), Edward Dentith (*Rutlidge*), Clifford Earl (*Branwell*), Pat Gorman, Derek Chaffer, John Spradbury, Terence Denville, Ralph Carrigan, Richard King, Peter Thornton (*Cybermen*) | **Crew:** Director: Douglas Camfield; Writer: Derrick Sherwin (from an idea by Kit Pedler); Music: Don Harper | **Broadcast:** 2 November–21 December 1968, 6.9m (N, 1985; DVD, 2006 [animated episodes 1 & 4]; CD, 2004)

Précis: London is invaded by Cybermen from the city's sewers . . .

Observations: The scenes of deserted London were filmed over ten days, mainly centring on the St Paul's area of the city. Regent's Canal was used for canoe scenes with the Doctor and Jamie. A Guinness brewery in Park Royal, London NW10, stood in for the IE site and a Hercules transporter plane at RAF Fairford in Gloucestershire became an itinerant UNIT base. Six new Cybermen costumes were constructed by Bill King (helmets) and Jack and John Lovell (bodies). Wendy Padbury was absent for episode three's studio recording and Frazer Hines likewise for the final episode.

Verdict: The exciting (that is, expensive) set pieces take place off-screen and it's at least four episodes too long. Kevin Stoney is wonderful though. 5/10

47. THE KROTONS (four episodes)

Cast: Philip Madoc (*Eelek*), Gilbert Wynne (*Thara*), James Copeland (*Selris*), Terence Brown (*Abu*), Madeleine Mills (*Vana*), Richard Ireson (*Axus*), James Cairncross (*Beta*), Maurice Selwyn (*Custodian*), Roy Skelton, Patrick Tull (*Kroton voices*), Robert La'Bassiere, Miles Northover (*Krotons*) | **Crew:** Director: David Maloney; Writer: Robert Holmes | **Broadcast:** 28 December 1968–18 January 1969, 8m (N, 1985; CD, 2008)

Précis: The Gonds have been enslaved by the crystalline Krotons . . .

Observations: This debut story by prolific contributor Robert Holmes was a last-minute replacement for an abandoned gender-swap satire by comedy writer Dick Sharples. Two Krotons were constructed from Perspex and fibreglass.

Verdict: Forgettable performances aside, *The Krotons* has a decent plot and some imaginative visuals. The Krotons' Brummie accents are . . . interesting. 6/10

48. THE SEEDS OF DEATH (six episodes)

Cast: Ronald Leigh-Hunt (*Radnor*), Philip Ray (*Eldred*), Louise Pajo (*Gia Kelly*), Terry Scully (*Fewsham*), Harry Towb (*Osgood*), Ric Felgate (*Brent*), Martin Cort (*Locke*), Christopher Coll (*Phipps*), Alan Bennion (*Slaar*), Hugh Morton (*Gregson*), Graham Leaman (*Grand Marshall*), Steve Peters, Tony Harwood, Sonny Caldinez (*Ice Warriors*) | **Crew:** Director: Michael Ferguson; Writers: Brian Hayles (1–2) & Terrance Dicks (3–6); Music: Dudley Simpson | **Broadcast:** 25 January–1 March 1969, 7.2m (N, 1986; DVD, 2011)

Précis: Ice Warriors invade a lunar transmat station, intent on sending deadly seeds to Earth . . .

Observations: The spreading fungus was filmed on Hampstead Heath, North London. The fungus itself was a product of the BBC's foam-generating machine, while the seeds were powder-filled balloons. The Ice Lord costume was made from rubber and fibreglass by Jack and John Lovell. Patrick Troughton was absent for episode four.

Verdict: The plot's fine, but a reliance on artsy direction and dull sets means the story never really gets off the ground. 4/10

49. THE SPACE PIRATES (six episodes)

Cast: Gordon Gostelow (*Milo Clancey*), Jack May (*Hermack*), Donald Gee (*Warne*), Dudley Foster (*Caven*), Edmond Knight (*Dom Issigri*), Lisa Daniely (*Madelaine Issigri*), Brian Peck (*Dervish*), George Layton

(*Penn*), Nik Zaran (*Sorba*) | **Crew:** Director: Michael Hart; Writer: Robert Holmes; Music: Dudley Simpson | **Broadcast:** 8 March–12 April 1969, 5.9m (N, 1990; DVD, 2004 [episode 2]; CD, 2003)

Précis: The Tardis crew join the International Space Corps on the trail of intergalactic pirates . . .

Observations: Ian Scoones and Nick Alder supervised the most model filming yet conducted for the series, assisted by John Horton who had worked on *2001: A Space Odyssey* (1968). Jack May was better known as Nelson Gabriel on BBC Radio 4's *The Archers*. The three regulars were all absent from the final episode's studio recording.

Verdict: An attempt to emulate the slick, Americanised *Thunderbirds*, this serial is a clinically directed, lamely acted flop in which the regulars hardly appear. 2/10

50. THE WAR GAMES (ten episodes)

Cast: Jane Sherwin (*Jennifer*), David Savile (*Carstairs*), Terence Bayler (*Barrington*), Brian Forster (*Willis*), Noel Coleman (*Smythe*), Hubert Rees (*Ransom*), Esmond Webb (*Burns*), Richard Steele (*Gorton*), David Valla (*Crane*), Gregg Palmer (*Lucke*), David Garfield (*Von Weich*), Bill Hutchinson (*Thompson*), Terry Adams (*Riley*), Edward Brayshaw (*War Chief*), Leslie Schofield (*Leroy*), Vernon Dobtcheff (*Scientist*), Rudolph Walker (*Harper*), Michael Lynch (*Spencer*), Graham Weston (*Russell*), James Bree (*Security Chief*), David Troughton (*Moor*), Philip Madoc (*War Lord*), Peter Craze (*Du Pont*), Michael Napier-Brown (*Arturo Villar*), Stephen Hubay (*Petrov*), Clare Jenkins (*Tanya*), Bernard Horsfall, Trevor Martin, Clyde Pollitt (*Time Lords*), Freddie Wilson (*Quark*), John Levene (*Yeti*), Tony Harwood (*Ice Warrior*), Roy Pearce (*Cyberman*), Robert Jewell (*Dalek*) | **Crew:** Director: David Maloney; Writers: Malcolm Hulke & Terrance Dicks; Music: Dudley Simpson | **Broadcast:** 19 April–21 June 1969, 4.9m (N, 1979; DVD, 2009; A, 2011)

Précis: A renegade of the Doctor's own race has trapped the Tardis crew in a variety of dangerous Earth war zones . . .

Observations: *The War Games* replaced two aborted storylines of six and four parts respectively. The Sheepcote rubbish tip in Brighton represented no man's land, while a farm in Seaford, East Sussex, was the site of the Roman chariot charge. Other locations were Clayton, West Dean and East Dean, all in West Sussex. Patrick Troughton's son, David, appeared in episode six and the serial was notable for revealing the Doctor's origins, although his home planet went unnamed. It was uncertain whether *Doctor Who* would continue into the next decade, so the final episode was left open-ended.

Verdict: Overlong, obviously, but there's no denying that this is a turning point in the show's history. The Doctor's riposte to the Time Lords is heady stuff, and the psychedelic sets and costumes are groovy. Just a shame there's no regeneration. 9/10

SEASON 7

Producers: Derrick Sherwin (51) & Barry Letts (52–54)
Script Editor: Terrance Dicks
Third Doctor: Jon Pertwee
Companions: Caroline John (*Liz Shaw*) & Nicholas
Courtney (*Brigadier Lethbridge-Stewart*)

51. SPEARHEAD FROM SPACE (four episodes)

Cast: Hugh Burden (*Channing*), John Woodnutt (*Hibbert*), Neil Wilson
(*Sam Seeley*), Betty Bowden (*Meg Seeley*), Derek Smee (*Ransome*),
John Breslin (*Munro*), Antony Webb (*Dr Henderson*), Hamilton Dyce
(*Scobie*), Talfryn Thomas (*Mullins*), George Lee (*Forbes*), Ivan Orton,
Hein Viljoen, Barry Ashton, Bob Williman, Arnold Chazen, Cy Town,
Keith Ashley (*Autons*) | **Crew:** Director: Derek Martinus; Writer: Robert
Holmes; Music: Dudley Simpson | **Broadcast:** 3–24 January 1970, 8.2m
(N, 1974; DVD, 2000; A, 2008)

Précis: The Doctor helps UNIT thwart an invasion of plastic facsimiles . . .
Observations: A studio strike allowed the story to be shot
entirely on film, a first for *Doctor Who*. Amongst the extensive
locations were the BBC Training Centre at Wood Norton in

Worcestershire, the rear of St Pancras Station (as UNIT HQ), Ealing Broadway (the famous shop dummies sequence), a doll factory in Holloway and Madame Tussaud's Waxworks. Bernard Lodge designed a new title sequence with monochrome electronic howlround filmed through coloured gels, while Pertwee's dandified costume was the creation of Christine Rawlins. The story was accompanied by a *Radio Times* cover.

Verdict: Stilted and often inaudible, this is really only notable for its iconic scenes of rampaging shop dummies. Repeated music cues, a crass comedy performance by Pertwee and a monster that would be more at home in *The Goodies* all conspire to drag the story down. 4/10

52. DOCTOR WHO AND THE SILURIANS

(seven episodes)

Cast: Peter Miles (*Lawrence*), Norman Jones (*Baker*), Fulton Mackay (*Quinn*), Thomasine Heiner (*Miss Dawson*), Paul Darrow (*Hawkins*), Geoffrey Palmer (*Masters*), Peter Halliday (*Silurian voices*), Dave Carter, Nigel Johns, Pat Gorman, Paul Barton, Simon Cain (*Silurians*) | **Crew:** Director: Timothy Combe; Writer: Malcolm Hulke; Music: Carey Blyton | **Broadcast:** 31 January–14 March 1970, 7.7m (N, 1974; DVD, 2008; CD, 2006)

Précis: Cave-dwelling Silurians are causing power losses in an underground atomic research station . . .

Observations: This was the first story to be shot on colour video and therefore the first to utilise Colour Separation Overlay (CSO) to combine pictures from more than one camera source. Filmwork mainly centred in Godalming and Milford, Surrey, and Marylebone Station, London. Bessie, the Doctor's yellow Edwardian car, appears here for the first time. Six PVC and latex Silurian costumes were constructed by James Ward.

Verdict: Stylishly directed and convincingly acted, this is an engrossing story spoiled only by Carey Blyton's awful music. 8/10

53. THE AMBASSADORS OF DEATH
(seven episodes)

Cast: Ronald Allen (*Cornish*), Michael Wisher (*Wakefield*), Robert Cawdron (*Taltalian*), John Abineri (*Carrington*), Ric Felgate (*Van Lyden/Alien*), Steve Peters (*Lefee/Alien*), Neville Simons (*Michaels/Alien*), Dallas Cavell (*Quinlan*), William Dysart (*Reegan*), Cyril Shaps (*Lennox*), John Levene (*Benton*), Peter Noel Cook (*Alien Captain*), Geoffrey Beevers (*Johnson*), Peter Halliday (*Aliens' voices*) | **Crew:** Director: Michael Ferguson; Writer: David Whitaker; Music: Dudley Simpson | **Broadcast:** 21 March–2 May 1970, 7.3m (N, 1987; CD, 2009)

Précis: The Doctor discovers that astronauts from a Mars probe have been replaced by aliens . . .
Observations: Film locations included Marlow Weir, Bucks; Southall Gasworks, Middx; and cement works in Northfleet, Kent. Uniquely, the title sequence was split either side of the recapped cliffhangers. Episode four was delayed by half an hour because of the FA Cup Final (a 2–2 draw). A trailer, with Pertwee directly addressing the viewer, aired immediately after the previous story.
Verdict: Too long, but it's interesting to see a *Doctor Who* story that relies on human villains instead of monsters. Flashy direction, convincing fight scenes and good incidental music add much-needed weight to a padded storyline with a very flat ending. 7/10

54. INFERNO (seven episodes)

Cast: Olaf Pooley (*Stahlman*), Sheila Dunn (*Petra Williams*), Derek Newark (*Greg Sutton*), Christopher Benjamin (*Keith Gold*), John Levene (*Benton/Primord*), Walter Randall (*Slocum*), Ian Fairbairn (*Bromley*), Derek Ware (*Wyatt*), Dave Carter, Pat Gorman, Philip Ryan, Peter Thompson, Walter Henry (*Primords*) | **Crew:** Directors: Douglas Camfield & Barry Letts; Writer: Don Houghton | **Broadcast:** 9 May–20 June 1970, 5.8m (N, 1984; DVD, 2006)

Précis: An experimental drilling project – here and on a parallel world – goes hideously wrong . . .

Observations: An industrial plant at Hoo St Werburgh, Kent, was used for Project Inferno. After Douglas Camfield collapsed with a heart murmur halfway through the production, most of the studio recording was completed by producer Barry Letts. Six actors were made up as Primords, with guttural screams courtesy of Brian Hodgson of the Radiophonic Workshop. *Inferno* was the last *Doctor Who* story not to have specially composed incidental music.

Verdict: The most intense *Doctor Who* story ever – the gradual build-up of tension is magnificently orchestrated and the ever-present noise of the drill means everyone has to shout to be heard. The cliffhanger to episode six is arguably the finest in the show's history. 10/10

SEASON 8

Producer: Barry Letts
Script Editor: Terrance Dicks
Third Doctor: Jon Pertwee
Companions: Katy Manning (*Jo Grant*), Nicholas
Courtney (*Brigadier Lethbridge-Stewart*), John Levene
(*Sergeant Benton*, 55–57, 59) & Richard Franklin (*Captain
Yates*, 55–57, 59)

55. TERROR OF THE AUTONS (four episodes)

Cast: Roger Delgado (*The Master*), Michael Wisher (*Rex Farrel*),
Harry Towb (*McDermott*), Stephen Jack (*John Farrel*), Barbara Leake
(*Mrs Farrel*), Roy Stewart (*Strong Man*), Dermot Tuohy (*Brownrose*),
John Baskcomb (*Luigi Rossini*), Christopher Burgess (*Phillips*), Frank
Mills (*Director*), David Garth (*Time Lord*), Terry Walsh, Pat Gorman
(*Autons*), Haydn Jones (*Auton voice*), Tommy Reynolds (*Troll Doll*) |
Crew: Director: Barry Letts; Writer: Robert Holmes; Music: Dudley
Simpson | Broadcast: 2–23 January 1971, 8m (N; A, 2010)

Précis: The Master, an evil renegade Time Lord, helps
the Nestene Consciousness to attempt another Earth
invasion . . .

Observations: Locations included Roberts Brothers Circus, Leyton, London, and Thermo Plastics, Dunstable, Beds. New assistant Jo Grant, arch-villain the Master and UNIT soldier Captain Mike Yates all made their debut appearances, with Delgado featuring prominently on a *Radio Times* cover to promote the new series.

Verdict: The Autons barely feature in this tackier, but more exciting, remake of *Spearhead from Space* (51). The various plastic-related killings are gleefully inventive. 8/10

56. THE MIND OF EVIL (six episodes)

Cast: Neil McCarthy (*Barnham*), William Marlowe (*Mailer*), Roger Delgado (*Keller/The Master*), Pik-Sen Lim (*Chin Lee*), Michael Sheard (*Summers*), Tommy Duggan (*Alcott*), Simon Lack (*Kettering*), Haydn Jones (*Vosper*), Patrick Godfrey (*Cosworth*), Kristopher Kum (*Fu Peng*), Eric Mason (*Green*), Roy Purcell (*Powers*), Fernanda Marlowe (*Bell*) | **Crew:** Director: Timothy Combe; Writer: Don Houghton; Music: Dudley Simpson | **Broadcast:** 30 January–6 March 1971, 7.6m (N, 1985; CD, 2009)

Précis: The Master uses prisoners to hijack a nerve-gas missile and blow up a peace conference . . .

Observations: Extensive use was made of Dover Castle, Kent, to represent Stangmoor Prison, with members of the production team padding out episode five's big fight sequence. London scenes were filmed in Kensington and the Ministry of Defence supplied a genuine Bloodhound missile.

Verdict: Unrelentingly grim, if a little repetitious, this throwback to Season 7's hard-edged narrative style has many effective moments and the Master excels as a Mafia-style boss. 8/10

57. THE CLAWS OF AXOS (four episodes)

Cast: Paul Grist (*Filer*), Donald Hewlett (*Hardiman*), Roger Delgado (*The Master*), Peter Bathurst (*Chinn*), David Savile (*Winser*), Derek Ware (*Pigbin Josh*), Bernard Holley (*Axon Man*), Patricia Gordino (*Axon Woman*), John Hicks (*Axon Boy*), Debbie Lee London (*Axon Girl*), Tim Pigott-Smith (*Harker*), Peter Holmes, Steve Smart, Pierce McAvoy, George Howse, Stuart Fell, Clinton Morris, Marc Boyle, Jack Cooper (*Axon Monsters*) | **Crew:** Director: Michael Ferguson; Writers: Bob Baker & Dave Martin; Music: Dudley Simpson | **Broadcast:** 13 March–3 April 1971, 7.4m (N, 1977; DVD, 2005)

Précis: Beautiful aliens offer the British Government a miraculous substance called Axonite . . .
Observations: Dungeness Beach and Power Station in Kent were the chosen locations. Odd weather conditions (snow, rain, sunshine and fog) were explained away by the Axons' arrival. Kenneth Sharp redesigned the Tardis interior, last seen in *The War Games* (50). Captions with the original title of *The Vampire from Space* were reshot shortly before transmission.
Verdict: Crass, but immensely likeable – a surfeit of undeveloped ideas jostling for attention against wildly variable effects and psychedelic direction. Pigbin Josh deserves a story all to himself. 9/10

58. COLONY IN SPACE (six episodes)

Cast: Roger Delgado (*Adjudicator/The Master*), David Webb (*Leeson*), John Ringham (*Ashe*), Helen Worth (*Mary*), Sheila Grant (*Jane*), Nicholas Pennell (*Winton*), Roy Skelton (*Norton*), Morris Perry (*Dent*), Tony Caunter (*Morgan*), Bernard Kay (*Caldwell*), John Herrington (*Holden*), Norman Atkyns (*Guardian*), Roy Heymann (*Alien Priest*), Peter Forbes-Robertson, John Baker, Graham Leaman (*Time Lords*), John Scott Martin (*IMC Robot*) | **Crew:** Director: Michael Briant; Writer: Malcolm Hulke; Music: Dudley Simpson | **Broadcast:** 10 April–15 May 1971, 8.5m (N, 1974; A, 2007)

Précis: Colonists fight against a ruthless mining company on a barren planet . . .

Observations: A china clay quarry near St Austell, Cornwall, provided the locations. The story marked the first interplanetary Tardis voyage since *The War Games* (50) and the last use of the photographic blow-up interior wall, as seen in the very first story.

Verdict: An intelligent morality play, saddled with dreary sets and locations. If you persevere, there are many fine moments. 6/10

59. THE DÆMONS (five episodes)

Cast: Damaris Hayman (*Miss Hawthorne*), Roger Delgado (*Magister/ The Master*), Robin Wentworth (*Horner*), David Simeon (*Alistair Fergus*), John Joyce (*Garvin*), Don McKillop (*Bert*), Rollo Gamble (*Winstanley*), Jon Croft (*Tom*), Alec Linstead (*Osgood*), Matthew Corbett (*Jones*), Stanley Mason (*Bok*), Stephen Thorne (*Azal*) | **Crew:** Director: Christopher Barry; Writer: 'Guy Leopold' (pseudonym for Barry Letts & Robert Sloman); Music: Dudley Simpson | **Broadcast:** 22 May–19 June 1971, 8.3m (N, 1974; A, 2008)

Précis: Devil's End is cut off from civilisation when an archaeological dig uncovers seemingly occult forces . . .

Observations: When filming took place in the Wiltshire village of Aldbourne, a late snowfall hampered shooting of the heat-barrier sequences. The shot of the exploding model church in episode five provoked complaints from naïve viewers who thought the BBC had destroyed a real building.

Verdict: This wannabe occult chiller gradually dissipates into a technobabble-filled damp squib. The UNIT 'family' do their stuff in civvies and the quintessentially English village is a pleasant backdrop, but much of the action now seems dated. 6/10

SEASON 9

Producer: Barry Letts
Script Editor: Terrance Dicks
Third Doctor: Jon Pertwee
Companions: Katy Manning (*Jo Grant*), Nicholas Courtney (*Brigadier Lethbridge-Stewart,* 60, 64), John Levene (*Sergeant Benton,* 60, 64) & Richard Franklin (*Captain Yates,* 60, 64)

60. DAY OF THE DALEKS (four episodes)

Cast: Wilfrid Carter (*Styles*), Aubrey Woods (*Controller*), Anna Barry (*Anat*), Jimmy Winston (*Shura*), Scott Fredericks (*Boaz*), Valentine Palmer (*Monia*), Andrew Carr (*Senior Guard*), Peter Hill (*Manager*), Alex MacIntosh (*Himself*), Oliver Gilbert, Peter Messaline (*Dalek voices*), John Scott Martin, Ricky Newby, Murphy Grumbar (*Daleks*), Rick Lester, Maurice Bush, David Joyce, Frank Menzies, Bruce Wells, Geoffrey Todd (*Ogrons*) | **Crew:** Director: Paul Bernard; Writer: Louis Marks; Music: Dudley Simpson | **Broadcast:** 1–22 January 1972, 9.6m (N, 1974; DVD, 2011)

Précis: Guerrillas from a Dalek-controlled twenty-second century travel back in time to prevent WWIII . . .

Observations: Dropmore House in Burnham, Bucks, was the location for the peace conference, while a railway bridge over the Paddington Branch of the Grand Union Canal, near Bull's Bridge in Hayes, Middx, was the site chosen as the time tunnel. The three 1960s Daleks were repainted – two dark grey and one gold – and had pupils added to their eyestalks. The Ogron half-masks, reminiscent of the *Planet of the Apes* films, were sculpted by John Friedlander. Frank Bellamy painted a *Radio Times* cover to advertise the story.

Verdict: This intelligently scripted *Terminator* prototype features a credible future world and an effective documentary-style approach to much of the present-day action. On the downside, the Daleks seem oddly static. 9/10

61. THE CURSE OF PELADON (four episodes)

Cast: David Troughton (*Peladon*), Geoffrey Toone (*Hepesh*), Stuart Fell (*Alpha Centauri*), Ysanne Churchman (*Alpha Centauri voice*), Terry Bale (*Arcturus voice*), Alan Bennion (*Izlyr*), Sonny Caldinez (*Ssorg*), Henry Gilbert (*Torbis*), Gordon St Clair (*Grun*), Nick Hobbs (*Aggedor*) | **Crew:** Director: Lennie Mayne; Writer: Brian Hayles; Music: Dudley Simpson | **Broadcast:** 29 January–19 February 1972, 9.4m (N, 1975; DVD, 2010; CD, 2007)

Précis: The ghost of Aggedor threatens to stop Peladon joining the Galactic Federation . . .

Observations: This story and its sequel, *The Monster of Peladon* (73), were the only two Pertwee serials not to have any location filming. Sonny Caldinez and Alan Bennion resumed roles similar to the ones they played in *The Seeds of Death* (48), although Bennion's Ice Lord costume was new. Alpha Centauri was given a cloak by director Lennie Mayne to disguise its phallic appearance.

Verdict: An adventure dripping with atmosphere and featuring a memorable cast of green-skinned monsters. Pertwee and Manning are on top form. 10/10

62. THE SEA DEVILS (six episodes)

Cast: Roger Delgado (*The Master*), Clive Morton (*Trenchard*), Edwin Richfield (*Hart*), June Murphy (*Blythe*), Declan Mulholland (*Clark*), Donald Sumpter (*Ridgeway*), Martin Boddey (*Walker*), Hugh Futcher (*Hickman*), Pat Gorman, Brian Nolan, Steve Ismay, Jeff Witherick, Frank Seton, Billy Horrigan, Mike Stephens, Mike Horsborough, Marc Boyle, Peter Brace, Stuart Fell, Terry Walsh (*Sea Devils*), Peter Forbes-Robertson (*Chief Sea Devil*) | **Crew:** Director: Michael Briant; Writer: Malcolm Hulke; Music: Malcolm Clarke | **Broadcast:** 26 February–1 April 1972, 8.2m (N, 1974; DVD, 2008; CD, 2006)

Précis: The Sea Devils, aquatic cousins of the Silurians, threaten to wipe out humanity . . .

Observations: Extensive location filming took place at various naval sites in Portsmouth, Hants, as well as Norris Castle and Whitecliff Bay on the Isle of Wight and a No Man's Land sea-fort in the Solent. Sequences were also taken from Royal Navy training films. Six Sea Devil costumes were made from latex by Maggie Fletcher, with turtle-like heads sculpted by John Friedlander. Peter Day's nuclear submarine model coincidentally resembled a top-secret prototype developed by Naval Intelligence.

Verdict: This gaudy rehash of *Doctor Who and the Silurians* (52) is on a par with *The Green Death* (69) as the Pertwee story everyone remembers. Disorientating direction and music provide plenty of chills, but ultimately this is nothing more than a glorified Naval recruitment film. Delgado, however, is sublime. 7/10

63. THE MUTANTS (six episodes)

Cast: Paul Whitsun-Jones (*Marshal*), Rick James (*Cotton*), Christopher Coll (*Stubbs*), Geoffrey Palmer (*Administrator*), James Mellor (*Varan*), Jonathan Sherwood (*Varan's son*), Garrick Hagon (*Ky*), George Pravda (*Jaeger*), John Hollis (*Sondergaard*), John Scott Martin, Mike Torres, Eddie Sommer, Laurie Goode, Nick Thompson Hill, Mike Mungarven, Rick Newby, Bill Gosling (*Mutts*) | **Crew:** Director: Christopher Barry;

Writers: Bob Baker & Dave Martin; Music: Tristram Cary | **Broadcast:** 8 April–13 May 1972, 7.8m (N, 1977, DVD, 2011)

Précis: On Solos the sadistic Marshal is exterminating the native mutant population . . .

Observations: Cave exteriors were shot at a quarry in Northfleet and cave interiors at Chislehurst Caves, both in Kent. Six Mutt costumes were made by freelance prop-builder Alistair Bowtell. Technological advances meant that five camera shots could be combined for complex special effects sequences, such as Ky's episode six transformation.

Verdict: An interesting concept padded out mercilessly for six episodes, with dire acting and terrible effects. The Mutants are stunning though. 4/10

64. THE TIME MONSTER (six episodes)

Cast: Roger Delgado (*Thascalos/The Master*), Wanda Moore (*Ruth*), Ian Collier (*Stuart*), John Wyse (*Dr Percival*), Donald Eccles (*Krasis*), Aidan Murphy (*Hippias*), George Cormack (*Dalios*), Ingrid Pitt (*Galleia*), Susan Penhaligon (*Lakis*), Dave Prowse (*Minotaur*), Ingrid Bower (*Kronos face*), Marc Boyle (*Kronos*) | **Crew:** Director: Paul Bernard; Writer: Robert Sloman; Music: Dudley Simpson | **Broadcast:** 20 May–24 June 1972, 7.4m (N, 1985; DVD, 2010)

Précis: The Master travels to Atlantis to unleash the power of Kronos the time eater . . .

Observations: Swallowfield Park in Berks was the ficti-tious Newton Institute, while Stratfield Saye Park, Hants, provided the backdrop to various scenes involving the Doctor's car and a UNIT convoy attacked by historical figures. Dave Prowse went on to become the Green Cross Code Man and Darth Vader in the *Star Wars* films. A new Tardis interior designed by Tim Gleeson made its first and only appearance.

Verdict: An unfunny *Doctor Who* spoof, in which pretty much everything fails. 2/10

SEASON 10

Producer: Barry Letts
Script Editor: Terrance Dicks
Third Doctor: Jon Pertwee
Companions: Katy Manning (*Jo Grant*), Nicholas
Courtney (*Brigadier Lethbridge-Stewart*, 65, 69), John
Levene (*Sergeant Benton*, 65, 69) & Richard Franklin
(*Captain Yates*, 65, 69)

65. THE THREE DOCTORS (four episodes)

Cast: William Hartnell (*First Doctor*), Patrick Troughton (*Second Doctor*), Rex Robinson (*Tyler*), Stephen Thorne (*Omega*), Laurie Webb (*Ollis*), Patricia Prior (*Mrs Ollis*), Roy Purcell (*President*), Clyde Pollitt (*Chancellor*), Graham Leaman (*Time Lord*), Cy Town, Rick Newby, Murphy Grumbar, John Scott Martin (*Gell Guards*), Alan Chuntz (*Omega's Champion*) | **Crew:** Director: Lennie Mayne; Writers: Bob Baker & Dave Martin; Music: Dudley Simpson | **Broadcast:** 30 December 1972–20 January 1973, 10.3m (N, 1975; DVD, 2003; A, 2010)

Précis: The Time Lords call on the first two Doctors to aid the current one in stopping stellar engineer Omega

– trapped inside a black hole – from causing universal destruction . . .

Observations: This story marked William Hartnell's final acting assignment. He appeared on pre-filmed inserts only, reading his lines off cue cards as memory loss prevented him taking part in the studio. UNIT HQ scenes were filmed at Halings House, Denham Green, Bucks, while Springwell Quarry in Rickmansworth, Herts, represented the black hole landscape. Four latex Gell Guards were made by Alistair Bowtell. Roger Liminton designed a new Tardis interior set, harking back to the original one in *An Unearthly Child* (1). New synthesised title music was arranged by Delia Derbyshire and Paddy Kingsland, but was scrapped just before transmission. Appropriately, a tenth *Radio Times* cover featured all three Doctors.

Verdict: An obvious idea done on the cheap. 4/10

66. CARNIVAL OF MONSTERS (four episodes)

Cast: Peter Halliday (*Pletrac*), Michael Wisher (*Kalik*), Terence Lodge (*Orum*), Leslie Dwyer (*Vorg*), Cheryl Hall (*Shirna*), Tenniel Evans (*Daly*), Ian Marter (*Andrews*), Jenny McCracken (*Claire*), Andrew Staines (*Captain*) | **Crew:** Director: Barry Letts; Writer: Robert Holmes; Music: Dudley Simpson | **Broadcast:** 27 January–17 February 1973, 9.2m (N, 1977; DVD, 2011)

Précis: Aboard a 1920s cargo ship, the Doctor and Jo contend with an anachronistic plesiosaur . . .

Observations: Filming took place on the Royal Fleet Auxiliary ship *Robert Dundas* as it sailed from Chatham to Sheerness on the River Medway in Kent. The Drashigs' hunting grounds were filmed on Tillingham Marshes, Essex. Three latex and foam Drashig puppets were made, with fox skulls as heads.

Verdict: Charming and timeless, this larger-than-life story mixes the absurd with the ordinary to great effect. Big concepts, scary monsters and a fast and witty script make this one of the most satisfying *Doctor Who* adventures ever. 10/10

67. FRONTIER IN SPACE (six episodes)

Cast: Michael Hawkins (*Williams*), Roger Delgado (*Sirius 4 Commissioner/The Master*), John Woodnutt (*Draconian Emperor*), Peter Birrel (*Draconian Prince*), Vera Fusek (*Earth President*), Richard Shaw (*Cross*), Harold Goldblatt (*Dale*), John Rees (*Hardy*), James Culliford (*Stewart*), Dennis Bowen (*Governor*), Stephen Thorne, Michael Kilgarriff, Rick Lester (*Ogrons*), Michael Wisher (*Dalek voices*), John Scott Martin, Murphy Grumbar, Cy Town (*Daleks*) | **Crew:** Director: Paul Bernard; Writer: Malcolm Hulke; Music: Dudley Simpson | **Broadcast:** 24 February–31 March 1973, 8m (N, 1976; DVD, 2009; A, 2008)

Précis: In the twenty-sixth century, Earth and Draconia are fighting for control of the galaxy . . .
Observations: Walkways around the Hayward Gallery and a house in Fitzroy Park, Highgate, provided the London locations, while a quarry in Redhill, Surrey, was the Ogrons' homeworld. Spacecraft for the story were reused from Gerry Anderson's *Thunderbirds* and *UFO*. This was Roger Delgado's last appearance as the Master – he was killed on 18 June 1973 in a car crash in Turkey. David Maloney reshot the ending to tie in more closely with his following Dalek story.
Verdict: An overlong and uninteresting space opera – a genre *Doctor Who* has never done well. Delgado's exit is particularly badly handled. 4/10

68. PLANET OF THE DALEKS (six episodes)

Cast: Bernard Horsfall (*Taron*), Tim Preece (*Codal*), Prentis Hancock (*Vaber*), Roy Skelton (*Wester*), Jane How (*Rebec*), Alan Tucker (*Latep*), Michael Wisher, Roy Skelton (*Dalek voices/Spiridon voices*), John Scott Martin, Cy Town, Murphy Grumbar (*Daleks*), Tony Starr (*Dalek Supreme*) | **Crew:** Director: David Maloney; Writer: Terry Nation;

Music: Dudley Simpson | **Broadcast:** 7 April–12 May 1973, 9.7m (N, 1976; DVD, 2009; A, 2004)

Précis: On Spiridon, a Thal commando team find a vast Dalek army hidden under an ice volcano . . .

Observations: Location filming was conducted in a quarry in Redhill, Surrey. Commercially sold Louis Marx toys provided the Dalek army, and the Dalek Supreme was a modified prop, loaned by Terry Nation, from the 1966 film *Daleks' Invasion Earth: 2150 AD* with a torch stuck onto its eyestalk.

Verdict: A believable jungle setting and ambitious (if unoriginal) ideas make this live-action comic-strip romp breeze along in fine style. 8/10

69. THE GREEN DEATH (six episodes)

Cast: Jerome Willis (*Stevens*), Stewart Bevan (*Clifford Jones*), Tony Adams (*Elgin*), Ben Howard (*Hinks*), Mostyn Evans (*Dai Evans*), Talfryn Thomas (*Dave*), Roy Skelton (*James*), Roy Evans (*Bert*), John Scott Martin (*Hughes*), Mitzi McKenzie (*Nancy*), John Rolfe (*Fell*), Brychan Powell (*PM*), John Dearth (*BOSS voice*) | **Crew:** Director: Michael Briant; Writer: Robert Sloman; Music: Dudley Simpson | **Broadcast:** 19 May–23 June 1973, 7.7m (N, 1975; DVD, 2004; A, 2008)

Précis: In Llanfairfach, pollution from Global Chemicals is creating giant maggots and deadly slime . . .

Observations: Ogilvie Colliery at Deri, near Glamorgan, stood in for the fictitious Llanfairfach Colliery. The RCA International factory in Brynmawr, Powys, was used for Global Chemicals (originally Universal Chemicals). The maggots were a mixture of water-filled condoms, glove and rod puppets, static props pulled along on wires, and live maggots on model sets. UNIT's aerial bombs were lavatory ballcocks. The unseen PM was named after Liberal Party leader Jeremy Thorpe.

Verdict: One of the very best UNIT stories, offering terrifying maggots, horrible green slime and some very scary cliffhangers. There is also real character development and an attempt to address adult themes in an adult way. Jo's departure is one of the series' saddest moments. 10/10

SEASON 11

Producer: Barry Letts
Script Editor: Terrance Dicks
Third Doctor: Jon Pertwee
Fourth Doctor: Tom Baker (74)
Companions: Elisabeth Sladen (*Sarah Jane Smith*),
Nicholas Courtney (*Brigadier Lethbridge-Stewart*, 70–71,
74), John Levene (*Sergeant Benton*, 71, 74), Richard
Franklin (*Captain Yates*, 71, 74)

70. THE TIME WARRIOR (four parts)

Cast: Kevin Lindsay (*Linx*), David Daker (*Irongron*), John J Carney
(*Bloodaxe*), Donald Pelmear (*Rubeish*), June Brown (*Lady Eleanor*),
Jeremy Bulloch (*Hal*), Alan Rowe (*Edward of Wessex*), Sheila Fay (*Meg*),
Bella Emberg, Mary Rennie (*Kitchen Hags*) | **Crew:** Director: Alan
Bromly; Writer: Robert Holmes; Music: Dudley Simpson | **Broadcast:**
15 December 1973–5 January 1974, 8.2m (N, 1978; DVD, 2007; A, 2008)

Précis: In the thirteenth century, a Sontaran is abducting
scientists to restore his crashed spaceship . . .
Observations: Location filming took place at Peckforton
Castle, Cheshire. A new 'slit-scan' animated title sequence

debuted with this story, designed by Bernard Lodge as a deliberate nod towards *2001: A Space Odyssey*'s stargate trip. Jeremy Bulloch found later fame as Bobba Fett in the *Star Wars* films, while June Brown is more famous as Dot from *EastEnders*. Linx's latex mask was modelled by John Friedlander and his quilted Lurex costume was designed by James Acheson. Pertwee and fans featured on a *Radio Times* cover. The Doctor's home planet was finally named as Gallifrey.

Verdict: A clever hybrid of history and science fiction. Linx is a chilling creation and, despite the hammy acting, there are some great moments. 8/10

71. INVASION OF THE DINOSAURS (six parts)

Cast: Noel Johnson (*Charles Grover*), Peter Miles (*Professor Whitaker*), Martin Jarvis (*Butler*), John Bennett (*General Finch*), Terence Wilton (*Mark*), Brian Badcoe (*Adam*), Carmen Silvera (*Ruth*), Gordon Reid (*Phillips*), George Bryson (*Ogden*), Trevor Lawrence (*Lodge*), Dave Carter (*Duffy*) | **Crew:** Director: Paddy Russell; Writer: Malcolm Hulke; Music: Dudley Simpson | **Broadcast:** 12 January–16 February 1974, 9.6m (N, 1976; A, 2007)

Précis: Dinosaurs terrorise London and Sarah uncovers a high-ranking plot to alter the course of time . . .

Observations: Rodney Fuller designed five puppet dinosaurs, usually filmed on model backgrounds, but sometimes inserted into studio footage via CSO (Colour Separation Overlay). Part one was entitled *Invasion* to maintain the surprise of the first cliffhanger. The Doctor's unnamed futuristic car, sometimes referred to as the Alien or the Whomobile, made its first appearance. London locations included Westminster Bridge, Whitehall, Trafalgar Square, Haymarket, Covent Garden, Moorfields, Southall and Wimbledon Common.

Verdict: An intelligent and atmospheric conspiracy tale, with a concept-heavy plot that's sufficiently well written to make up for some of the poorer effects work. The fake colony ship is a wonderfully cynical idea and the scenes of deserted London are fabulously eerie. 10/10

72. DEATH TO THE DALEKS (four parts)

Cast: Neil Seiler (*Stewart*), Duncan Lamont (*Galloway*), John Abineri (*Railton*), Julian Fox (*Hamilton*), Joy Harrison (*Tarrant*), Arnold Yarrow (*Bellal*), Michael Wisher (*Dalek voices*), John Scott Martin, Cy Town, Murphy Grumbar (*Daleks*), Mostyn Evans (*High Priest*) | **Crew:** Director: Michael Briant; Writer: Terry Nation; Music: Carey Blyton | **Broadcast:** 23 February–16 March 1974, 9.4m (N, 1978)

Précis: Drained of power, the Tardis lands on a barren planet where the Doctor and Sarah are caught in a power struggle between humans and Daleks . . .

Observations: Filming took place in a quarry at Gallows Hill, Dorset. The four Daleks (one sans operator) were repainted silver to bring them more in line with their original colour and moved around the quarry on camera dolly tracks. Ten Exxilon costumes were made from calico and terylene wadding, while their city was a large, carved polystyrene model.

Verdict: Carey Blyton's score is, as you'd expect, awful, but there are some atmospheric model shots and the Exxilons are very creepy. The opening ten minutes are superb. 7/10

73. THE MONSTER OF PELADON (six parts)

Cast: Frank Gatliff (*Ortron*), Nina Thomas (*Queen Thalira*), Donald Gee (*Eckersley*), Ralph Watson (*Ettis*), Michael Crane (*Blor*), Sonny Caldinez (*Sskel*), Alan Bennion (*Azaxyr*), Nick Hobbs (*Aggedor*), Stuart Fell (*Alpha Centauri*), Ysanne Churchman (*Alpha Centauri voice*), Rex Robinson (*Gebek*), Gerald Taylor (*Vega Nexos*), David Cleeve, Kevin Moran, Alan Lenoir, Terence Denville (*Ice Warriors*) | **Crew:** Director: Lennie Mayne; Writer: Brian Hayles; Music: Dudley Simpson | **Broadcast:** 23 March–27 April 1974, 7.7m (N, 1980; DVD, 2010; CD, 2008)

Précis: The populace of Peladon is once more in fear of Aggedor's vengeful spirit . . .

Observations: Many people working on this story had also been employed on *The Curse of Peladon* (61). Costumes from that story were reused, along with three Ice Warriors previously seen in *The Ice Warriors* (39) and *The Seeds of Death* (48).

Verdict: Everything that made the previous Peladon tale so wonderful is sadly absent from this dull rehash. 2/10

74. PLANET OF THE SPIDERS (six parts)

Cast: John Dearth (*Lupton*), Cyril Shaps (*Clegg*), Kevin Lindsay (*Cho-je*), John Kane (*Tommy*), Ysanne Churchman, Kismet Delgado, Maureen Morris (*Spider voices*), George Cormack (*K'Anpo*), Carl Forgione (*Land*), Terence Lodge (*Moss*), Christopher Burgess (*Barnes*), Geoffrey Morris (*Sabor*), Gareth Hunt (*Arak*), Ralph Arliss (*Tuar*), Jenny Laird (*Neska*), Joanna Munro (*Rega*), Chubby Oates (*Policeman*) | **Crew:** Director: Barry Letts; Writer: Robert Sloman; Music: Dudley Simpson | **Broadcast:** 4 May–8 June 1974, 9m (N, 1975; A, 2009)

Précis: Giant spiders try to invade Earth through the pliable minds of meditating humans . . .

Observations: Filming took place at Tidmarsh and Stratfield Mortimer, Berks; Membury Airfield and Le Marchant Barracks, Wilts; and on the River Severn, Glos. The part-two chase involved Bessie, a (CSO) flying Whomobile, a gyrocopter, a hovercraft and a speedboat. Ian Scoones and Steve Bowman constructed approximately twenty latex-covered spiders. The original Great One prop was deemed too horrific and so was substituted with the Queen Spider version prior to studio recording.

Verdict: With its avant-garde editing, ridiculously OTT chase and gems of witty dialogue (especially from Tommy), this story is a fitting paean to the Pertwee era. Funny, sad, scary and thought-provoking, even Jenny Laird's terrible acting can't spoil this heady brew. 10/10

SEASON 12

Producers: Barry Letts (75) & Philip Hinchcliffe (76–79)
Script Editor: Robert Holmes
Third Doctor: Jon Pertwee (75)
Fourth Doctor: Tom Baker
Companions: Elisabeth Sladen (*Sarah Jane Smith*) & Ian
Marter (*Harry Sullivan*)

75. ROBOT (four parts)

Cast: Nicholas Courtney (*Brigadier*), John Levene (*Benton*), Alec
Linstead (*Jellicoe*), Patricia Maynard (*Hilda Winters*), Edward Burnham
(*Kettlewell*), Michael Kilgarriff (*K1 Robot*), Timothy Craven (*Stride*) |
Crew: Director: Christopher Barry; Writer: Terrance Dicks; Music:
Dudley Simpson | **Broadcast:** 28 December 1974–18 January 1975, 10m
(N, 1975; DVD, 2007; A, 2007)

Précis: A peaceful robot is reprogrammed to steal codes for
the world's nuclear weapons . . .
Observations: Mirroring Jon Pertwee's introductory story,
the locations this time recorded on OB (Outside Broadcast
Video) were centred round the BBC Training Centre at Wood
Norton. Bernard Lodge designed a new, simplified, title

sequence. Jim Acheson created Tom Baker's new costume, influenced by the French artist Toulouse-Lautrec and Baker's flatmate Christopher Tranchell.

Verdict: Stylishly put together, this action-packed adventure still works brilliantly. The robot is a wonderful creation and there are some stunning moments. 9/10

76. THE ARK IN SPACE (four parts)

Cast: Kenton Moore (*Noah*), Wendy Williams (*Vira*), Christopher Masters (*Libri*), Richardson Morgan (*Rogin*), John Gregg (*Lycett*), Brian Jacobs (*Dune*), Gladys Spencer (*High Minister's voice*), Stuart Fell, Nick Hobbs (*Wirrn*) | **Crew:** Director: Rodney Bennett; Writer: Robert Holmes; Music: Dudley Simpson | **Broadcast:** 25 January–15 February 1975, 11m (N, 1977; DVD, 2002)

Précis: On space station Nerva, parasitic Wirrn have started taking over the last of the human race . . .

Observations: Studio sets were shared with *Revenge of the Cybermen* (79). The Wirrn larva was made from the cutting-edge new material of bubble wrap. This and the following story were last-minute replacements for an abandoned six-part serial by John Lucarotti. Producer Philip Hinchcliffe heavily edited the part three scene of Noah begging to be killed, fearing it was unsuitable for young children.

Verdict: A harrowing tale of possession, the explicit horror is made all the more disturbing by the story's clinically white visual style. 10/10

77. THE SONTARAN EXPERIMENT (two parts)

Cast: Kevin Lindsay (*Styre/Marshal*), Donald Douglas (*Vural*), Terry Walsh (*Zake*), Peter Walshe (*Erak*), Glyn Jones (*Krans*), Peter Rutherford (*Roth*), Brian Ellis (*Prisoner*) | **Crew:** Director: Rodney Bennett; Writers: Bob Baker & Dave Martin; Music: Dudley Simpson | **Broadcast:** 22 February–1 March 1975, 10.7m (N, 1978; DVD, 2006)

Précis: On Earth, a Sontaran is conducting experiments on human colonists prior to invasion . . .

Observations: The first story to be shot entirely on exterior locations, OB videoing was carried out around Hound Tor on Dartmoor, Devon. Tom Baker slipped and broke his collarbone, necessitating stuntman Terry Walsh doubling for him in long shots and fight sequences. John Friedlander sculpted a new Sontaran mask for Styre, although the costume was reused from *The Time Warrior* (70).

Verdict: Very atmospheric, although the story makes absolutely no sense. Styre is a magnificent creation, thanks mainly to Kevin Lindsay's chillingly sadistic performance. 8/10

78. GENESIS OF THE DALEKS (six parts)

Cast: Peter Miles (*Nyder*), Michael Wisher (*Davros*), Roy Skelton (*Dalek voices*), John Scott Martin, Cy Town, Keith Ashley (*Daleks*), Dennis Chinnery (*Gharman*), Guy Siner (*Ravon*), Richard Reeves (*Kaled Leader*), Stephen Yardley (*Sevrin*), James Garbutt (*Ronson*), Tom Georgeson (*Kavell*), Ivor Roberts (*Mogran*), Harriet Philpin (*Bettan*), John Franklyn-Robbins (*Time Lord*) | **Crew:** Director: David Maloney; Writer: Terry Nation; Music: Dudley Simpson | **Broadcast:** 8 March–12 April 1975, 9.6m (N, 1976; DVD, 2006; CD, 2001)

Précis: The Time Lords send the Doctor to Skaro to stop the crippled genius Davros creating the Daleks . . .

Observations: Betchworth Quarry in Surrey represented Skaro. Davros' wheelchair, based on the lower half of a Dalek, was designed by Peter Day, his mask sculpted by John Friedlander and his costume created by Barbara Kidd. Seven Daleks were used, but only three were equipped with operators.

Verdict: The first half is very strong, the second less so. Lashings of atmosphere make up for the repetitious nature of the plot, although at times it's all rather talky. Peter Miles and Michael Wisher give chilling performances, but there is a distinct lack of Dalek action. 8/10

79. REVENGE OF THE CYBERMEN (four parts)

Cast: Jeremy Wilkin (*Kellman*), Ronald Leigh-Hunt (*Stevenson*), William Marlowe (*Lester*), Alec Wallis (*Warner*), David Collings (*Vorus*), Michael Wisher (*Magrik*), Kevin Stoney (*Tyrum*), Brian Grellis (*Sheprah*), Christopher Robbie (*Cyber Leader*), Melville Jones, Tony Lord, Pat Gorman (*Cybermen*) | **Crew:** Director: Michael Briant; Writer: Robert Holmes (from an idea by Gerry Davis); Music: Carey Blyton & Peter Howell | **Broadcast:** 19 April–10 May 1975, 9.3m (N, 1976; DVD, 2010)

Précis: Returning to Nerva in the past, the Doctor discovers Cybermats have poisoned the crew . . .
Observations: The interior of Voga was filmed at Wookey Hole Caves in Somerset. For Nerva, redressed sets were used from *The Ark in Space* (76). New Cybermats were designed by Jim Ward, while Alistair Bowtell built four 1970s-style Cybermen costumes, complete with flares.
Verdict: A good first part and the cave locations are excellent. But Christopher Robbie is a very emotive Cyberman and the effects are variable. 5/10

SEASON 13

Producer: Philip Hinchcliffe
Script Editor: Robert Holmes
Fourth Doctor: Tom Baker
Companions: Elisabeth Sladen (*Sarah Jane Smith*) & Ian
Marter (*Harry Sullivan*, 80, 83)

80. TERROR OF THE ZYGONS (four parts)

Cast: Nicholas Courtney (*Brigadier*), John Levene (*Benton*), John
Woodnutt (*Duke/Broton*), Angus Lennie (*Angus*), Tony Sibbald
(*Huckle*), Robert Russell (*Caber*), Lillias Walker (*Sister Lamont*), Hugh
Martin (*Munro*), Keith Ashley, Ronald Gough, David Selby (*Zygons*) |
Crew: Director: Douglas Camfield; Writer: Robert Banks Stewart;
Music: Geoffrey Burgon | Broadcast: 30 August–20 September 1975,
7.5m (N, 1976)

Précis: The Doctor discovers that the Loch Ness Monster
is no myth . . .
Observations: Charlton and Climping Beach, West Sussex,
were chosen to represent the Scottish Highlands. Some
shots of the Skarasen were achieved with stop-motion
animation. The three Zygon costumes, made by James

Acheson and John Friedlander, were based on human embryos.

Verdict: Creepy, dark and Scottish, this is a terrific tale that sadly falls to bits when it goes south of the border. 8/10

81. PLANET OF EVIL (four parts)

Cast: Frederick Jaeger (*Sorenson*), Ewen Solon (*Vishinsky*), Michael Wisher (*Morelli*), Prentis Hancock (*Salamar*), Graham Weston (*De Haan*), Louis Mahoney (*Ponti*), Terence Brook (*Braun*), Tony McEwan (*Baldwin*), Haydn Wood (*O'Hara*), Melvyn Bedford (*Reig*), Mike Lee Lane (*Antimatter Monster*) | **Crew:** Director: David Maloney; Writer: Louis Marks; Music: Dudley Simpson | **Broadcast:** 27 September– 18 October 1975, 9.9m (N, 1977; DVD; 2007)

Précis: On Zeta Minor, a Morestran expedition is menaced by an energy force from a black pit . . .

Observations: The extensive Zeta Minor jungle set was designed by Roger Murray-Leach and filmed at the BBC Film Studios, Ealing. The Antimatter Monster was based on the similar-looking Id Monster from *Forbidden Planet* (1956).

Verdict: A claustrophobic horror story with a palpable sense of menace around every corner. 9/10

82. PYRAMIDS OF MARS (four parts)

Cast: Peter Maycock (*Namin*), Bernard Archard (*Marcus Scarman*), Peter Copley (*Warlock*), Michael Sheard (*Laurence Scarman*), George Tovey (*Clements*), Gabriel Woolf (*Sutekh*), Michael Bilton (*Collins*), Vic Tablian (*Ahmed*), Nick Burnell, Melvyn Bedford, Kevin Selway (*Mummies*) | **Crew:** Director: Paddy Russell; Writer: 'Stephen Harris' (pseudonym for Robert Holmes & Paddy Russell, from an idea by Lewis Greifer); Music: Dudley Simpson | **Broadcast:** 25 October–15 November 1975, 10.7m (N, 1976; DVD, 2004; A, 2008)

Précis: A possessed Edwardian attempts to free an imprisoned Egyptian deity . . .

Observations: Stargrove Manor in East End, Hants (owned by Mick Jagger), was the chosen film location. John Friedlander fashioned three mummy costumes from fibreglass shells overlaid with fabric bandages. Christine Ruscoe designed a new version of the Tardis interior.

Verdict: Splendid for the first three episodes, then it all goes pear-shaped. Sutekh looks and sounds great, although his inability to move is a major weakness. Still, the mummies are terrifying, the music is generally excellent and the trip to a ravaged 1980s Earth provides a memorable moment. 8/10

83. THE ANDROID INVASION (four parts)

Cast: John Levene (*Benton*), Milton Johns (*Crayford*), Patrick Newell (*Faraday*), Dave Carter (*Grierson*), Heather Emmanuel (*Tessa*), Hugh Lund (*Matthews*), Martin Friend (*Styggron*), Roy Skelton (*Chedaki*), Max Faulkner (*Adams*), Peter Welch (*Morgan*), Stuart Fell (*Kraal*) | **Crew:** Director: Barry Letts; Writer: Terry Nation; Music: Dudley Simpson | **Broadcast:** 22 November–13 December 1975, 11.7m (N, 1978)

Précis: The quaint English village of Devesham seems to be populated by alien-controlled zombies . . .

Observations: East Hagbourne and the nearby National Radiological Protection Board at Harwell, both in Oxfordshire, stood in for Devesham and the Space Defence Station. Three rhinocerotic Kraal costumes were made, with masks sculpted by Lauri Warburton.

Verdict: Eerie, with a tangible sense of dislocation, this is an effective stab at something other than Gothic horror. Unfortunately, any mystery is made redundant by the title. 7/10

84. THE BRAIN OF MORBIUS (four parts)

Cast: Philip Madoc (*Solon*), Colin Fay (*Condo*), Cynthia Grenville (*Maren*), Gilly Brown (*Ohica*), Stuart Fell (*Monster*), Michael Spice (*Morbius voice*), John Scott Martin (*Kriz*), Sue Bishop, Janie Kells,

Gabrielle Mowbray, Veronica Ridge (*Sisterhood*) | **Crew:** Director: Christopher Barry; Writer: 'Robin Bland' (pseudonym for Terrance Dicks & Robert Holmes); Music: Dudley Simpson | **Broadcast:** 3–24 January 1976, 9.8m (N, 1977; DVD, 2008; A, 2008)

Précis: Mad surgeon Solon has created a headless body for the brain of a Time Lord criminal . . .

Observations: Utilising elements from his 1974 stage play *Doctor Who and the Daleks in Seven Keys to Doomsday* (see Spin-offs), Terrance Dicks originally scripted Solon as a robot. When this aspect was altered without his knowledge, he requested his name be removed from the story. Various members of the production team can be seen during part four's mind-bending contest.

Verdict: A flawless spoof of *Frankenstein*, notable for its unflinching horror and graphic depiction of violence. Philip Madoc is dynamite. 10/10

85. THE SEEDS OF DOOM (six parts)

Cast: Tony Beckley (*Harrison Chase*), John Challis (*Scorby*), Kenneth Gilbert (*Dunbar*), Michael McStay (*Moberley*), John Gleeson (*Winlett*), Hubert Rees (*Stevenson*), Seymour Green (*Hargreaves*), Michael Barrington (*Thackeray*), Mark Jones (*Keeler*), Sylvia Coleridge (*Amelia Ducat*), John Acheson (*Beresford*), Ray Barron (*Henderson*), Ronald Gough, Keith Ashley (*Krynoid*) | **Crew:** Director: Douglas Camfield; Writer: Robert Banks Stewart; Music: Geoffrey Burgon | **Broadcast:** 31 January–6 March 1976, 9m (N, 1977; DVD, 2010)

Précis: An insane botanist steals a flesh-eating Krynoid pod in a bid to wipe out animalkind . . .

Observations: Chase's stately home was Athelhampton House in Dorset, while the icy wastes of Antarctica were filmed in a quarry in Buckland, Surrey. BBC Television Centre stood in for the World Ecology Bureau. The Krynoid in its early stages was a reused Axon costume from *The Claws of Axos* (57) painted green.

Verdict: Remorselessly violent, this is one of the series' most accomplished dramas. Tony Beckley is wonderful, while his sidekick Scorby undergoes genuine character development. Keeler's Krynoid transformation is almost unwatchable and the final gigantic monster is remarkably effective. 10/10

SEASON 14

Producer: Philip Hinchcliffe
Script Editor: Robert Holmes
Fourth Doctor: Tom Baker
Companions: Elisabeth Sladen (*Sarah Jane Smith*, 86–87)
& Louise Jameson (*Leela*, 89–91)

86. THE MASQUE OF MANDRAGORA
(four parts)

Cast: Gareth Armstrong (*Giuliano*), John Laurimore (*Federico*), Tim Pigott-Smith (*Marco*), Norman Jones (*Hieronymous*), Antony Carrick (*Rossini*), Robert James (*High Priest*), Peter Tuddenham (*Titan voice*), Pat Gorman (*Soldier*) | **Crew:** Director: Rodney Bennett; Writer: Louis Marks; Music: Dudley Simpson | **Broadcast:** 4–25 September 1976, 9.5m (N, 1977; DVD, 2010)

Précis: In Renaissance Italy, Mandragora energy tries to drag the world back into the Dark Ages . . .
Observations: The 1920s Italianate-inspired village of Portmeirion, Wales, stood in for Italy. Costumes were reused from the 1954 film version of *Romeo and Juliet*.

Barry Newbery designed a new Secondary Console Room, built from plywood lined with wood-veneer wallpaper to suggest wooden panels and a new, simplified police box exterior prop with a flatter roof.

Verdict: A sumptuous historical with a serious message about free will. On the downside, the Mandragora Helix is poorly conceived, the ending is confusing and musician Dudley Simpson has a rare off-day. 6/10

87. THE HAND OF FEAR (four parts)

Cast: Rex Robinson (*Carter*), Glyn Houston (*Watson*), Roy Boyd (*Driscoll*), Judith Paris (*Eldrad*), Stephen Thorne (*Kastrian/Eldrad*), Roy Skelton (*King Rokon*), Roy Pattison (*Zazzka*), David Purcell (*Tom Abbott*), Renu Setna (*Doctor*), Frances Pidgeon (*Miss Jackson*), John Cannon (*Elgin*) | **Crew:** Director: Lennie Mayne; Writers: Bob Baker & Dave Martin; Music: Dudley Simpson | **Broadcast:** 2–23 October 1976, 11m (N, 1979; DVD, 2006)

Précis: Sarah, possessed by a fossilised hand, seizes control of a nuclear reactor . . .

Observations: Oldbury Nuclear Power Station, Glos, provided the main location, with the Doctor depositing Sarah in a cul-de-sac in nearby Thornbury. Eldrad's hand was a glove with a fake wrist, worn by Steve Drewett and made to move by CSO, or by inserting it through a hole in specially made props.

Verdict: Judith Paris and Elisabeth Sladen positively shine in this fast-moving contemporary thriller, although the part four Kastria scenes are tacky. Sarah's departure is beautifully underplayed by the two leads. 8/10

88. THE DEADLY ASSASSIN (four parts)

Cast: Angus Mackay (*Borusa*), Bernard Horsfall (*Goth*), Derek Seaton (*Hilred*), George Pravda (*Spandrell*), Erik Chitty (*Engin*), Hugh Walters (*Runcible*), Maurice Quick (*Gold Usher*), Peter Pratt (*The Master*) |

Crew: Director: David Maloney; Writer: Robert Holmes; Music: Dudley Simpson | **Broadcast:** 30 October–20 November 1976, 12.2m (N, 1977; DVD, 2009)

Précis: On Gallifrey, the Doctor is framed for the President's murder . . .

Observations: Part three's Matrix scenes were filmed in Betchworth Quarry and the Royal Alexandra & Albert School, Merstham, both in Surrey, while biplane-strafing shots were taken at Wycombe Air Park, Bucks. The cliffhanger, a freeze-frame of the Doctor's head held under-water, was criticised by the late Mary Whitehouse, leading to its excision from the 1977 repeat. Alistair Bowtell made the Master's disfigured face mask.

Verdict: The Doctor's first solo story, *The Deadly Assassin* is a stunning piece of television. The virtual reality scenes are compellingly nasty and Gallifrey's rotten core has never been more cynically portrayed. 10/10

89. THE FACE OF EVIL (four parts)

Cast: Leslie Schofield (*Calib*), David Garfield (*Neeva*), Victor Lucas (*Andor*), Brendan Price (*Tomas*), Colin Thomas (*Sole*), Leon Eagles (*Jabel*), Mike Elles (*Gentek*), Tom Baker (*Xoanon*), Tom Baker, Rob Edwards, Pamela Salem, Anthony Frieze, Roy Herrick (*Xoanon voices*) | **Crew:** Director: Pennant Roberts; Writer: Chris Boucher; Music: Dudley Simpson | **Broadcast:** 1–22 January 1977, 11.2m (N, 1978)

Précis: The Sevateem tribe worship Xoanon, in reality a computer driven mad by the Doctor . . .

Observations: Leela's name originated from Palestinian terrorist Leila Khaled. Her minimal suede costume was designed by John Bloomfield, with actress Louise Jameson given red contact lenses to turn her naturally blue eyes brown. The five-week gap prior to this story was bridged with compilation repeats of *Pyramids of Mars* (82) and *The Brain of Morbius* (84).

Verdict: A clever story, boringly told. There's too much technobabble and the characters are unsympathetic. 3/10

90. THE ROBOTS OF DEATH (four parts)

Cast: Russell Hunter (*Uvanov*), Pamela Salem (*Toos*), Brian Croucher (*Borg*), David Bailie (*Dask*), Tania Rogers (*Zilda*), Tariq Yunus (*Cass*), David Collings (*Poul*), Miles Fothergill (*SV7*), Gregory de Polnay (*D84*), Rob Edwards (*Chub*), John Bleasdale, Mark Cooper, Peter Langtry, Jeremy Ranchev, Richard Seager, Mark Blackwell Baker (*Robots*) | **Crew:** Director: Michael Briant; Writer: Chris Boucher; Music: Dudley Simpson | **Broadcast:** 29 January–19 February 1977, 12.7m (N, 1979; DVD, 2000)

Précis: Robot servants are killing off the crew of an alien Sandminer . . .
Observations: Designer Kenneth Sharp and costumier Elizabeth Waller worked together to ensure that all the visuals, including the nine robots, had a strong Art Deco influence. Mention is made of Isaac Asimov's Three Laws of Robotics, formulated in 1941, while Taren Capel's name deliberately mirrors the Czech writer Karel Capek who, with his brother Josef, first coined the word 'robot' in his 1923 play *R.U.R.*
Verdict: Fabulous design work, hugely suspenseful music and a very believable scenario make this one of the programme's most durable tales. The killer may be obvious, but the tension is wrung out to the bitter end. 10/10

91. THE TALONS OF WENG-CHIANG (six parts)

Cast: John Bennett (*Chang*), Michael Spice (*Weng-Chiang/Greel*), Trevor Baxter (*Litefoot*), Christopher Benjamin (*Jago*), Deep Roy (*Mr Sin*), Tony Then (*Lee*), Chris Gannon (*Casey*), Vincent Wong (*Ho*), Joseph Buller (*Alan Butler*), David McKall (*Kyle*), Stuart Fell (*Rat*) | **Crew:** Director: David Maloney; Writer: Robert Holmes; Music: Dudley Simpson | **Broadcast:** 26 February–2 April 1977, 10.3m (N, 1977; DVD, 2010)

Précis: The Doctor and Leela investigate horrific murders in Victorian London . . .

Observations: Location work on film and video took place in Wapping, London, and the Royal Theatre, Northants. The giant rat sequences were achieved by having a genuine rodent on model sets and a full-size prop, built by John Bloomfield and Michaeljohn Harris, in the studio. After the last part, Melvyn Bragg's BBC2 series *The Lively Arts* featured a programme called *Whose Doctor Who*, which detailed the making of this story.

Verdict: Groaning under the weight of so much clichéd Victoriana, *Talons* emerges as a garish hybrid of science fiction and literary pastiche. If watched in one go, the lack of subtlety can be draining. 7/10

Producer: Graham Williams
Script Editors: Robert Holmes (92–95) & Anthony Read
(96–97)
Fourth Doctor: Tom Baker
Companions: Louise Jameson (*Leela*) & John Leeson (*K-9
voice*, 93, 95–97)

92. HORROR OF FANG ROCK (four parts)

Cast: Colin Douglas (*Reuben*), John Abbott (*Vince*), Ralph Watson
(*Ben*), Sean Caffery (*Palmerdale*), Annette Woollett (*Adelaide*), Rio
Fanning (*Harker*), Alan Rowe (*Skinsale*) | **Crew:** Director: Paddy
Russell; Writer: Terrance Dicks; Music: Dudley Simpson | **Broadcast:**
3–24 September 1977, 8.4m (N, 1978; DVD, 2005)

Précis: The occupants of a fogbound Victorian lighthouse
are being murdered one by one . . .
Observations: A last-minute replacement for a vampire
story (later resurrected as *State of Decay*, 112), the realistically cramped lighthouse scenes were shot at Pebble Mill
Studios, Birmingham – the first time the series had ventured

from its London studio base. Louise Jameson stopped using her red contact lenses due to their discomfort.

Verdict: Strong on atmosphere, this is a tense, scary tale that makes a virtue of its small cast and claustrophobic locale. Superlative in every way. 10/10

93. THE INVISIBLE ENEMY (four parts)

Cast: Brian Grellis (*Safran*), Jay Neill (*Silvey*), Edmund Pegge (*Meeker*), Michael Sheard (*Lowe*), Frederick Jaeger (*Marius*), Roy Herrick (*Parsons*), Nell Curran (*Nurse*), John Leeson (*Nucleus voice*), John Scott Martin (*Nucleus*) | **Crew:** Director: Derrick Goodwin; Writers: Bob Baker & Dave Martin; Music: Dudley Simpson | **Broadcast:** 1–22 October 1977, 8.1m (N, 1979; DVD, 2008)

Précis: The Doctor is possessed by an intelligent virus . . .
Observations: This effects-intensive story required two visual-effects designers: Ian Scoones for the modelwork and Tony Harding for studio effects. The radio-controlled K-9 prop was designed by Harding and operated by Nigel Brackley. The original console room was reintroduced (with minor alterations) after the plywood flats of the Secondary Console Room, last seen in *The Robots of Death* (90), had warped in storage.
Verdict: Plenty of good ideas and a strong first episode, but the plot loses coherence when it shifts to the Bi-Al Foundation. With the exception of the giant prawn, the effects are generally top-notch. 6/10

94. IMAGE OF THE FENDAHL (four parts)

Cast: Denis Lill (*Fendelman*), Wanda Ventham (*Ransome*), Scott Fredericks (*Stael*), Edward Arthur (*Colby*), Edward Evans (*Ted Moss*), Derek Martin (*Mitchell*), Geoffrey Hinsliff (*Jack*), Daphne Heard (*Granny*), Peter Wragg (*Fendahleen*) | **Crew:** Director: George Spenton-Foster; Writer: Chris Boucher; Music: Dudley Simpson | **Broadcast:** 29 October–19 November 1977, 7.8m (N, 1979; DVD, 2009)

Précis: Experiments on a primeval skull allow the Fendahl to once again terrorise the Earth . . .

Observations: As with *Pyramids of Mars* (82), Stargrove Manor in Hants doubled as the priory. A 7ft-high foam rubber and latex Fendahleen was built by Colin Mapson, while the embryonic versions were operated like glove puppets. Louise Jameson wore a new costume made from chamois leather.

Verdict: This last stab at Gothic horror almost succeeds, were it not for the aimless padding of part three and a weak resolution. 7/10

95. THE SUN MAKERS (four parts)

Cast: Richard Leech (*Gatherer Hade*), Michael Keating (*Goudry*), Roy Macready (*Cordo*), Jonina Scot (*Marn*), William Simons (*Mandrel*), Adrienne Burgess (*Veet*), Henry Woolf (*Collector*), David Rowlands (*Bisham*), Derek Crewe (*Synge*), Colin McCormack (*Commander*) | **Crew:** Director: Pennant Roberts; Writer: Robert Holmes; Music: Dudley Simpson | **Broadcast:** 26 November–17 December 1977, 8.8m (N, 1982)

Précis: The Company is taxing the inhabitants of Pluto's Megropolis One into the ground . . .

Observations: Filming took place on the roof of the Wills Tobacco Factory in Bristol, with Camden Town deep tube shelters, London NW1, forming the city's tunnels. The Collector's costume was a cross between a City banker and a Middle Eastern businessman, while the Consumcard was based on a Barclaycard.

Verdict: A witty script with plenty of jokes at the expense of the Inland Revenue, *The Sun Makers* hits most of its intended targets. Good filmwork, imaginative sets and the wonderfully oleaginous Henry Woolf offset some of the more obvious budgetary shortcomings. 8/10

96. UNDERWORLD (four parts)

Cast: Imogen Bickford-Smith (*Tala*), James Maxwell (*Jackson*), Jonathan Newth (*Orfe*), Alan Lake (*Herrick*), Jimmy Gardner (*Idmon*), Norman Tipton (*Idas*), James Marcus (*Rask*), Godfrey James (*Tarn*), Frank Jarvis (*Ankh*), Richard Shaw (*Lakh*), Stacey Tendeter (*Naia*), Christine Pollon (*Oracle voice*) | **Crew:** Director: Norman Stewart; Writers: Bob Baker & Dave Martin; Music: Dudley Simpson | **Broadcast:** 7–28 January 1978, 9.7m (N, 1980; DVD, 2010)

Précis: The Minyans are hunting for their lost colony ship, now the core of a new planet . . .
Observations: As a cost-cutting exercise, all of the cave sequences were achieved by placing actors in miniature sets by means of CSO. Characters' names were based on those from the Greek legend of Jason and the Argonauts, such as Herrick (Heracles) and the ship *P7E* (Persephone).
Verdict: Excellent modelwork in part one, but overall a dull story with an obvious lack of monsters. It's a pity that the extensive use of CSO is limited to caves (*Doctor Who*'s stock-in-trade) and not something more imaginative. 5/10

97. THE INVASION OF TIME (six parts)

Cast: John Arnatt (*Borusa*), Milton Johns (*Kelner*), Dennis Edwards (*Gomer*), Christopher Tranchell (*Andred*), Stan McGowan (*Vardan Leader*), Tom Kelly (*Vardan*), Charles Morgan (*Gold Usher*), Hilary Ryan (*Rodan*), Max Faulkner (*Nesbin*), Ray Callaghan (*Ablif*), Gai Smith (*Presta*), Michael Mundell (*Jasko*), Derek Deadman (*Stor*), Stuart Fell (*Sontaran*) | **Crew:** Director: Gerald Blake; Writer: 'David Agnew' (pseudonym for Graham Williams & Anthony Read); Music: Dudley Simpson | **Broadcast:** 4 February–11 March 1978, 10.5m (N 1980; DVD, 2008)

Précis: The Doctor returns to Gallifrey, assumes the role of President and lets the Vardans invade . . .
Observations: This story, a hurried replacement for an unworkable script by David Weir, lost two studio sessions

due to a BBC strike. Location recording on film and video took place at St Anne's Hospital (for the Tardis interiors) and a nearby sandpit, both in Redhill, Surrey, and a swimming pool at British Oxygen's HQ, Hammersmith Broadway, London. A new, lightweight Sontaran mask was made for Stor.

Verdict: The disorientating mix of film, OB video and studio work is jarring, as is the Tardis with its brick-walled cellars and hospital corridors. Some good moments (especially episode four's cliffhanger) marginally offset the endless padding, and the Sontarans aren't too bad. 6/10

SEASON 16

Producer: Graham Williams
Script Editor: Anthony Read
Fourth Doctor: Tom Baker
Companions: Mary Tamm (*Romana*) & John Leeson (*K-9 II voice*, 98–101, 103)

98. THE RIBOS OPERATION (four parts)

Cast: Iain Cuthbertson (*Garron*), Nigel Plaskitt (*Unstoffe*), Paul Seed (*Graff Vynda-K*), Robert Keegan (*Sholakh*), Prentis Hancock (*Captain*), Cyril Luckham (*White Guardian*), Ann Tirard (*Seeker*), Timothy Bateson (*Binro*), Nick Wilkinson, Stuart Fell (*Shrivenzale*) | Crew: Director: George Spenton-Foster; Writer: Robert Holmes; Music: Dudley Simpson | Broadcast: 2–23 September 1978, 8.1m (N, 1979; DVD, 2009; A, 2011)

Précis: A galactic conman is trying to 'sell' the planet Ribos to a deposed tyrant . . .
Observations: Producer Graham Williams originally mooted the idea of a season-long Key to Time quest in 1976. A 1978 BBC/Time-Life co-production of *Anna Karenina* provided many of the sets and costumes for this story. Dave Havard

made two copies of the six-segment Key to Time prop. K-9 (supposedly a copy of the original) was repainted charcoal grey and fitted with a quieter motor.

Verdict: A beautifully made character piece, with Holmes' skill for dialogue clearly showcased, this is atmospherically directed (especially the candlelit catacombs), convincingly acted and sometimes very funny. 10/10

99. THE PIRATE PLANET (four parts)

Cast: Bruce Purchase (*Captain*), Rosalind Lloyd (*Nurse*), Andrew Robertson (*Mr Fibuli*), Vi Delmar (*Queen Xanxia*), David Sibley (*Pralix*), Ralph Michael (*Balaton*), Primi Townsend (*Mula*), David Warwick (*Kimus*), Adam Kurakin (*Guard*), Bernard Finch (*Mentiad*) | **Crew:** Director: Pennant Roberts; Writer: Douglas Adams; Music: Dudley Simpson | **Broadcast:** 30 September–21 October 1978, 8.3m (DVD, 2009)

Précis: An insane cyborg is materialising his hollow world around others to drain them of their energy . . .

Observations: Douglas Adams wrote this, his first *Doctor Who* script, simultaneously with the first Radio 4 series of *The Hitchhiker's Guide to the Galaxy*. Location filming took place at Berkley Power Station, Glos, and caves in Powys, Wales. Tom Baker's lip sported a visible wound due to a dog bite received during recording on the previous story. Tony Oxley built K-9's opponent, the Polyphase Avatron, which was seen to fly courtesy of CSO.

Verdict: The big concepts are intriguing, K-9 gets to fight a robot parrot and Tom Baker plays it straight. But the direction's flat and the acting is generally disappointing. 6/10

100. THE STONES OF BLOOD (four parts)

Cast: Beatrix Lehmann (*Professor Rumford*), Susan Engel (*Vivien Fay*), Nicholas McArdle (*De Vries*), Elaine Ives-Cameron (*Martha*), Gerald Cross, David McAlister (*Megara voices*), James Murray, Shirin Taylor

(*Campers*) | **Crew:** Director: Darrol Blake; Writer: David Fisher; Music: Dudley Simpson | **Broadcast:** 28 October–18 November 1978, 8m (N, 1980; DVD, 2009)

Précis: In twentieth-century rural England, an ancient stone circle seems to have a life of its own . . .

Observations: To celebrate *Doctor Who*'s hundredth programme, a scene featuring a surprise party for the Doctor's birthday was planned, but cut at the last minute. Location OB videoing took place at the Rollright Stones and Little Rollright Quarry, Oxon, as well as Reed College in Little Compton, Worcs.

Verdict: The first two parts are wonderfully dark and menacing. Unfortunately, the last two are deathly dull, with the Ogri consigned to the background and Tom Baker out-hamming everyone in sight. Still, Beatrix Lehmann is delightful and the story has an unusually strong female cast. 7/10

101. THE ANDROIDS OF TARA (four parts)

Cast: Peter Jeffrey (*Grendel*), Neville Jason (*Reynart*), Paul Lavers (*Farrah*), Simon Lack (*Zadek*), Lois Baxter (*Lamia*), Declan Mulholland (*Till*), Cyril Shaps (*Archimandrite*), Roy Lavender (*Wood Beast*) | **Crew:** Director: Michael Hayes; Writer: David Fisher; Music: Dudley Simpson | **Broadcast:** 25 November–16 December 1978, 9.1m (N, 1980; DVD, 2009)

Précis: Count Grendel is plotting to steal the Taran throne from its rightful owner, using Romana – or her android double – as an accomplice . . .

Observations: Leeds Castle in Kent stood in for Castle Gracht. Characters' swords were supposed to be electrically charged, but most of the flashes and sparks were not added later due to disruption caused by industrial action.

Verdict: Charmingly and confidently played by all concerned, the clichés of the genre enrich the narrative with their emotive pull and the late Peter Jeffrey is excellent. It's got a great swordfight too. 10/10

102. THE POWER OF KROLL (four parts)

Cast: Neil McCarthy (*Thawn*), Philip Madoc (*Fenner*), John Leeson (*Dugeen*), Glyn Owen (*Rohm-Dutt*), John Abineri (*Ranquin*), Carl Rigg (*Varlik*), Graham Mallard (*Harg*), Terry Walsh (*Mensch*) | **Crew:** Director: Norman Stewart; Writer: Robert Holmes; Music: Dudley Simpson | **Broadcast:** 23 December 1978–13 January 1979, 9.4m (N, 1980; DVD, 2009)

Précis: The Doctor and Romana are caught between native Swampies and power-hungry humans as a mile-wide squid emerges from its swamp . . .

Observations: Filming took place on the reed beds of the Maltings and Iken Cliff in Snape, Suffolk. Steve Drewett designed the latex and foam Kroll model, which had a 12ft tentacle span, but due to a technical error the obvious join between location footage and modelwork film reduced its impact. The Swampies were painted with water-resistant green body make-up that proved extremely difficult to remove.

Verdict: The cast look bored rigid, the direction is as flat as the horizon and the story is uninspiring. But Kroll looks good and the watery location is at least an attempt to do something different. 5/10

103. THE ARMAGEDDON FACTOR (six parts)

Cast: John Woodvine (*Marshal*), Lalla Ward (*Astra*), Davyd Harries (*Shapp*), William Squire (*Shadow*), Ian Saynor (*Merak*), Barry Jackson (*Drax*), Valentine Dyall (*Black Guardian*), Pat Gorman (*Pilot*), Stephen Calcutt (*Mute*) | **Crew:** Director: Michael Hayes; Writers: Bob Baker & Dave Martin; Music: Dudley Simpson | **Broadcast:** 20 January–24 February 1979, 8.5m (N, 1980; DVD, 2009)

Précis: Twin planets are at war, but the puppet of the Black Guardian, the Shadow, is guiding the conflict for his own evil ends . . .

Observations: Work commitments prevented Cyril Luckham reprising his role as the White Guardian for this studio-only conclusion to the Key to Time series. Incoming script editor Douglas Adams' first work on *Doctor Who* was to clarify the story's ending.

Verdict: After a promising start, the story soon falters. There is far too much padding, characters come and go as they please and there is no clear structure to the narrative. A hugely disappointing finale. 3/10

SEASON 17

Producer: Graham Williams
Script Editor: Douglas Adams
Fourth Doctor: Tom Baker
Companions: Lalla Ward (*Romana II*) & David Brierley
(*K-9 II voice*, 106–109)

---

104. DESTINY OF THE DALEKS (four parts)

Cast: David Gooderson (*Davros/Dalek voices*), Tim Barlow (*Tyssan*),
Peter Straker (*Sharrel*), Suzanne Danielle (*Agella*), Tony Osoba (*Lan*),
Penny Casdagli (*Jall*), David Yip (*Veldan*), Roy Skelton (*Dalek voices/K-9
voice*), Cy Town, Mike Mungarven, Toby Byrne, Tony Starr (*Daleks*),
Lee Richards (*Short Romana*), Maggie Armitage (*Tall Romana*), Yvonne
Gallagher (*Buxom Romana*) | **Crew:** Director: Ken Grieve; Writer: Terry
Nation; Music: Dudley Simpson | **Broadcast:** 1–22 September 1979, 13.5m
(N, 1979; DVD, 2007).

Précis: On Skaro, the Doctor and the newly regenerated
Romana are caught between Daleks and Movellans intent
on exhuming Davros . . .
Observations: Two Dorset locations – Winspit Quarry in
Worth Matravers and Binnegar Heath in Wareham – were

chosen to represent Skaro. A Steadicam was used on location for the first time in the series' history. Michael Wisher was on tour in Australia and so David Gooderson replaced him as Davros. The original costume and wheelchair from *Genesis of the Daleks* (78) were reused, despite being in poor condition. The story utilised four Daleks, with vacuum-formed dummies featuring in part four's explosive climax.

Verdict: Despite its well-designed sets and crisp location footage, this story is often compared unfavourably with its Season 12 predecessor. Tatty Daleks aside though, this is a polished adventure that skilfully balances humour with action. 7/10

105. CITY OF DEATH (four parts)

Cast: Julian Glover (*Scarlioni/Scaroth/Tancredi*), Catherine Schell (*Countess Scarlioni*), David Graham (*Kerensky*), Kevin Flood (*Hermann*), Tom Chadbon (*Duggan*), Peter Halliday (*Soldier*), John Cleese, Eleanor Bron (*Art lovers*), Pat Gorman, Peter Kodak, Anthony Powell, Mike Finbar (*Henchmen*) | **Crew:** Director: Michael Hayes; Writer: 'David Agnew' (pseudonym for Douglas Adams & Graham Williams); Music: Dudley Simpson | **Broadcast:** 29 September–20 October 1979, 14.5m (DVD, 2005)

Précis: In Paris, Count Scarlioni is selling off Mona Lisas to fund dangerous time experiments . . .

Observations: For the programme's first overseas location shoot, Parisian landmarks included the Eiffel Tower, the Place de la Concorde, the Louvre and the Avenue des Champs Elysées. The 'art gallery visitors' scene in part four was a late addition after Douglas Adams discovered that Cleese and Bron were in the BBC TV Centre at the time of recording. Because of an unprecedented 75-day ITV strike, the story received *Doctor Who*'s highest ever ratings.

Verdict: As a light comedy drama, *City of Death* is flawless. The cast are at the height of their powers and the dialogue is lovely. 10/10

106. THE CREATURE FROM THE PIT (four parts)

Cast: Myra Frances (*Adrasta*), Eileen Way (*Karela*), Geoffrey Bayldon (*Organon*), John Bryans (*Torvin*), Edward Kelsey (*Edu*), Tim Munro (*Ainu*), Morris Barry (*Tollund*), Terry Walsh (*Doran*) | **Crew:** Director: Christopher Barry; Writer: David Fisher; Music: Dudley Simpson | **Broadcast:** 27 October–17 November 1979, 10m (N, 1981; DVD, 2010; A, 2008)

Précis: On Chloris, the wicked Lady Adrasta keeps a fearsome monster in her Pit . . .

Observations: Erato, the titular creature, was designed by Mat Irvine and consisted of meteorological balloons covered with a latex skin. Its appearance was regarded as a failure by the production team. Actor Morris Barry had previously directed three Patrick Troughton stories. Mat Irvine designed the five radio-controlled wolf weeds.

Verdict: The filmed jungle scenes are wonderful, but the story loses any gravitas the moment we see the phallic creature itself. Geoffrey Bayldon turns in an acutely unfunny performance, while the excellent Myra Frances is killed off far too soon. 3/10

107. NIGHTMARE OF EDEN (four parts)

Cast: David Daker (*Rigg*), Lewis Fiander (*Tryst*), Geoffrey Bateman (*Dymond*), Barry Andrews (*Stott*), Jennifer Lonsdale (*Della*), Stephen Jenn (*Secker*), Geoffrey Hinsliff (*Fisk*), Peter Craze (*Costa*), James Muir, Derek Suthern, David Korff, Jan Murzynowski, Robert Goodman (*Mandrels*) | **Crew:** Director: Alan Bromly; Writer: Bob Baker; Music: Dudley Simpson | **Broadcast:** 24 November–15 December 1979, 9.3m (N, 1980)

Précis: Two spaceships crash during a hyperspace jump and hordes of Mandrels escape from their holographic zoo . . .

Observations: The name of the addictive drug was changed from Zip to Vraxoin to make it less appealing to children. Five Mandrels were made by Rupert Jarvis. A special trailer was recorded for the season on the Eden jungle set.

Verdict: Serious themes battle against flippant acting and cheap production values, but the end product is surprisingly entertaining. 7/10

108. THE HORNS OF NIMON (four parts)

Cast: Graham Crowden (*Soldeed*), Simon Gipps-Kent (*Seth*), Janet Ellis (*Teka*), Michael Osborne (*Sorak*), Bob Hornery (*Pilot*), Malcolm Terris (*Co-Pilot*), John Bailey (*Sezom*), Clifford Norgate (*Nimons' voices*), Robin Sherringham, Bob Appleby, Trevor St John Hacker (*Nimons*) | **Crew:** Director: Kenny McBain; Writer: Anthony Read; Music: Dudley Simpson | **Broadcast:** 22 December 1979–12 January 1980, 8.8m (N, 1980; DVD 2010)

Précis: Skonnos youths are being sacrificed to the bull-headed Nimon, in return for which their empire will be returned to its former glory . . .

Observations: Three Nimon costumes were constructed, using fake leather imported from Germany. The Nimon actors wore 12in-high platform sandals to increase their height. Story names reflect the Greek Minotaur legend (Skonnos instead of Knossos, for instance). Director Kenny McBain created the phenomenally successful *Morse* series for ITV; Janet Ellis became a *Blue Peter* presenter.

Verdict: A serious story, played for laughs by Graham Crowden. The Nimons – with their impressive voices – tower above the cast, while Tom Baker and Lalla Ward are at their most assured. Technically, it's all rather impressive. 7/10

SEASON 18

Producer: John Nathan-Turner
Executive Producer: Barry Letts
Script Editor: Christopher H Bidmead
Fourth Doctor: Tom Baker
Fifth Doctor: Peter Davison (115)
Companions: Lalla Ward (*Romana II*, 109–113), John
Leeson (*K-9 II voice*, 109–113), Matthew Waterhouse
(*Adric* 111–115), Sarah Sutton (*Nyssa*, 114–115) & Janet
Fielding (*Tegan Jovanka*, 115)

109. THE LEISURE HIVE (four parts)

Cast: Laurence Payne (*Morix*), David Haig (*Pangol*), John Collin (*Brock*),
Ian Talbot (*Klout*), Adrienne Corri (*Mena*), Martin Fisk (*Vargos*), Nigel
Lambert (*Hardin*), Roy Montague (*Guide*), David Allister (*Stimson*),
Clifford Norgate (*Generator voice*) | **Crew:** Director: Lovett Bickford;
Writer: David Fisher; Music: Peter Howell | **Broadcast:** 30 August–
20 September 1980, 5.1m (N, 1982; DVD, 2004)

Précis: The Argolins' holiday resort is infiltrated by the
reptilian Foamasi . . .
Observations: Peter Howell arranged a new synthesised
version of the title music, while a radically different starfield

title sequence was animated by Sid Sutton, together with a new neon logo. A new, more authentic, police box prop was also constructed. The serial saw the debut of a digital image manipulator called Quantel 5000, which, in this case, enabled the image to zoom out as the Tardis materialised. June Hudson redesigned the Doctor's costume, giving him a more sombre look, and location filming was carried out on Brighton Beach. Tom Baker's gaunt appearance was due to an illness he got in Australia; it plagued him for the rest of the season. Scheduled opposite American SF series *Buck Rogers in the 25th Century*, the story's ratings were disastrous.

Verdict: Visually stunning, technically astounding, frenetically paced and overloaded with technobabble. Underneath all the gloss, though, is a very old-fashioned story. 8/10

110. MEGLOS (four parts)

Cast: Jacqueline Hill (*Lexa*), Edward Underdown (*Zastor*), Bill Fraser (*Grugger*), Colette Gleeson (*Caris*), Frederick Treves (*Brotadac*), Christopher Owen (*Earthling*), Crawford Logan (*Deedrix*), Tom Baker (*Meglos*) | **Crew:** Director: Terence Dudley; Writers: John Flanagan & Andrew McCulloch; Music: Paddy Kingsland & Peter Howell | **Broadcast:** 27 September–18 October 1980, 4.7m (N, 1983; DVD, 2011)

Précis: An evil cactus impersonates the Doctor and steals the sacred Dodecahedron from Tigella . . .

Observations: Former companion Jacqueline Hill played Lexa in this story, which saw the first use of Scene-Sync, a state-of-the-art motion-control system that produced a composite image from two moving sources. Parts two to four came in well under the programme's twenty-five–minute norm.

Verdict: The main thing going for *Meglos* is its mercifully short running time. Cutting-edge effects aside, the comedy is heavily signposted and an ill-looking Tom Baker gives a lacklustre performance as the Doctor, although his Meglos is great. 5/10

111. FULL CIRCLE (four parts)

Cast: George Baker (*Login*), James Bree (*Nefred*), Leonard Maguire (*Draith*), Tony Calvin (*Dexeter*), Richard Willis (*Varsh*), Bernard Padden (*Tylos*), Andrew Forbes (*Omril*), June Page (*Keara*), Alan Rowe (*Garif*), Norman Bacon (*Marshchild*), Adrian Gibbs (*Rysik*), Steve Kelly (*Marsh Leader*), Barney Lawrence, Graham Cole, Keith Guest, James Jackson, Stephen Watson, Stephen Calcutt (*Marshmen*) | **Crew:** Director: Peter Grimwade; Writer: Andrew Smith; Music: Paddy Kingsland | **Broadcast:** 25 October–15 November 1980, 5.3m (N, 1982; DVD, 2009)

Précis: In a pocket universe, the Tardis arrives on Alzarius during Mistfall, a time when strange creatures emerge from the swamps . . .

Observations: Eighteen-year-old *Doctor Who* fan Andrew Smith wrote this story, the first of a trilogy set in Exo-Space (usually shortened to E-Space). 'Adric' was an anagram of the surname of English physicist Paul Dirac. Filming took place at Black Park, Bucks, site of many Hammer horror films. Eight Marshmen costumes were made from latex-covered wetsuits.

Verdict: A stylish and confident story, saddled with an irritating gang of youths (of which Matthew Waterhouse is the least offensive) and a confused resolution. 8/10

112. STATE OF DECAY (four parts)

Cast: Emrys James (*Aukon*), William Lindsay (*Zargo*), Rachel Davies (*Camilla*), Clinton Greyn (*Ivo*), Iain Rattray (*Habris*), Thane Bettany (*Tarak*), Rhoda Lewis (*Marta*), Arthur Hewlett (*Kalmar*), Stacy Davies (*Veros*), Stuart Fell (*Roga*), Stuart Blake (*Zoldaz*) | **Crew:** Director: Peter Moffatt; Writer: Terrance Dicks; Music: Paddy Kingsland | **Broadcast:** 22 November–13 December 1980, 5.2m (N, 1981; DVD, 2009; A, 1981)

Précis: Vampires on a medieval planet are trying to revive the Great Vampire himself, mortal enemy of the Time Lords . . .

Observations: A revised version of *The Witch Lords* (the Season 15 story replaced by *Horror of Fang Rock*, 92); filming took place in Burnham Beeches, Bucks. Stock footage of bats was combined with mechanical toys. The RSPCA complained about their vampiric depiction in the story.

Verdict: A limply directed vampire tale that doesn't really gel – the horror should be more explicit, the vampirism more obvious. One feels the production team deliberately didn't want to plagiarise Hammer, which, considering the Hammeresque script, seems a mistake. 6/10

113. WARRIORS' GATE (four parts)

Cast: Clifford Rose (*Rorvik*), Kenneth Cope (*Packard*), Freddie Earlle (*Aldo*), Harry Waters (*Royce*), Vincent Pickering (*Sagan*), David Weston (*Biroc*), Jeremey Gittins (*Lazlo*), David Kincaid (*Lane*), Marianne Lawrence (*Servant*), Erika Spotswood (*Tharil Child*) | **Crew:** Director: Paul Joyce; Writer: Steve Gallagher; Music: Peter Howell | **Broadcast:** 3–24 January 1981, 7.5m (N, 1981; DVD, 2009)

Précis: Searching for a way out of E-Space, the Tardis materialises in a white void . . .

Observations: Monochrome stills of Powis Castle in Powys, Wales, were used to represent the world behind the mirrors. June Hudson designed the leonine Tharil costumes. The complex nature of Steve Gallagher's storyline and the inability of director Paul Joyce to appreciate the limitations of a multi-camera studio set-up led to a particularly fraught time during recording.

Verdict: Beautiful, violent and ultimately puzzling conclusion to the E-Space trilogy. Joyce's direction is exceptional, bar some questionable comic moments, and the script and acting display unusual maturity. 9/10

114. THE KEEPER OF TRAKEN (four parts)

Cast: John Woodnutt (*Seron*), Denis Carey (*Keeper*), Sheila Ruskin (*Kassia*), Anthony Ainley (*Tremas/The Master*), Margot Van Der Burgh (*Katura*), Robin Soans (*Luvic*), Roland Oliver (*Neman*), Geoffrey Beevers (*Melkur voice/The Master*), Graham Cole (*Melkur*) | **Crew:** Director: John Black; Writer: Johnny Byrne; Music: Roger Limb | **Broadcast:** 31 January–21 February 1981, 6.3m (N, 1982; DVD, 2007)

Précis: Traken is a refuge of peace and harmony until the arrival of the Melkur . . .
Observations: The Master's emaciated mask was virtually unaltered from *The Deadly Assassin* (88), bar the removal of fake eyes to allow more expression. Peter Logan moulded the Melkur from plastic, basing his design on a 1913 sculpture by Futurist artist Umberto Boccioni.
Verdict: This fairytale is a welcome respite from the so-called 'hard' science of Season 18. Oddly, its studio-bound artificiality makes it more effective. 8/10

115. LOGOPOLIS (four parts)

Cast: Anthony Ainley (*The Master*), Dolore Whiteman (*Aunt Vanessa*), Tom Georgeson (*Detective Inspector*), John Fraser (*Monitor*), Adrian Gibbs (*Watcher*), Christopher Hurst (*Guard*), Ray Knight (*Policeman*) | **Crew:** Director: Peter Grimwade; Writer: Christopher H Bidmead; Music: Paddy Kingsland | **Broadcast:** 28 February–21 March 1981, 6.7m (N, 1982; DVD, 2007; A, 2010)

Précis: The Master and the Doctor discover that a planet of mathematicians is holding the Universe together . . .
Observations: London film locations featured Ursula Street, Battersea, and Cadogan Pier and Albert Bridge, Chelsea. The BBC Receiving Station at Crowsley Park, Berks, was used as the Pharos Project. The old police box prop (last used in the cancelled *Shada*, see 'Spin-offs') was erected in a lay-by on the A413 near Denham, Bucks, together with the

current one, so that two Tardises could be shown together.
The story culminated in two extensive flashback sequences
showing Tom Baker's companions and enemies.

Verdict: Virtually plotless, *Logopolis* impresses because
of its weighty subject matter and the enormous scale of its
threat. The regeneration is particularly well handled. 10/10

SEASON 19

Producer: John Nathan-Turner
Script Editors: Eric Saward (116, 118, 120, 122) & Antony Root (117, 119, 121)
Fourth Doctor: Tom Baker (116)
Fifth Doctor: Peter Davison
Companions: Matthew Waterhouse (*Adric*, 116–121), Sarah Sutton (*Nyssa*) & Janet Fielding (*Tegan Jovanka*)

116. CASTROVALVA (four parts)

Cast: Anthony Ainley (*Portreeve/The Master*), Dallas Cavell (*Head of Security*), Michael Sheard (*Mergrave*), Derek Waring (*Shardovan*), Frank Wylie (*Ruther*), Souska John (*Child*) | **Crew:** Director: Fiona Cumming; Writer: Christopher H Bidmead; Music: Paddy Kingsland | **Broadcast:** 4–12 January 1982, 9.6m (N, 1983; DVD, 2007; A, 2010)

Précis: The Master deposits the Tardis near the seemingly tranquil city of Castrovalva . . .
Observations: Filming was done at Buckhurst Park and Harrison's Rocks, Groombridge, both East Sussex. Due to Season 18's poor ratings and to test the waters for new soap opera *EastEnders* (whose audience was considered

similar to *Doctor Who*'s), this was the first season to be transmitted in a bi-weekly slot rather than on a Saturday. Peter Davison's cricketing costume was designed by Colin Lavers. The story's visual elements were influenced by the paintings of MC Escher, notably 'Castrovalva' (1930) and 'Up and Down' (1947).

Verdict: Peter Davison exudes energy and the cerebral plot features a wonderfully realised alien culture, but the story suffers in its early stages from a lack of direction. 7/10

117. FOUR TO DOOMSDAY (four parts)

Cast: Stratford Johns (*Monarch*), Paul Shelley (*Persuasion*), Annie Lambert (*Enlightenment*), Philip Locke (*Bigon*), Burt Kwouk (*Lin Fitu*), Illarrio Bisi (*Kurkutji*), Nadia Hammam (*Villagra*) | **Crew:** Director: John Black; Writer: Terence Dudley; Music: Roger Limb | **Broadcast:** 18–26 January 1982, 8.9m (N, 1983; DVD, 2008)

Précis: Aboard a vast spaceship filled with human ethnic groups, Monarch has delusions of divinity . . .

Observations: This studio-bound story featured dance sequences choreographed by Sue Lefton. Monarch's spaceship was a 6ft model built by outside contractor Unit 22.

Verdict: Daft, but visually stunning. 5/10

118. KINDA (four parts)

Cast: Simon Rouse (*Hindle*), Richard Todd (*Sanders*), Nerys Hughes (*Todd*), Mary Morris (*Panna*), Adrian Mills (*Aris*), Sarah Prince (*Karuna*), Anna Wing (*Anatta*), Jeffrey Stewart (*Dukkha*), Roger Milner (*Annica*), Lee Cornes (*Trickster*), Stephen Calcutt (*Mara*) | **Crew:** Director: Peter Grimwade; Writer: Christopher Bailey; Music: Peter Howell | **Broadcast:** 1–9 February 1982, 8.8m (N, 1984; DVD, 2011; A, 2004)

Précis: In the lush forests of Deva Loka, the snake-like Mara has invaded Tegan's mind . . .

Observations: Nyssa only appeared in parts one and four because her contract didn't stretch to the whole season. Part four's giant snake was built by Stephen Greenfield and suspended from the studio lighting rig. Mara is the Buddhist term for 'temptation'.

Verdict: A chilling psychodrama with a remarkably strong cast. The dialogue, performances and direction are razor sharp. Even the snake's not *that* bad. 10/10

119. THE VISITATION (four parts)

Cast: John Savident (*Squire John*), Anthony Calf (*Charles*), Valerie Fyfer (*Elizabeth*), Michael Robbins (*Richard Mace*), Michael Melia (*Terileptil Leader*), Peter Van Dissel (*Android*), David Sumner, Michael Leader (*Terileptils*), John Baker (*Ralph*), James Charlton (*Miller*), Neil West (*Poacher*), Eric Dodson (*Headman*), Jeff Wayne (*Scythe Man*) | **Crew:** Director: Peter Moffatt; Writer: Eric Saward; Music: Paddy Kingsland | **Broadcast:** 15–23 February 1982, 9.6m (N, 1982; DVD, 2004)

Précis: In 1666, crash-landed alien fugitives plan to release plague-carrying rats . . .

Observations: Three latex and fibreglass Terileptil costumes were made, based on tropical fish bodies. The leader's mask saw the programme's first use of animatronics. The sonic screwdriver was destroyed until its reappearance fourteen years later in *Doctor Who* (156). Location filming took place in Black Park, Bucks, and Tithe Barn, Hurley, Berks.

Verdict: A flatly directed story that fails to generate much tension. The emphasis on dialogue is more suited to radio and the surprise ending is utterly predictable. 4/10

120. BLACK ORCHID (two parts)

Cast: Michael Cochrane (*Charles Cranleigh*), Barbara Murray (*Lady Cranleigh*), Gareth Milne (*George Cranleigh*), Moray Watson (*Robert Muir*), Ahmed Khalil (*Latoni*), Sarah Sutton (*Ann Talbot*), David Wild (*Digby*), Timothy Block (*Tanner*), Ivor Salter (*Markham*), Andrew

Tourell (*Cummings*) | **Crew:** Director: Ron Jones; Writer: Terence Dudley; Music: Roger Limb | **Broadcast:** 1–2 March 1982, 10m (N, 1986; DVD, 2008; A, 2008)

Précis: Accused of murder during a 1925 costume ball, the Doctor must prove his innocence and discover the identity of the disfigured man in the locked room . . .

Observations: Filming took place at Buckhurst Park, East Sussex, and Quainton, Bucks. Stuntman Gareth Milne injured himself jumping off the false flat roof in part two.

Verdict: This charming Margery Allingham-style mystery is a breath of fresh air. The studio sets are sumptuous and there is a plethora of small, beautiful moments. 10/10

121. EARTHSHOCK (four parts)

Cast: James Warwick (*Scott*), Clare Clifford (*Kyle*), June Bland (*Berger*), Beryl Reid (*Briggs*), Alec Sabin (*Ringway*), Steve Morley (*Walters*), Suzi Arden (*Snyder*), Ann Holloway (*Mitchell*), David Banks (*Cyber Leader*), Mark Hardy (*Cyber Lieutenant*), Jeff Wayne, Peter Gates-Fleming, Steve Ismay, Norman Bradley, Graham Cole, David Bache (*Cybermen*), Carolyn Mary Simmonds, Barney Lawrence (*Androids*) | **Crew:** Director: Peter Grimwade; Writer: Eric Saward; Music: Malcolm Clarke | **Broadcast:** 8–16 March 1982, 9.3m (N, 1983; DVD, 2003)

Précis: The Cybermen try to destroy Earth, first with a bomb, then with a colliding spaceship . . .

Observations: Twenty-fifth century Earth was briefly represented by Springwell Quarry, Rickmansworth, Herts. Richard Gregory constructed eight new Cybermen costumes from aircraft pilot suits, each sporting updated fibreglass helmets with transparent jaws. Because of Adric's shock death, part four's end titles were rolled in silence.

Verdict: A dynamically directed action story, much praised at the time, although the plot has huge holes and the dialogue is often lousy. 8/10

122. TIME-FLIGHT (four parts)

Cast: Anthony Ainley (*The Master/Kalid*), Richard Easton (*Stapley*), Keith Drinkel (*Scobie*), Michael Cashman (*Bilton*), Nigel Stock (*Hayter*), John Flint (*Urquhart*), Judith Byfield (*Angela Clifford*), Hugh Hayes (*Anithon*), André Winterton (*Zarak*), Barney Lawrence (*Dave Culshaw*) | **Crew:** Director: Ron Jones; Writer: Peter Grimwade; Music: Roger Limb | **Broadcast:** 22–30 March 1982, 8.9m (N, 1983; DVD, 2007)

Précis: The Master is dragging Concordes back to the Pleistocene Era . . .
Observations: Filming took place at Heathrow Airport, Middx. British Airways allowed a Concorde to be used for the first time in a BBC drama, in return for product placement. Freelance props firm Unit 22 made five Plasmatons by pouring expanded polyurethane liquid over mail sacks.
Verdict: Inexplicable, boring and very badly written. 2/10

SEASON 20

Producer: John Nathan-Turner
Script Editor: Eric Saward
Fifth Doctor: Peter Davison
Companions: Janet Fielding (*Tegan Jovanka*), Sarah
Sutton (*Nyssa*, 123–126) & Mark Strickson (*Turlough*
125–128)

123. ARC OF INFINITY (four parts)

Cast: Michael Gough (*Hedin*), Leonard Sachs (*Borusa*), Ian Collier, Peter Davison (*Omega*), Colin Baker (*Maxil*), Paul Jerricho (*Castellan*), Elspet Gray (*Thalia*), Neil Daglish (*Damon*), Andrew Boxer (*Robin Stuart*), Alastair Cumming (*Colin Frazer*) | **Crew:** Director: Ron Jones; Writer: Johnny Byrne; Music: Roger Limb | **Broadcast:** 3–12 January 1983, 7m (N, 1983; DVD, 2007)

Précis: Omega has escaped from his anti-matter world and needs the Doctor's body to survive . . .
Observations: Overseas filming was conducted in Amsterdam due to its link with the BBC soap opera *Triangle* (1981–83). Future Sixth Doctor actor Colin Baker appeared as Maxil. Richard Gregory made Omega's mask

and the Ergon costume, which had a head based on a ptero-dactyl skull.

Verdict: Bland direction, awful music, stilted dialogue, wooden acting. Its only saving grace is Davison's portrayal of Omega in the final part. 2/10

124. SNAKEDANCE (four parts)

Cast: Martin Clunes (*Lon*), Colette O'Neil (*Tanha*), John Carson (*Ambril*), Preston Lockwood (*Dojjen*), Brian Miller (*Dugdale*), Johnathon Morris (*Chela*), Hilary Sester (*Fortune Teller*), Barry Smith (*Puppeteer*), Brian Grellis (*Megaphone Man*) | **Crew:** Director: Fiona Cumming; Writer: Christopher Bailey; Music: Peter Howell | **Broadcast:** 18–26 January 1983, 7.1m (N, 1984; DVD, 2011)

Précis: On Manussa, the Mara plans to return on the five-hundredth anniversary of its exile . . .

Observations: This sequel to *Kinda* (118) used real non-poisonous snakes on its single filming day at Ealing Studios. Four prop snakes were made, one of which was a hydrauli-cally operated head seen in part four.

Verdict: While less experimental than *Kinda*, there are still some good moments. Martin Clunes and Colette O'Neil are the best things in it. 7/10

125. MAWDRYN UNDEAD (four parts)

Cast: Nicholas Courtney (*Brigadier*), David Collings (*Mawdryn*), Valentine Dyall (*Black Guardian*), Angus MacKay (*Headmaster*), Stephen Garlick (*Ibbotson*), Roger Hammond (*Runciman*), Sheila Gill (*Matron*), Peter Warmsley, Brian Darnley (*Mutants*), Sian Pattenden (*Tegan as child*), Lucy Baker (*Nyssa as child*) | **Crew:** Director: Peter Moffatt; Writer: Peter Grimwade; Music: Paddy Kingsland | **Broadcast:** 1–9 February 1983, 7m (N, 1983; DVD, 2009)

Précis: The Brigadier suffers amnesia, while the mutated occupants of a spaceship are doomed to live for ever . . .

Observations: Middlesex Polytechnic in Cockfosters, London, was the site chosen as Turlough's public school. A sepia flashback sequence in part two featured foes from the Brigadier's past. Eight Mutant costumes with distended skulls were designed by Amy Roberts. The Brigadier's retirement date of 1977 clashed with the generally accepted view that the UNIT stories had taken place during the late 1970s or early 1980s.

Verdict: The whole story consists of characters running from one place to another. If there is a plot, it is well disguised. But David Collings, the best Doctor we never had, excels. 5/10

126. TERMINUS (four parts)

Cast: Liza Goddard (*Kari*), Dominic Guard (*Olvir*), Andrew Burt (*Valgard*), Martin Potter (*Eirak*), Tim Munro (*Sigurd*), Peter Benson (*Bor*), RJ Bell (*Garm*), Valentine Dyall (*Black Guardian*), Rachel Weaver (*Inga*), Martin Muncaster (*Tannoy voice*) | **Crew:** Director: Mary Ridge; Writer: Steve Gallagher; Music: Roger Limb | **Broadcast:** 15–23 February 1983, 7m (N, 1983; DVD, 2009)

Précis: Terminus Inc, a refuge for lazar victims, appears to have cosmic significance . . .

Observations: A complaint was received from a lecturer at a school of tropical medicine objecting to the story's depiction of leprosy ('lazar' is an archaic word for leprosy). BAFTA-nominated actress Kathy Burke appeared as an extra. The five Vanir costumes were influenced by Middle Ages woodcuts, while the lazar patients wore shrouds in the style of Black Death victims.

Verdict: The depressing subject matter and monotonous spaceship interiors make for minimal enjoyment, while the shock revelation is patently absurd. 3/10

127. ENLIGHTENMENT (four parts)

Cast: Keith Barron (*Striker*), Christopher Brown (*Marriner*), Tony Caunter (*Jackson*), Leee John (*Mansell*), Lynda Baron (*Wrack*), James McClure (*First Officer*), Clive Kneller (*Collier*), Pat Gorman (*Grogan*), Byron Sotiris (*Critas*), Valentine Dyall (*Black Guardian*), Cyril Luckham (*White Guardian*) | **Crew:** Director: Fiona Cumming; Writer: Barbara Clegg; Music: Malcolm Clarke | **Broadcast:** 1–9 March 1983, 6.8m (N, 1984; DVD, 2009)

Précis: The Tardis materialises aboard an Edwardian racing yacht in space . . .

Observations: Mike Kelt supervised the extensive model-work for this story, filmed on 35mm (rather than 16mm) at Ealing Studios. Sessions were delayed by several months due to strike action, which meant that Peter Sallis and David Rhule, originally cast as Striker and Mansell respectively, were unavailable for the remount.

Verdict: Beautifully directed, with a real sense of wonder. Keith Barron is surprisingly good as the soulless eternal wanderer and there are some genuinely exciting sequences. 9/10

128. THE KING'S DEMONS (two parts)

Cast: Frank Windsor (*Ranulf*), Gerald Flood (*King John/Kamelion voice*), Isla Blair (*Isabella*), Anthony Ainley (*The Master/Estram*), Christopher Villiers (*Hugh*), Michael J Jackson (*Geoffrey*) | **Crew:** Director: Tony Virgo; Writer: Terence Dudley; Music: Jonathan Gibbs & Peter Howell | **Broadcast:** 15–16 March 1983, 6.5m (N, 1986; DVD, 2010)

Précis: The Master, helped by his shape-changing robot Kamelion, wants to prevent the signing of the Magna Carta . . .

Observations: Filming took place at Bodiam Castle, East Sussex. Mike Power created Kamelion as a functioning automation for an advertising campaign, but the robot's future appearances were severely curtailed when Power died shortly afterwards in a boating accident.

Verdict: A pedestrian effort that can't even sustain itself for two parts. 2/10

SPECIAL

Producer: John Nathan-Turner
Script Editor: Eric Saward
Fifth Doctor: Peter Davison
Companions: Janet Fielding (*Tegan Jovanka*) & Mark Strickson (*Turlough*)

129. THE FIVE DOCTORS (90m)

Cast: Richard Hurndall (*First Doctor*), Carole Ann Ford (*Susan*), Patrick Troughton (*Second Doctor*), Frazer Hines (*Jamie McCrimmon*), Wendy Padbury (*Zoe Heriot*), Jon Pertwee (*Third Doctor*), Elisabeth Sladen (*Sarah Jane Smith*), John Leeson (*K-9 III voice*), Nicholas Courtney (*Brigadier*), Richard Franklin (*Yates*), Caroline John (*Liz Shaw*), Anthony Ainley (*The Master*), Philip Latham (*Borusa*), Paul Jerricho (*Castellan*), Dinah Sheridan (*Flavia*), Richard Mathews (*Rassilon*), Roy Skelton (*Dalek voice*), John Scott Martin (*Dalek*), David Banks (*Cyber Leader*), Mark Hardy (*Cyber Lieutenant*), Lee Woods, Richard Naylor, Mark Whincup, Gilbert Gillan, Emyr Morris Jones, Stuart Fell, Graham Cole, Alan Riches, Ian Marshall-Fisher, Mark Bessenger (*Cybermen*), Keith Hodiak (*Raston Robot*) | **Crew:** Director: Peter Moffatt; Writer: Terrance Dicks; Music: Peter Howell | **Broadcast:** 25 November 1983, 7.7m (N, 1983; DVD, 2008)

Précis: Scooping Doctors, companions and foes from their own time-streams, President Borusa hopes to cross the Death Zone on Gallifrey, enter the Dark Tower and discover the secret of eternal life . . .

Observations: As well as various quarries in Gwynedd, Wales, filming also took place in Upper Denham, Bucks, and Uxbridge, Middx, for this ABC/BBC co-produced twentieth-anniversary special. Inserts from the unscreened story *Shada* covered Tom Baker's absence. Malcolm Thornton designed a radically updated Tardis console, and a *Radio Times* artwork cover by Andrew Skilleter accompanied the programme's broadcast during the BBC's *Children in Need* charity telethon. A special edition was later released in 1995 by Paul Vanezis, completely re-edited with CGI replacing the original effects, alternate takes and a newly created 5.1 soundtrack.

Verdict: Despite the all-star cast and the workable plot, *The Five Doctors* still manages to be dull. Too many ingredients and flaccid direction combine to produce a curiously uninvolving 'celebration'. 5/10

SEASON 21

Producer: John Nathan-Turner
Script Editor: Eric Saward
Fifth Doctor: Peter Davison (130–135)
Sixth Doctor: Colin Baker (135–136)
Companions: Janet Fielding (*Tegan Jovanka*, 130–133),
Mark Strickson (*Turlough*, 130–134) & Nicola Bryant (*Peri Brown*, 134–136)

130. WARRIORS OF THE DEEP (four parts)

Cast: Tom Adams (*Vorshak*), Ian McCulloch (*Nilson*), Ingrid Pitt (*Solow*), Martin Neil (*Maddox*), Nigel Humphreys (*Bulic*), Tara Ward (*Preston*), Norman Comer (*Icthar*), Vincent Brimble (*Tarpok*), Stuart Blake (*Scibus*), Christopher Farries (*Sauvix*), Steve Kelly, Chris Wolff, Jules Walters, Mike Brayburn, Dave Ould (*Sea Devils*), William Perrie, John Asquith (*Myrka*) | **Crew:** Director: Pennant Roberts; Writer: Johnny Byrne; Music: Jonathan Gibbs | **Broadcast:** 5–13 January 1984, 7.2m (N, 1984; DVD, 2008; CD, 2006; A, 2004)

Précis: In 2084, the Silurians and Sea Devils invade Sea Base Four in order to start a nuclear war . . .

Observations: Interior location filming was conducted at the Royal Engineers' Diving Establishment at Marchwood, Hants. Richard Gregory and Mat Irvine made six Sea Devil and four Silurian costumes. The two operators of the Myrka also played Dobbin, the pantomime horse in *Rentaghost* (1975–84).

Verdict: Visually striking, the story's downfall is the linear plot, the sluggish invaders and the tinny music. The Myrka, despite much criticism, is no worse than any other large, lumbering *Doctor Who* monster. 7/10

131. THE AWAKENING (two parts)

Cast: Denis Lill (*Hutchinson*), Polly James (*Jane Hampden*), Glyn Houston (*Wolsey*), Keith Jayne (*Will*), Jack Galloway (*Willow*), Frederick Hall (*Verney*), Christopher Saul, Christopher Wenner (*Troopers*), John Kearns (*Plague Victim*) | **Crew:** Director: Michael Owen Morris; Writer: Eric Pringle; Music: Peter Howell | **Broadcast:** 19–20 January 1984, 14.5m (N, 1985; A, 2010)

Précis: For the inhabitants of Little Hodcombe, a Civil War re-enactment becomes all too real . . .

Observations: Filming took place in three villages: Tarrant Monkton and Shapwick, Dorset, and Martin, Hants. A beheading scene was slightly trimmed prior to transmission and a brief scene featuring Kamelion was edited out completely. Peter Davison was given a new, slightly altered, costume.

Verdict: An atmospheric little gem with a creepy central premise, well directed by Michael Owen Morris. 9/10

132. FRONTIOS (four parts)

Cast: Jeff Rawle (*Plantagenet*), Peter Gilmore (*Brazen*), Lesley Dunlop (*Norna*), William Lucas (*Range*), Maurice O'Connell (*Cockerill*), John Beardmore (*Revere*), John Gillett (*Gravis*), Raymond Murtagh (*Retrograde*), Jim Dowdall (*Warnsman*), George Campbell, Michael Malcolm, Stephen

Speed, William Bowen, Hedi Khursandi (*Tractators*) | **Crew:** Director: Ron Jones; Writer: Christopher H Bidmead; Music: Paddy Kingsland | **Broadcast:** 26 January–3 February 1984, 6.8m (N, 1984)

Précis: An Earth colony is attacked by meteors, while insect-like Tractators suck people into the ground . . .

Observations: Six Tractator costumes, based on woodlice, were designed by Dave Havard. Planned shots of them curling into a ball were abandoned due to their restrictive nature. Originally, Peter Arne was to play Dr Range, but he was murdered days before recording.

Verdict: Although the action sequences are rather clumsy, this is an imaginative story with excellent production values and an intriguing race of monsters. 8/10

133. RESURRECTION OF THE DALEKS

(two × 50m parts)

Cast: Maurice Colbourne (*Lytton*), Terry Molloy (*Davros*), Rodney Bewes (*Stien*), Rula Lenska (*Styles*), Del Henney (*Archer*), Chloe Ashcroft (*Laird*), Philip McGough (*Calder*), Jim Findley (*Mercer*), Leslie Grantham (*Kiston*), Adrian Scott (*Chemist*), Sneh Gupta (*Osborn*), Brian Miller, Royce Mills (*Dalek voices*), John Scott Martin, Cy Town, Tony Starr, Toby Byrne (*Daleks*) | **Crew:** Director: Matthew Robinson; Writer: Eric Saward; Music: Malcolm Clarke | **Broadcast:** 8–15 February 1984, 7.7m (DVD, 2011)

Précis: Davros escapes from his space prison to help deactivate a Movellan virus stored in London . . .

Observations: Butler's Wharf, Curlew Street, Lafone Street and Shad Thames were the locations chosen in London's Docklands. Davros' new mask was sculpted by Stan Mitchell and a flashback scene of all the Doctor's companions (minus Leela) featured in part two. The story was transmitted in two double-length parts to make way for the 1984 Winter Olympics from Sarajevo, an event which also pushed the Daleks off the cover of the *Radio Times*.

Verdict: An ultra-violent, soulless remake of *Earthshock* (121). Beneath the technobabble, endless continuity references, silly hats and abysmally acted death scenes, there's no sign of a plot. 2/10

134. PLANET OF FIRE (four parts)

Cast: Peter Wyngarde (*Timanov*), Anthony Ainley (*The Master*), Dallas Adams (*Howard*), Barbara Shelley (*Sorasta*), Gerald Flood (*Kamelion voice*), James Bate (*Amyand*), Jonathan Caplan (*Roskal*), Edward Highmore (*Malkon*), Max Arthur (*Zuko*) | **Crew:** Director: Fiona Cumming; Writer: Peter Grimwade; Music: Peter Howell | **Broadcast:** 23 February–2 March 1984, 7m (N, 1984; DVD, 2010)

Précis: A miniaturised Master gets Kamelion to restore his size in a planet's volcano . . .

Observations: Filming in Lanzarote was conducted at various locations in Montanas del Fuego, Mirador del Rio, Papagoyo Bay and Orzola. Kamelion was finally written out because of operating problems, despite not appearing since his introduction in *The King's Demons* (128).

Verdict: Despite energetic direction and breathtaking location photography, the highlight of this story is probably still Nicola Bryant in a skimpy bikini. 6/10

135. THE CAVES OF ANDROZANI (four parts)

Cast: Christopher Gable (*Sharaz Jek*), Maurice Roëves (*Stotz*), John Normington (*Morgus*), Robert Glenister (*Salateen*), Martin Cochrane (*Chellak*), Roy Holder (*Krelper*), Barbara Kinghorn (*Timmin*), David Neal (*President*), Colin Taylor (*Magma Creature*) | **Crew:** Director: Graeme Harper; Writer: Robert Holmes; Music: Roger Limb | **Broadcast:** 8–16 March 1984, 7.3m (N, 1984; DVD, 2010)

Précis: Dying of spectrox poisoning, the Doctor and Peri are caught in a futile war on Androzani Minor . . .

Observations: Location filming was done at Masters Quarry in Wareham, Dorset. Part four's effects-heavy regeneration sequence featured a specially shot montage of past companions and the Master. Sharaz Jek's leather mask was based on that of a Zulu warrior.

Verdict: A visceral war story, brilliantly directed, edited and acted, with a marvellously doom-laden musical score. 10/10

136. THE TWIN DILEMMA (four parts)

Cast: Dennis Chinnery (*Sylvest*), Maurice Denham (*Edgeworth/ Azmael*), Kevin McNally (*Lang*), Edwin Richfield (*Mestor*), Seymour Green (*Chamberlain*), Barry Stanton (*Noma*), Oliver Smith (*Drak*), Gavin Conrad (*Romulus*), Andrew Conrad (*Remus*), Helen Blatch (*Fabian*), Steve Wickham, Ridgewell Hawkes (*Gastropods*) | **Crew:** Director: Peter Moffatt; Writer: Anthony Steven; Music: Malcolm Clarke | **Broadcast:** 22–30 March 1984, 7.1m (N, 1985; DVD, 2009)

Précis: A giant slug kidnaps twin mathematical geniuses . . .

Observations: Quarries in Rickmansworth, Herts, and Gerrards Cross, Bucks, were used for filming. The Sixth Doctor's tasteless costume was designed by Pat Godfrey, with Sid Sutton and Terry Handley creating a more colourful version of the title sequence to accompany it. Four gastropod costumes were built by Richard Gregory.

Verdict: An old-fashioned *TV Comic*-style plot isn't helped by terrible production values and a misjudged central performance. 2/10

SEASON 22

Producer: John Nathan-Turner
Script Editor: Eric Saward
Sixth Doctor: Colin Baker
Companion: Nicola Bryant (*Peri Brown*)

137. ATTACK OF THE CYBERMEN (two × 45m parts)

Cast: Maurice Colbourne (*Lytton*), Terry Molloy (*Russell*), Brian Glover (*Griffiths*), James Beckett (*Payne*), Jonathan David (*Stratton*), Michael Attwell (*Bates*), Sarah Greene (*Varne*), Sarah Berger (*Rost*), Esther Freud (*Threst*), Faith Brown (*Flast*), David Banks (*Cyber Leader*), Michael Kilgarriff (*Cyber Controller*), Brian Orrell (*Cyber Lieutenant*), John Ainley, Ian Marshall-Fisher, Roger Pope, Thomas Lucy, Ken Barker, Pat Gorman (*Cybermen*) | **Crew:** Director: Matthew Robinson; Writer: 'Paula Moore' (pseudonym for Eric Saward and Paula Woolsey, from a story by Ian Levine); Music: Malcolm Clarke | **Broadcast:** 5–12 January 1985, 8m (N, 1989; DVD, 2009)

Précis: The Cybermen plan to crash Halley's Comet into the Earth . . .
Observations: Transmission was moved back to Saturday for this, and the following, season. London scenes were

filmed in Acton and Shepherd's Bush and the same Gerrards Cross quarry represented Telos as it did for *The Tomb of the Cybermen* (37). The Tardis briefly changed its outward appearance to a pipe organ and a pair of ornate gates. Eight Cyberman costumes were reused from *Earthshock* (121) and *The Five Doctors* (129). The Cryon costumes consisted of white leotards under cellophane jumpsuits.

Verdict: Badly written and continuity-obsessed, with a predilection towards needless violence. 3/10

138. VENGEANCE ON VAROS (two × 45m parts)

Cast: Nabil Shaban (*Sil*), Martin Jarvis (*Governor*), Jason Connery (*Jondar*), Forbes Collins (*Chief Officer*), Sheila Reid (*Etta*), Stephen Yardley (*Arak*), Geraldine Alexander (*Areta*), Owen Teale (*Maldak*), Nicholas Chagrin (*Quillam*), Graham Cull (*Bax*), Keith Skinner (*Rondel*), Gareth Milne, Roy Alon (*Mortuary Attendants*) | **Crew:** Director: Ron Jones; Writer: Philip Martin; Music: Jonathan Gibbs | **Broadcast:** 19–26 January 1985, 7.1m (N, 1988; DVD, 2001)

Précis: On Varos, a sadistic government transmits torture scenes as entertainment . . .

Observations: Born with osteogenesis imperfecta, Nabil Shaban was co-founder of the disabled actors' theatre group, Graeae. His Sil costume was made from latex by Charles Jeanes. Letters to the *Radio Times* and *Points of View* criticised the perceived level of violence in this story and the previous one.

Verdict: A brave idea, hindered by a plodding narrative and wooden performances. The notorious acid bath scene, in which the Doctor makes a flippant comment after watching two men die, is deeply problematic. 6/10

139. THE MARK OF THE RANI (two × 45m parts)

Cast: Kate O'Mara (*The Rani*), Anthony Ainley (*The Master*), Terence Alexander (*Lord Ravensworth*), Gawn Grainer (*George Stephenson*),

Gary Cady (*Luke Ward*), Peter Childs (*Jack Ward*), Kevin White (*Sam Rudge*) | **Crew:** Director: Sarah Hellings; Writers: Pip & Jane Baker; Music: Jonathan Gibbs | **Broadcast:** 2–9 February 1985, 6.8m (N, 1986; DVD, 2006)

Précis: The Rani is extracting brain fluid from miners during the Luddite uprising . . .

Observations: An extra week's filming was allocated to this story, which utilised Blists Hill Open Air Museum, Coalport China Works and Granville Colliery Spoil Heaps, Shropshire. A remount due to bad weather took place at Park Wood, Ruislip, Middx. The interior of the Rani's Tardis was designed by David Barton.

Verdict: Excitingly directed by newcomer Sarah Hellings, this is nonetheless a meandering story with some very stupid moments and the inclusion of one too many panto-mime villains. 4/10

140. THE TWO DOCTORS (three × 45m parts)

Cast: Patrick Troughton (*Second Doctor*), Frazer Hines (*Jamie*), Laurence Payne (*Dastari*), John Stratton (*Shockeye*), Jacqueline Pearce (*Chessene*), James Saxon (*Oscar*), Carmen Gomez (*Anita*), Clinton Greyn (*Stike*), Tim Raynham (*Varl*) | **Crew:** Director: Peter Moffatt; Writer: Robert Holmes; Music: Peter Howell | **Broadcast:** 16 February–2 March 1985, 6.3m (N, 1985; DVD, 2003)

Précis: Sontarans take the Second Doctor to Spain where they plan to dissect him and steal the secrets of time travel . . .

Observations: The story's location was originally New Orleans in Louisiana, but this fell through when American co-financier Lionheart pulled out. Instead, Spanish filming was conducted in Seville and a hacienda between Gerena and El Garrobo. The two Sontarans were redesigned by Jan Wright and Richard Gregory. The story's cannibalistic overtones were heavily criticised by BBC1 Controller Michael Grade, along with similar elements in *Attack of the*

Cybermen (137) and *Vengeance on Varos* (138), leading to a nine-month postponement for Season 23.

Verdict: A *Doctor Who* version of *Last of the Summer Wine* as sponsored by the Vegetarian Society. 7/10

141. TIMELASH (two × 45m parts)

Cast: Paul Darrow (*Tekker*), Jeananne Crowley (*Vena*), Eric Deacon (*Mykros*), David Chandler (*HG Wells*), Robert Ashby (*The Borad*), Denis Carey (*Old Man*), David Ashton (*Kendron*), Dicken Ashworth (*Sezon*), Dean Hollingsworth (*Android*), Peter Robert Scott (*Brunner*), Neil Hallet (*Maylin Renis*) | **Crew:** Director: Pennant Roberts; Writer: Glen McCoy; Music: Liz Parker | **Broadcast:** 9–16 March 1985, 7m (N, 1985; DVD, 2007)

Précis: Those who oppose the Borad's tyrannical rule are thrown into the Timelash . . .

Observations: Stan Mitchell sculpted the Borad half-mask from fine foam rubber, enabling it to move with Robert Ashby's facial expressions. The Timelash's interior was a wall studded with hexagonal wooden rods covered with tinsel and lit by disco lights. Part two was found to be under-running, so an extra Tardis scene was recorded during the following Dalek story.

Verdict: An unfairly maligned homage to HG Wells and bad 'B' movies, *Timelash* is good, old-fashioned entertainment in a season brimming with macho portentousness. It all goes pear-shaped towards the end, but on the way there's plenty of fun to be had. 7/10

142. REVELATION OF THE DALEKS
(two × 45m parts)

Cast: Clive Swift (*Jobel*), Jenny Tomasin (*Tasembeker*), Eleanor Bron (*Kara*), Hugh Walters (*Vogel*), Terry Molloy (*Davros*), Alexei Sayle (*DJ*), William Gaunt (*Orcini*), John Ogwen (*Bostock*), Stephen Flynn (*Grigory*), Bridget Lynch-Blosse (*Natasha*), Trevor Cooper (*Takis*),

Colin Spaull (*Lilt*), Royce Mills, Roy Skelton (*Dalek voices*), John Scott Martin, Cy Town, Tony Starr, Toby Byrne (*Daleks*) | **Crew:** Director: Graeme Harper; Writer: Eric Saward; Music: Roger Limb | **Broadcast:** 23–30 March 1985, 7.6m (DVD, 2005)

Précis: Davros, posing as the Great Healer, is raiding a mortuary on Necros to breed new Daleks . . .

Observations: IBM UK, Cosham, and Queen Elizabeth Park, Petersfield, both Hants, were chosen as filming locations. Six new cream and gold Daleks were constructed, along with a hollow Perspex version made by outside contractor Dennys. Davros' mask and chair were also newly made. Film scenes involving flying Daleks (catapulted from a spring-loaded platform) were abandoned due to heavy snowfall. Colin Baker's deleted final word, 'Blackpool', was a reference to *The Nightmare Fair* by Graham Williams, a Celestial Toymaker story that was to have opened Season 23 prior to its postponement.

Verdict: An incredibly violent black comedy. Harper's direction is visceral, the actors are having a whale of a time and it's all held together by Roger Limb's spine-chilling music. The only thing missing is a plot. 8/10

SEASON 23

Producer: John Nathan-Turner
Script Editor: Eric Saward (143a–143b, 143d)
Sixth Doctor: Colin Baker
Companions: Nicola Bryant (*Peri Brown*, 143a–143b, 143d) & Bonnie Langford (*Melanie Bush*, 143c–143d)

143. THE TRIAL OF A TIME LORD (14 parts)

143A | PARTS 1–4

Cast: Michael Jayston (*The Valeyard*), Lynda Bellingham (*The Inquisitor*), Tony Selby (*Glitz*), Joan Sims (*Katryca*), Glen Murphy (*Dibber*), Tom Chadbon (*Merdeen*), Roger Brierley (*Drathro voice*), Paul McGuinness (*Drathro*), Mike Ellis (*L1 Service Robot*), David Rodigan (*Broken Tooth*), Adam Blackwood (*Balazar*), Sion Tudor Owen (*Tandrell*), Billy McColl (*Humker*) | **Crew:** Director: Nick Mallett; Writer: Robert Holmes; Music: Dominic Glynn | **Broadcast:** 6–27 September 1986, 4.6m (N, 1987; DVD, 2008)

Précis: On trial by the Time Lords, the Doctor is shown a recent adventure on Ravolox in which conmen steal secrets held by a giant robot . . .

Observations: Producer John Nathan-Turner decided to reflect the real-life crisis facing the show by reformatting this new, shortened season into one full-length story. The opening computer-controlled model shot of the space station cost £8,000 – the show's most expensive special effect to date. Location videotaping took place at Butser Hill and Queen Elizabeth Country Park, both Hants. Dominic Glynn arranged a new, more sinister, version of the theme music.

Verdict: Despite good performances all round, the story goes nowhere, says little and ultimately comes to nothing. The supposedly humorous ending is woeful. 4/10

143B | PARTS 5–8

Cast: Michael Jayston (*The Valeyard*), Lynda Bellingham (*The Inquisitor*), Patrick Ryecart (*Crozier*), Brian Blessed (*Yrcanos*), Nabil Shaban (*Sil*), Christopher Ryan (*Kiv*), Trevor Laird (*Frax*), Thomas Branch (*Lukoser*), Gordon Warnecke (*Tuza*), Alibe Parsons (*Matrona Kani*), Russell West (*Raak*), Richard Henry (*Mentor*) | **Crew:** Director: Ron Jones; Writer: Philip Martin; Music: Richard Hartley | **Broadcast:** 4–25 October 1986, 4.9m (N, 1989; DVD, 2008)

Précis: On Thoros Beta, Sil's boss Kiv needs a brain transplant – but the Doctor has been brainwashed and Peri is chosen as Kiv's new host . . .

Observations: Location videoing took place at Telscombe Cliffs, near Brighton; new digital image processor 'Harry' coloured the sky green and the sea pink. Peri became the fourth companion to be killed (although this is later denied in part thirteen). Nabil Shaban wore his original Sil costume, albeit with a more comfortable headpiece, while Peter Wragg made four more Mentor costumes.

Verdict: Excellent music, imaginative design, a stunning final cliffhanger and the presence of Sil make this a memorable tale. Of the supporting cast, top marks go to Thomas Branch as the Lukoser. 9/10

143C | PARTS 9–12

Cast: Michael Jayston (*The Valeyard*), Lynda Bellingham (*The Inquisitor*), Honor Blackman (*Lasky*), Michael Craig (*Commodore*), Denys Hawthorne (*Rudge*), Tony Scoggo (*Grenville*), Malcolm Tierney (*Doland*), David Allister (*Bruchner*), Simon Slater (*Edwardes*), Yolande Palfrey (*Janet*), Arthur Hewlett (*Kimber*), Sam Howard (*Atza*), Leon Davis (*Ortezo*), Barbara Ward (*Ruth*), Peppi Borza, Bob Appleby, Gess Whitfield, Paul Hillier, Bill Perrie, Jerry Manley (*Vervoids*) | **Crew:** Director: Chris Clough; Writers: Pip & Jane Baker; Music: Malcolm Clarke | **Broadcast:** 1–22 November 1986, 5.1m (N, 1987; DVD, 2008)

Précis: In the near future, the Doctor and new companion Mel land on a spaceliner whose passengers are threatened by sentient plants . . .
Observations: To indicate this was a future story, Colin Baker wore a different tie and waistcoat. Six latex and rubber Vervoid costumes were constructed, with masks based on Venus flytraps. Citing artistic differences, script editor Eric Saward left midway through production.
Verdict: An archetypal studio-bound *Who*-dunnit, which might have worked had the sets been more realistic and the direction less flat. Impressive (albeit very rude) monsters and *great* cliffhangers though. 6/10

143D | PARTS 13–14

Cast: Michael Jayston (*The Valeyard*), Lynda Bellingham (*The Inquisitor*), Anthony Ainley (*The Master*), Tony Selby (*Glitz*), Geoffrey Hughes (*Popplewick*), James Bree (*The Keeper*) | **Crew:** Director: Chris Clough; Writers: Robert Holmes (13), Pip & Jane Baker (14); Music: Dominic Glynn | **Broadcast:** 29 November–6 December 1986, 5m (N, 1988; DVD, 2008)

Précis: The Doctor battles for his life in the strange world of the Matrix . . .
Observations: Robert Holmes died before finishing the last part, so Eric Saward completed it. But after disagreements

with Nathan-Turner over the ending (the Doctor and the Valeyard in mortal combat in the Matrix), he withdrew permission to use his version, thus Pip and Jane Baker were called in at the last minute to pen an alternative conclusion. Videoing took place at Camber Sands, East Sussex, and Gladstone Pottery Museum, Stoke-on-Trent, Staffs. Due to the intricacies of resolving so many plot threads, part 14 was allowed a five-minute extension.

Verdict: Revisiting the surreal Matrix of *The Deadly Assassin* (88) is a good idea, but the Dickensian setting is limiting and the minuscule cast gives the impression that the money has run out. The ending is chaotic and confused. 4/10

SEASON 24

Producer: John Nathan-Turner
Script Editor: Andrew Cartmel
Seventh Doctor: Sylvester McCoy
Companions: Bonnie Langford (*Melanie Bush*) & Sophie Aldred (*Ace*, 147)

144. TIME AND THE RANI (four parts)

Cast: Kate O'Mara (*The Rani*), Donald Pickering (*Beyus*), Wanda Ventham (*Faroon*), Karen Clegg (*Sarn*), Mark Greenstreet (*Ikona*), Richard Gauntlett (*Urak*), John Segal (*Lanisha*), Peter Tuddenham, Jackie Webb (*Voices*) | **Crew:** Director: Andrew Morgan; Writers: Pip & Jane Baker; Music: Keff McCulloch | **Broadcast:** 7–28 September 1987, 4.6m (N, 1987; DVD, 2010)

Précis: The Rani kidnaps the newly regenerated Doctor for his brainpower . . .

Observations: Having been sacked by the BBC the previous year, Colin Baker refused to appear in the pre-credits regeneration sequence, so McCoy donned a curly wig to impersonate him. Ken Trew created the Seventh Doctor's costume, based on a 1930s golfing design, and a new CGI title sequence was designed by Oliver Elmes and executed by Gareth Edwards of CAL Videographics, with the theme music rearranged by Keff McCulloch. Three quarries in Frome, Somerset, stood in for Lakertya.

Verdict: It may be childish at times, but there's a real sense of energy in the storytelling and it's got some fabulous special effects. 7/10

145. PARADISE TOWERS (four parts)

Cast: Richard Briers (*Chief Caretaker*), Clive Merrison (*Deputy*), Howard Cooke (*Pex*), Annabel Yuresha (*Bin Liner*), Julie Brennon (*Fire Escape*), Catherine Cusack (*Blue Kang Leader*), Astra Sheridan (*Yellow Kang*), Joseph Young (*Young Caretaker*), Brenda Bruce (*Tilda*), Elizabeth Spriggs (*Tabby*), Judy Cornwell (*Maddy*) | **Crew:** Director: Nicholas Mallett; Writer: Stephen Wyatt; Music: Keff McCulloch | **Broadcast:** 5–26 October 1987, 4.9m (N, 1988)

Précis: A block of flats occupied by street gangs and cannibalistic geriatrics is ruled by a dictatorial caretaker and his cronies . . .

Observations: The (unheated) swimming pool sequences were shot in Elmswell House, Chalfont St Giles. Three fibreglass Cleaner robots were designed by Simon Taylor, along with the lobster-like pool-cleaning robot.

Verdict: The script is a cross between Alans Bennett and Ayckbourn, while Clive Merrison and Richard Briers are hilarious as the Hitleresque caretakers with their 'fingers under nose' salutes. Paradise Towers itself is brilliantly realised and the story's strength lies in its expert balancing of humour and horror (which goes slightly awry in part four). 9/10

146. DELTA AND THE BANNERMEN (three parts)

Cast: Belinda Mayne (*Delta*), Don Henderson (*Gavrok*), David Kinder (*Billy*), Sara Griffiths (*Ray*), Stubby Kaye (*Weismuller*), Morgan Deare (*Hawk*), Richard Davies (*Burton*), Hugh Lloyd (*Goronwy*), Johnny Dennis (*Murray*), Ken Dodd (*Tollmaster*), Brian Hibbard (*Keillor*), Martyn Geraint (*Vinny*) | **Crew:** Director: Chris Clough; Writer: Malcolm Kohll; Music: Keff McCulloch | **Broadcast:** 2–16 November 1987, 5.3m (N, 1989; DVD, 2009)

Précis: Gavrok and his Bannermen chase the last of the Chimerons to a Welsh holiday camp in 1959 . . .

Observations: As well as Springwell Quarry in Rickmansworth, Herts, various South Wales sites were used for this location-only story, centring around the Yellow Camp area of the Majestic Holiday Camp on Barry Island. Keff McCulloch provided cover versions of all the rock and roll music in the show and also appeared in part one playing in backing group The Lorells. The Bannerman spaceship was built by Mike Tucker.

Verdict: A confident, summery musical comedy with violent overtones, *Delta* divides opinion like no other *Doctor Who* story. But it's hard not to admire its sheer cheek. 8/10

147. DRAGONFIRE (three parts)

Cast: Edward Peel (*Kane*), Patricia Quinn (*Belazs*), Tony Osoba (*Kracauer*), Stephanie Fayerman (*McLuhan*), Stuart Organ (*Bazin*), Nigel Miles-Thomas (*Pudovkin*), Ian Mackenzie (*Anderson*), Tony Selby (*Glitz*), Shirin Taylor (*Customer*), Miranda Borman (*Stellar*), Leslie Meadows (*Creature*) | **Crew:** Director: Chris Clough; Writer: Ian Briggs; Music: Dominic Glynn | **Broadcast:** 23 November–7 December 1987, 5.1m (N, 1989)

Précis: On the frozen planet of Svartos, the cadaverous Kane is hunting for treasure . . .

Observations: Characters were named after prominent film theorists, such as Béla Belázs and Marshall McLuhan, while the baddie's appellation came from *Citizen Kane* (1941). Kane's melting head in part three was achieved by pointing hot-air guns at a wax cast of Edward Peel, while pipes pumped out gunge from inside. *Dragonfire* was promoted, erroneously, as *Doctor Who*'s 150th story in the *Radio Times*.

Verdict: Sylvester McCoy gives a ludicrous performance in a story that can't decide whether it's all-out horror, or slapstick comedy. Edward Peel is suitably menacing and Sophie Aldred refreshingly naturalistic, but the production as a whole is inconsistent and sports one of the most baffling cliffhangers in the programme's history. 6/10

SEASON 25

Producer: John Nathan-Turner
Script Editor: Andrew Cartmel
Seventh Doctor: Sylvester McCoy
Companion: Sophie Aldred (*Ace*)

148. REMEMBRANCE OF THE DALEKS
(four parts)

Cast: George Sewell (*Ratcliffe*), Simon Williams (*Gilmore*), Dursley McLinden (*Mike*), Pamela Salem (*Rachel*), Karen Gledhill (*Allison*), Michael Sheard (*Headmaster*), Harry Fowler (*Harry*), Joseph Marcell (*John*), Jasmine Breaks (*Girl*), Peter Halliday (*Vicar*), John Evans (*Undertaker*), Terry Molloy (*Emperor Dalek/Davros*), Royce Mills, Roy Skelton, Brian Miller, John Leeson (*Dalek voices*), Hugh Spight, John Scott Martin, Tony Starr, Cy Town, David Harrison, Norman Bacon, Nigel Wild (*Daleks*) | **Crew:** Director: Andrew Morgan; Writer: Ben Aaronovitch; Music: Keff McCulloch | **Broadcast:** 5–26 October 1988, 5.4m (N, 1990; DVD, 2009)

Précis: Arriving in 1963 London to reclaim the Hand of Omega, the Doctor is caught between two rival Dalek factions . . .

Observations: London locations included Theed Street and environs; Kew Bridge Steam Museum, Green Dragon Lane; Willesden Lane Cemetery; and St John's School in Hammersmith. Eight Daleks were used in total: four old props (as the renegades) and four new, slightly modified ones (Imperials). The Dalek Supreme was a BBC Enterprises prop made by Stuart Wilkie, while the Special Weapons Dalek was designed by Stuart Brisdon and built by Dave Becker. A Dalek was seen to levitate up a staircase for the first time, courtesy of a chairlift-like device disguised by an electronic red glow.

Verdict: With well-constructed cliffhangers, revelations aplenty and an epic feel to it, the story is undeniably exciting. But it sags under the weight of Dalek continuity and McCoy is largely incoherent. 8/10

149. THE HAPPINESS PATROL (three parts)

Cast: Sheila Hancock (*Helen A*), Ronald Fraser (*Joseph C*), Harold Innocent (*Gilbert M*), Lesley Dunlop (*Susan Q*), David John Pope (*Kandy Man*), Georgina Hale (*Daisy K*), Rachel Bell (*Priscilla P*), Richard D Sharp (*Earl Sigma*), John Normington (*Trevor Sigma*), Jonathan Burn (*Silas P*), Tim Barker (*Harold V*), Philip Neave (*Wences*), Ryan Freedman (*Wulfric*), Steve Swinscoe, Mark Carroll (*Snipers*), Cy Town (*Victim*) | **Crew:** Director: Chris Clough; Writer: Graeme Curry; Music: Dominic Glynn | **Broadcast:** 2–16 November 1988, 5.1m (N, 1990; A, 2009)

Précis: On Terra Alpha, sadness is illegal . . .

Observations: The Kandy Man was built by outside contractor Artem using an aluminium exoskeleton covered with fibreglass, latex and foam. Bassett Foods' chairman complained that the BBC had copied its Bertie Bassett character.

Verdict: This odd blend of whimsy and violence has a uniquely rundown feel to it – although one can't help but wonder whether it's by accident or design. Surprisingly, the Kandy Man is rather sinister. 7/10

150. SILVER NEMESIS (three parts)

Cast: Anton Diffring (*De Flores*), Fiona Walker (*Lady Peinforte*), Gerard Murphy (*Richard*), Metin Yenal (*Karl*), David Banks (*Cyber Leader*), Mark Hardy (*Cyber Lieutenant*), Brian Orrell, Danny Boyd, Paul Barrass, Scott Mitchell, Tony Carlton, Bill Malin (*Cybermen*), Leslie French (*Mathematician*), Courtney Pine (*Himself*), Delores Gray (*Mrs Remington*), John Ould, Dave Ould (*Walkmen*) | **Crew:** Director: Chris Clough; Writer: Kevin Clarke; Music: Keff McCulloch | **Broadcast:** 23 November–7 December 1988, 5.5m (N, 1989; DVD, 2010)

Précis: Nazis, Cybermen and a seventeeth-century sorceress are all after the deadly Nemesis statue . . .
Observations: Videoing took place at Greenwich Gasworks, London (now the site of the Millennium Dome); Arundel Castle, Bramber and Goring-by-Sea, West Sussex; and Black Jack's Mill Restaurant, Harefield, Middx. For the Cybermen, modified helmets and chest units from *Attack of the Cybermen* (137) were used, with new bodies made from WWII parachute G-suits.
Verdict: The story's all over the shop, but the action scenes are terrific. 5/10

151. THE GREATEST SHOW IN THE GALAXY (four parts)

Cast: Ricco Ross (*Ringmaster*), TP McKenna (*Captain*), Jessica Martin (*Mags*), Daniel Peacock (*Nord*), Ian Reddington (*Chief Clown*), Christopher Guard (*Bellboy*), Dee Sadler (*Flowerchild*), Peggy Mount (*Stallslady*), Gian Sammarco (*Whizzkid*), Deborah Manship (*Morgana*), Chris Jury (*Deadbeat*), Janet Hargreaves (*Mum*), David Ashford (*Dad*), Kathryn Ludlow (*Girl*) | **Crew:** Director: Alan Wareing; Writer: Stephen Wyatt; Music: Mark Ayres | **Broadcast:** 14 December 1988–4 January 1989, 5.4m (N, 1989)

Précis: On Segonax, Ace and the Doctor visit the infamous Psychic Circus . . .
Observations: Warmwell Quarry, Dorset, was the venue for the circus (a model and a full-size entrance). Due to an

asbestos scare at Television Centre, the interior was filmed in a tent in the car park of BBC's Elstree Studios. Robert Allsopp and Susan Moore made the Gods of Ragnarok from foam-rubber cladding.

Verdict: Extraordinary images, a cast to die for, great music and a narrative that treads the finest of lines between humour and horror. 10/10

SEASON 26

Producer: John Nathan-Turner
Script Editor: Andrew Cartmel
Seventh Doctor: Sylvester McCoy
Companion: Sophie Aldred (*Ace*)

152. BATTLEFIELD (four parts)

Cast: Jean Marsh (*Morgaine*), Angela Bruce (*Bambera*), Christopher Bowen (*Mordred*), Marcus Gilbert (*Ancelyn*), Ling Tai (*Shou Yuing*), Nicholas Courtney (*Brigadier*), Angela Douglas (*Doris*), June Bland (*Elizabeth Rowlinson*), Noel Collins (*Pat Rowlinson*), James Ellis (*Peter Warmsly*), Marek Anton (*The Destroyer*) | **Crew:** Director: Michael Kerrigan; Writer: Ben Aaronovitch; Music: Keff McCulloch | **Broadcast:** 6–27 September 1989, 3.7m (N, 1991; DVD, 2008)

Précis: The Brigadier is called out of retirement when knights from another dimension converge on a nuclear missile convoy . . .

Observations: Location videoing took place in Fulmer and Black Park, Bucks; Hambleton, Leics; and Twyford Woods, Lincs. Sophie Aldred was involved in a potentially fatal accident when the water tank she was inside cracked and flooded the studio. The suits of armour were originally used in *Excalibur* (1981).

Verdict: Snappy editing aside, this is a confused mess of a story. Cheap knights fly through the air, the music's ghastly and a good monster stands there doing nothing. 3/10

153. GHOST LIGHT (three parts)

Cast: Ian Hogg (*Josiah Smith*), Carl Forgione (*Nimrod*), Sylvia Sims (*Mrs Pritchard*), Katharine Schlesinger (*Gwendoline*), Sharon Duce (*Control*), John Hallam (*Light*), Michael Cochrane (*Fenn-Cooper*), Frank Windsor (*Mackenzie*), John Nettleton (*Matthews*), Brenda Kempner (*Mrs Grose*) | **Crew:** Director: Alan Wareing; Writer: Marc Platt; Music: Mark Ayres | **Broadcast:** 4–18 October 1989, 4.1m (N, 1990; DVD, 2004)

Précis: Strange creatures lurk in the basement of Gabriel Chase . . .

Observations: A house in Weymouth, Dorset, featured as Gabriel Chase, videoed during the recording of *Survival* (155). Mike Tucker and Paul McGuinness made the two husks, while costume designer Ken Trew gave the Doctor a darker jacket.

Verdict: A powerful statement about embracing change is spoilt by incomprehensible editing. 5/10

154. THE CURSE OF FENRIC (four parts)

Cast: Dinsdale Landen (*Dr Judson*), Alfred Lynch (*Commander Millington*), Tomek Bork (*Sorin*), Nicholas Parsons (*Reverend Wainwright*), Janet Henfrey (*Miss Hardaker*), Joann Kenny (*Jean*), Joanne Bell (*Phyllis*), Marek Anton (*Vershinin*) | **Crew:** Director: Nicholas Mallett; Writer: Ian Briggs; Music: Mark Ayres | **Broadcast:** 25 October–15 November 1989, 4.1m (N, 1990; DVD, 2003)

Précis: Yorkshire, 1943, and a Viking curse looks like it's about to come true . . .

Observations: Locations doubling for Yorkshire were found in Hawkhurst, Kent; Crowborough Training Camp, East Essex; and Lulworth Cove, Dorset. The Haemovore masks were sculpted from latex by Susan Moore and Stephen Mansfield.

Verdict: Hugely atmospheric, with Nicholas Parsons giving a fine performance, but the plotting is sometimes cloudy. 7/10

155. SURVIVAL (three parts)

Cast: Anthony Ainley (*The Master*), Julian Holloway (*Paterson*), Will Barton (*Midge*), Lisa Bowerman (*Karra*), Sakuntala Ramanee (*Shreela*), Kate Eaton (*Ange*), David John (*Derek*), Adele Silva (*Squeak*), Gareth Hale (*Harvey*), Norman Pace (*Len*), Lee Towsey, Basil Peton, Leslie Meadows, Emma Darrell, Samantha Leverette, Adel Jackson, Susan Goode, Damon Jeffrey (*Cheetahs*) | **Crew:** Director: Alan Wareing; Writer: Rona Munro; Music: Dominic Glynn | **Broadcast:** 22 November–6 December 1989, 4.9m (N, 1990; DVD, 2007)

Précis: In present-day Perivale, Ace's friends are disappearing one by one . . .

Observations: Extensive videoing took place in Perivale and Sudbury Hill, West London, and Warmwell Quarry, Dorset. Ken Trew designed a new suit for the Master. When the show was not renewed for Season 27, an epilogue was dubbed onto the closing moments.

Verdict: A beautifully written story, dealing with big themes in an adult way. The clever mix of normality and exoticism is wonderful, as is the music. 9/10

SPECIAL

Producer: Peter V Ware
Script Supervisor: Jessica Clothier
Seventh Doctor: Sylvester McCoy
Eighth Doctor: Paul McGann
Companion: Daphne Ashbrook (*Grace Holloway*)

---

156. DOCTOR WHO (90m)

Cast: Eric Roberts (*The Master*), Yee Jee Tso (*Chang Lee*), Dave Hurtubise (*Wragg*), William Sasko (*Pete*), Eliza Roberts (*Miranda*), Delores Drake (*Curtis*), Michael David Simms (*Swift*) | **Crew:** Director: Geoffrey Sax; Writer: Matthew Jacobs; Music: John Debney | **Broadcast:** 27 May 1996, 9.1m (N, 1996; DVD, 2010; A, 2004)

Précis: In 1999 San Francisco, a newly regenerated Doctor tries to stop the Master from ending the world . . .
Observations: This Universal Television/BBC Worldwide co-production utilised many locations in Vancouver, Canada, to represent San Francisco. Richard Hudolin designed a huge new Jules Verne-style Tardis interior and the sonic screwdriver (last seen in *The Visitation*, 119)

reappeared. John Debney scored a new version of the theme music, while Northwest Imaging created a CGI title sequence incorporating the logo from Seasons 7–10. Cuts were made to an early gunfight scene in the wake of March's Dunblane school massacre, later reinstated in the DVD release. The *Radio Times* promoted the story with a cover and sixteen-page supplement.

Verdict: Way too many continuity references, but McGann is exceptional and the whole thing (plot holes and all) is a wonderfully slick entertainment. 8/10

SEASON 27

Executive Producers: Mal Young, Julie Gardner & Russell T Davies
Producer: Phil Collinson
Script Editors: Helen Raynor & Elwen Rowlands
Ninth Doctor: Christopher Eccleston
Tenth Doctor: David Tennant (166)
Companions: Billie Piper (*Rose Tyler*), Bruno Langley (*Adam*, 161–162), John Barrowman (*Captain Jack*, 164–166) & Noel Clarke (*Mickey Smith*, 157, 160, 165–166)

157. ROSE (one × 45m part)

Cast: Camille Coduri (*Jackie*), Mark Benton (*Clive*), Elli Garnett (*Caroline*), Alan Ruscoe, David Sant, Paul Kasey, Elizabeth Fost, Helen Otway, Holly Lumsden (*Autons*) | **Crew:** Director: Keith Boak; Writer: Russell T Davies; Music: Murray Gold | **Broadcast:** 26 March 2005, 10.8m (DVD, 2005)

Précis: The Autons are planning their third Earth invasion . . .

Observations: For the first episode in this new BBC Wales series, extensive night-time location videoing took place in the city centre of Cardiff, while brief London scenes included the Embankment, Westminster Bridge and the Brandon Estate in Walworth. A new arrangement of the theme music was composed by Murray Gold, accompanying a 'vortex' title sequence by MillTv (the television arm of visual effects company The Mill), together with a new elliptical logo designed by BBC Wales. A new, larger police box prop was constructed and the Tardis interior was totally redesigned by Edward Thomas, based on organic concept designs by Bryan Hitch. The Autons (unnamed as such in the story) were designed by Neill Gorton, while the Nestene Consciousness itself was a CGI creation by MillTv, which provided all the digital effects for the season. Lucinda Wright created the Ninth Doctor's minimalist costume of leather jacket and V-necked jumper. Because the story ran short, it incorporated a 'Next Week' trailer at the end (a trend that would continue for virtually every story thereafter). The *Radio Times* promoted the new series with a gatefold Tardis cover and a sixteen-page supplement. *Doctor Who Confidential*, a series of behind-the-scenes programmes looking at the making of the show, began transmitting on BBC3 immediately after each episode.

Verdict: Bright, brash and fast-moving, this is a perfect start to the Doctor's twenty-first century revival. Eccleston has real screen charisma and Billie Piper is charmingly naturalistic. The inclusion of the Autons, however, is less satisfying – reduced to 'monster of the week' status, their presence comes across as a cynical marketing ploy. 9/10

158. THE END OF THE WORLD (one × 45m part)

Cast: Simon Day (*Steward*), Yasmin Bannerman (*Jabe*), Jimmy Vee (*Moxx of Balhoon*), Zoë Wanamaker (*Cassandra voice*), Beccy Armory (*Raffalo*), Camille Coduri (*Jackie*) | **Crew:** Director: Euros Lyn; Writer: Russell T Davies; Music: Murray Gold | **Broadcast:** 2 April 2005, 8m (DVD, 2005)

Précis: On a space station observing the Earth's dying moments, a killer is at large . . .

Observations: Cardiff's Temple of Peace and Health was used as the interior of Platform One. Cassandra's skin, eyes and mouth were provided courtesy of CGI (as were the spider robots), while the rest of the aliens were realised by Neill Gorton's company, Millennium Effects. A pre-credits sequence made its first regular appearance.

Verdict: A woefully unfunny attempt to parody Douglas Adams, this is an obvious satire with little in the way of dramatic tension. The interiors are clearly terrestrial and the aliens are generally unconvincing. 3/10

159. THE UNQUIET DEAD (one × 45m part)

Cast: Simon Callow (*Charles Dickens*), Alan David (*Sneed*), Huw Rhys (*Redpath*), Eve Myles (*Gwyneth*), Jennifer Hill (*Mrs Peace*), Wayne Cater (*Stage Manager*), Zoe Thorne (*Gelth*) | **Crew:** Director: Euros Lyn; Writer: Mark Gatiss; Music: Murray Gold | **Broadcast:** 9 April 2005, 8.9m (DVD, 2005)

Précis: Cardiff, 1869, and the recently departed are just not staying in their coffins . . .

Observations: Night shooting was conducted around Swansea's maritime quarter and parts of Monmouth. Simon Callow had already portrayed Dickens in his one-man play, *The Mystery of Charles Dickens*.

Verdict: A beautifully made Victorian ghost story, with believable performances by the entire cast and some genuinely frightening moments. Gatiss' dialogue sparkles throughout. 10/10

160. ALIENS OF LONDON/ WORLD WAR THREE (two × 45m parts)

Cast: Camille Coduri (*Jackie*), Annette Badland (*Margaret Blaine*), Penelope Wilton (*Harriet Jones*), Rupert Vansittart (*Asquith*), David Verrey (*Green*), Eric Potts (*Charles*), Andrew Marr (*Himself*), Matt Baker (*Himself*), Navin Chowdhry (*Ganesh*), Steve Speirs (*Strickland*),

Naoko Mori (*Sato*), Morgan Hopkins (*Price*), Elizabeth Fost, Alan Ruscoe, Paul Kasey (*Slitheens*) | **Crew:** Director: Keith Boak; Writer: Russell T Davies; Music: Murray Gold | **Broadcast:** 16–23 April 2005, 7.8m (DVD, 2005)

Précis: A spaceship crashes into Big Ben and 10 Downing Street is overrun by baby-faced aliens . . .

Observations: Extensive filming was conducted on the Brandon Estate in London and Hensol Castle, Glamorgan, South Wales. The latter site represented the interior of 10 Downing Street, while a partially demolished house in Newport was used for its eventual demise. Cardiff Royal Infirmary became Albion Hospital. Rob Mayor and Neill Gorton made three fibreglass and latex Slitheen costumes with remote-controlled faces, while MillTv created CGI versions for action sequences.

Verdict: An oddly childish political spoof, with as many good moments as bad. Farting jokes, silly aliens, CBBC acting and a grossly naïve view of politics all drag it down. But the second part is more focused and the story has a neat, if rather unlikely, resolution. 7/10

161. DALEK (one × 45m part)

Cast: Corey Johnson (*Henry Van Statten*), Anna-Louise Plowman (*Goddard*), Steven Beckingham (*Polkowski*), Nigel Whitmey (*Simmons*), John Schwab (*Bywater*), Jana Carpenter (*De Maggio*), Joe Montana (*Commander*), Barnaby Edwards (*Dalek*), Nicholas Briggs (*Dalek voice*) | **Crew:** Director: Joe Ahearne; Writer: Robert Shearman; Music: Murray Gold | **Broadcast:** 30 April 2005, 8.6m (DVD, 2005)

Précis: In Utah, a millionaire's eccentric collection contains a deceptively harmless 'Metaltron' . . .

Observations: Based loosely on Robert Shearman's Big Finish audio play *Jubilee* (2003), most of this story was videoed in the basement corridors of Cardiff's Millennium Stadium. The redesigned Dalek incorporated many new features, most obviously an independently swivelling mid-section. MillTv were responsible for its ability to hover, while the tentacled mutant inside was made from silicone rubber by Neill Gorton.

Verdict: A dynamic reintroduction of the series' main foe, sadly hampered in the closing moments by an overdose of sentimentality. However, the Dalek itself is a thing of beauty and there are some fine scenes of death and destruction. The less said about Bruno Langley the better. 9/10

162. THE LONG GAME (one × 45m part)

Cast: Simon Pegg (*Editor*), Tamsin Greig (*Nurse*), Christine Adams (*Cathica*), Anna Maxwell-Martin (*Suki*), Colin Prockter (*Head Chef*), Judy Holt (*Adam's mum*) | **Crew:** Director: Brian Grant; Writer: Russell T Davies; Music: Murray Gold | **Broadcast:** 7 May 2005, 8m (DVD, 2005)

Précis: In AD 200,000, news broadcasts are being manipulated by a mysterious entity . . .

Observations: This studio-bound story featured a totally CGI monster in the form of the Mighty Jagrafess. Comic actor Simon Pegg was narrator of BBC 3 companion series *Doctor Who Confidential*.

Verdict: Probably intended as a satire of twenty-first-century news gathering, the simplistic plot and generally unconvincing set design conspire to give the story a cheap and rushed feel. Simon Pegg is muted and the climactic 'revelation' is a big disappointment. 4/10

163. FATHER'S DAY (one × 45m part)

Cast: Camille Coduri (*Jackie*), Shaun Dingwall (*Pete Tyler*), Christopher Llewellyn (*Stuart*), Frank Rozelaar-Green (*Sonny*), Natalie Jones (*Sarah*), Eirlys Bellin (*Bev*), Rhian James (*Suzie*), Julia Joyce (*Young Rose*), Casey Dyer (*Young Mickey*) | **Crew:** Director: Joe Ahearne; Writer: Paul Cornell; Music: Murray Gold | **Broadcast:** 14 May 2005, 8.1m (DVD, 2005)

Précis: Rose saves her father from a fatal road accident – with disastrous results for the world . . .

Observations: St Paul's Church in Grangetown, Cardiff, was the main location for this story. Originally intended as cloaked figures, the Reapers were brought to life by MillTv from Bryan Hitch's concept drawings.

Verdict: Billie Piper's finest forty-five minutes, this is a real attempt to widen the series' remit in terms of character-led storylines. It's a pity, then, that this intimate tale is saddled with a generic 'end of the world' threat. 8/10

164. THE EMPTY CHILD/ THE DOCTOR DANCES (two × 45m parts)

Cast: Florence Hoath (*Nancy*), Richard Wilson (*Constantine*), Albert Valentine (*Child*), Noah Johnson (*Child's voice*), Damian Samuels (*Mr Lloyd*), Cheryl Fergison (*Mrs Lloyd*), Luke Perry (*Timothy*), Robert Hands (*Algy*), Joseph Tremain (*Jim*), Jordan Murphy (*Ernie*), Martin Hodgson (*Jenkins*), Brandon Miller (*Alf*), Vilma Hollingbery (*Mrs Harcourt*), Dian Perry (*Computer voice*) | **Crew:** Director: James Hawes; Writer: Steven Moffat; Music: Murray Gold | **Broadcast:** 21–28 May 2005, 7m (DVD, 2005)

Précis: During the Blitz, an unearthly child in a gas mask roams the streets of London . . .

Observations: Cardiff was the main location for this story, while Barry Island's railway station saw scenes involving the crashed Chula ship. As with *Aliens of London* (160), Cardiff's Royal Infirmary once again appeared as Albion Hospital.

Verdict: Told entirely at night, the Blitz is brilliantly realised, thanks to some great CGI, and the atmosphere is consistently spooky. Iconic images abound – the gas-masked plague victims will probably live long in many children's nightmares. Scary, funny and exciting, only the heavy-handed references to 'dancing' (that is, sex) seem superfluous to the mix. 10/10

165. BOOM TOWN (one × 45m part)

Cast: Annette Badland (*Margaret Blaine*), William Thomas (*Cleaver*), Aled Pedrick (*Idris*), Mali Harries (*Cathy*), Alan Ruscoe (*Slitheen*) | **Crew:** Director: Joe Ahearne; Writer: Russell T Davies; Music: Murray Gold | **Broadcast:** 4 June 2005, 7.7m (DVD, 2005)

Précis: A lone Slitheen attempts to open a dimensional rift in the centre of Cardiff . . .

Observations: Extensive location videoing was carried out in Cardiff city centre, including the plaza outside the Millennium Centre, Cardiff Bay and Cardiff University's Glamorgan Building, seen as the interior of City Hall.

Verdict: There's probably a fascinating discourse on the nature of justice at the heart of this dull, unfunny exercise in padding, but you'd be hard pressed to find it. 1/10

166. BAD WOLF/ THE PARTING OF THE WAYS (two × 45m parts)

Cast: Anne Robinson (*Ann Droid voice*), Alan Ruscoe (*Ann Droid*), Davina McCall (*Davinadroid voice*), Trinny Woodall (*Trine-E voice*), Susannah Constantine (*Zu-Zana voice*), Martha Cope (*Controller*), Jo Joyner (*Lynda*), Jamie Bradley (*Strood*), Abi Eniola (*Crosbie*), Paterson Joseph (*Rodrick*), Dominic Burgess (*Agorax*), Karren Winchester (*Fitch*), Kate Loustau (*Colleen*), Camille Coduri (*Jackie*), Jo Stone Fewings (*Male Programmer*), Nisha Nayar (*Female Programmer*), Barnaby Edwards, Nicholas Pegg, David Hankinson (*Daleks*), Nicholas Briggs (*Dalek voices*) | **Crew:** Director: Joe Ahearne; Writer: Russell T Davies; Music: Murray Gold | **Broadcast:** 11–18 June 2005, 6.8m (DVD, 2005)

Précis: The Doctor ends up on *Big Brother* while the Daleks prepare to invade Earth . . .

Observations: A new Dalek Emperor was built by Mike Tucker, loosely based on the one seen in *The Evil of the Daleks* (36). Hordes of Daleks flying through space were CGI creations by MillTv. A sequence showing John Barrowman's naked backside was shot but never used.

Various false endings and scripts were leaked in order to keep the true resolution a secret.

Verdict: An odd amalgam of two stylistically opposing episodes, the whole is perhaps slightly less impressive than the sum of its parts. The Daleks and their retro 1960s spaceships look magnificent, but there is little plot development in the final episode and the way in which they are despatched by Rose's 'vortex' powers is akin to waving a magic wand. 9/10

SPECIAL

> **Executive Producers:** Julie Gardner & Russell T Davies
> **Producer:** Phil Collinson
> **Script Editor:** Helen Raynor
> **Tenth Doctor:** David Tennant
> **Companions:** Billie Piper (*Rose Tyler*) & Noel Clarke
> (*Mickey Smith*)

167. THE CHRISTMAS INVASION (60m)

Cast: Camille Coduri (*Jackie*), Penelope Wilton (*PM Harriet Jones*), Adam Garcia (*Alex*), Daniel Evans (*Danny Llewellyn*), Sean Gilder (*Sycorax leader*), Chu Omambala (*Major Blake*), Anita Briem (*Sally*) | **Crew:** Director: James Hawes; Writer: Russell T Davies; Music: Murray Gold | **Broadcast:** 25 December 2005, 9.8m (DVD, 2006)

Précis: A massive rock-shaped spaceship appears over London . . .

Observations: David Tennant's pinstripe suit was designed by Louise Page. A new version of the closing music was performed by the BBC National Orchestra of Wales. London locations included Walworth's Brandon Estate and the Tower of London. The UNIT base was actually the loading dock of Cardiff's Millennium Stadium. Clearwell Caves in Glos were used for the Sycorax spaceship interiors, while the exterior sword fight took place on Barry Island. Neill Gorton made the fibreglass Sycorax helmets, with the costumes inspired by Masai warriors. A seven-minute 'teaser' scene in the Tardis was shown on the BBC's *Children in Need* appeal on 3 November 2005. A *Radio Times* Christmas cover (the first for *Doctor Who*) promoted the show.

Verdict: Everything learnt over the previous year has been put to good use in this thoroughly enjoyable story. Fluidly directed, with an intelligent script by Davies and wonderful performances throughout, the whole thing looks amazing. 10/10

SEASON 28

Executive Producers: Julie Gardner & Russell T Davies
Producer: Phil Collinson
Script Editors: Helen Raynor & Simon Winstone
Tenth Doctor: David Tennant
Companions: Billie Piper (*Rose Tyler*), Noel Clarke
(*Mickey Smith,* 168, 170–172, 177) & Catherine Tate
(*Donna Noble,* 177)

168. NEW EARTH (one × 45m part)

Cast: Camille Coduri (*Jackie*), Zoë Wanamaker (*Cassandra voice/
Cassandra*), Sean Gallagher (*Chip*), Dona Croll (*Casp*), Michael Fitzgerald
(*Duke of Manhattan*), Lucy Robinson (*Frau Clovis*), Adjoa Andoh (*Jatt*),
Anna Hope (*Hame*), Simon Ludders (*Patient*), Struan Rodgers (*Face of
Boe voice*) | **Crew:** Director: James Hawes; Writer: Russell T Davies;
Music: Murray Gold | **Broadcast:** 15 April 2006, 8.6m (DVD, 2006)

Précis: Hideous experiments are being conducted in a
futuristic hospital . . .
Observations: A loose sequel to *The End of the World*
(158), location shooting was conducted on the Gower
Peninsula, while the interior of the hospital was, variously,

the Millennium Centre foyer, a basement in Newport's Tredegar House and a disused Cardiff paper mill previously seen in *Rose* (157). Three feline mask appliances were created by Neill Gorton. Debuting with this episode were children's companion series *Totally Doctor Who* on BBC1 and a series of mobile phone and Internet teasers called Tardisodes. A *Radio Times* wraparound cover heralded the new season.

Verdict: A very lame opening episode, this dismal attempt at 'body swap' comedy is neither funny, exciting nor original. 1/10

169. TOOTH AND CLAW (one × 45m part)

Cast: Pauline Collins (*Queen Victoria*), Derek Riddell (*Sir Robert*), Jamie Sives (*Captain Reynolds*), Ian Hanmore (*Father Angelo*), Ron Donachie (*Steward*), Tom Smith (*The Host*), Ruthie Milne (*Flora*) | **Crew:** Director: Euros Lyn; Writer: Russell T Davies; Music: Murray Gold | **Broadcast:** 22 April 2006, 9.2m (DVD, 2006)

Précis: 1879, and a werewolf is on the prowl in the Scottish Highlands . . .

Observations: Pauline Collins had previously been asked to play a companion after her appearance in *The Faceless Ones* (35) in 1967. Torchwood House was an amalgam of Tredegar House, Newport; Treowen Manor, Monmouth; Llansannor Court, Glamorgan; and Penllyn Castle, Cowbridge. The werewolf was a CGI creation by MillTv.

Verdict: A beautiful-looking, pacily edited horror story with great performances and a tangible sense of place, which even has time to set up spin-off series *Torchwood*. 10/10

170. SCHOOL REUNION (one × 45m part)

Cast: Elisabeth Sladen (*Sarah Jane Smith*), John Leeson (*K-9 III/ IV voice*), Anthony Head (*Finch*), Rod Arthur (*Parsons*), Eugene Washington (*Wagner*), Heather Cameron (*Nina*), Joe Pickley (*Kenny*),

Benjamin Smith (*Luke*), Clem Tibber (*Milo*), Lucinda Dryzek (*Melissa*) |
Crew: Director: James Hawes; Writer: Toby Whithouse; Music: Murray
Gold | **Broadcast:** 29 April 2006, 8.3m (DVD, 2006)

Précis: Winged aliens are eating the pupils of Deffry Vale
High School . . .

Observations: Two locations were used as the school:
Fitzalan High School, Cardiff, and Duffryn High School,
Newport. Sarah Jane Smith and K-9 had last been seen in
The Five Doctors (129). The rusted K-9 was a new prop
built by Nick Kool and Alan Brannan, while the 'rejuven-
ated' version was the original 1977 model first seen in *The
Invisible Enemy* (93).

Verdict: A bright, summery adventure that never seems
to go quite far enough in its satire and ends up feeling
rather rushed. Sarah's angst at being left behind seems odd,
considering she'd already returned *twice* to the *Doctor Who*
universe. 7/10

171. THE GIRL IN THE FIREPLACE
(one × 45m part)

Cast: Sophia Myles (*Reinette*), Jessica Atkins (*Young Reinette*), Ben
Turner (*Louis XV*), Angel Coulby (*Katherine*), Gareth Wyn Griffiths
(*Manservant*), Paul Kasey (*Clockwork Man*), Ellen Thomas (*Clockwork
Woman*), Arthur/Bolero (*Horse*) | **Crew:** Director: Euros Lyn; Writer:
Steven Moffat; Music: Murray Gold | **Broadcast:** 6 May 2006, 7.9m
(DVD, 2006)

Précis: An abandoned spaceship houses gateways to eight-
eenth-century France . . .

Observations: Neill Gorton and Louise Page designed the
clockwork robots, based on a real-life 1769 chess-playing
'clockwork' hoax called the Turk. Locations included
Tredegar House, Newport; Dyffryn Gardens, Glamorgan;
and Ragley Hall, Warwickshire. The story marked Mickey's
first trip in the Tardis. The climactic mirror scene had

stuntman Peter Miles' head digitally replaced by Tennant's.
Verdict: Superbly written romantic fantasy with a surreal
and frightening atmosphere and a devastating conclusion.
Myles gives a muted performance, but the attention to
detail is stunning, as is the music. 9/10

172. RISE OF THE CYBERMEN/ THE AGE OF STEEL (two × 45m parts)

Cast: Camille Coduri (*Jackie*), Shaun Dingwall (*Pete*), Noel Clarke
(*Rickey*), Roger Lloyd-Pack (*John Lumic*), Andrew Hayden-Smith
(*Jake*), Don Warrington (*President*), Helen Griffin (*Mrs Moore*), Colin
Spaull (*Crane*), Mona Hammond (*Rita-Anne*), Paul Antony-Barber
(*Kendrick*), Duncan Duff (*Newsreader*), Paul Kasey (*Cyber Leader/
Cyber Controller*), Nicholas Briggs (*Cybermen voices*) | **Crew:** Director:
Graeme Harper; Writer: Tom MacRae; Music: Murray Gold | **Broadcast:**
13–20 May 2006, 8.4m (DVD, 2006)

Précis: Cybermen are being created on a parallel Earth . . .
Observations: The story was loosely based on Marc
Platt's 2002 audio play *Spare Parts*, for which he received
a credit. Neill Gorton and Edward Thomas designed the
newly imagined Art Deco Cybermen. They were made
from fibreglass, upgraded with powdered metal, with silicone hands and necks. Tear ducts and 'handlebars' were
retained from previous appearances. As well as London's
Battersea Power Station and Lambeth Pier, Welsh locations included Uskmouth Power Station and the Riverside
Arts Centre, Newport; Cardiff Heliport, Ely Papermill
and Cardiff Docks, Cardiff; and a Stella Artois brewery in
Monmouthshire. A *Radio Times* cover promoted the story.
Verdict: An unashamedly continuity-obsessed *Earthshock*
(121) for the twenty-first century, this is a wildly ambitious
reimagining of what made the Cybermen so popular. The
alternate universe aspect seems unnecessary, though, and
Lloyd-Pack's performance is deeply embarrassing. 7/10

173. THE IDIOT'S LANTERN (one × 45m part)

Cast: Maureen Lipman (*The Wire*), Ron Cook (*Magpie*), Jamie Foreman (*Eddie Connolly*), Debra Gillett (*Rita Connolly*), Rory Jennings (*Tommy Connolly*), Margaret John (*Grandma*), Sam Cox (*DI Bishop*), Ieuan Rhys (*Crabtree*) | **Crew:** Director: Euros Lyn; Writer: Mark Gatiss; Music: Murray Gold | **Broadcast:** 27 May 2006, 6.8m (DVD, 2006)

Précis: 1953 London, and an alien entity is inhabiting television sets . . .

Observations: Some videoing was done at Alexandra Palace, London, although Florizel Street (the working title for *Coronation Street*, 1960–present) was actually Florentia Street in Cardiff. Lipman recorded all her scenes in one morning.

Verdict: A rather dull 1950s pastiche that drowns a potentially creepy idea under a surfeit of technobabble. Most of the imagery is borrowed from *Sapphire and Steel* anyway. 5/10

174. THE IMPOSSIBLE PLANET/ THE SATAN PIT (two × 45m parts)

Cast: Shaun Parkes (*Zachary*), Danny Webb (*Jefferson*), Claire Rushbrook (*Ida*), Will Thorp (*Toby*), Ronny Jhutti (*Danny*), MyAnna Buring (*Scooti*), Paul Kasey (*Ood*), Gabriel Woolf (*Beast voice*), Silas Carson (*Ood voice*) | **Crew:** Director: James Strong; Writer: Matt Jones; Music: Murray Gold | **Broadcast:** 3–10 June 2006, 6.2m (DVD, 2006)

Précis: On a planet orbiting a black hole, a satanic creature is awakening . . .

Observations: Some Sanctuary Base interiors were shot at Mamhilad Park Industrial Estate in Pontypool, the cavern was Wenvoe Quarry (the first time the new series used this typically *Doctor Who* location), and sequences in the Pit itself took place at Clearwell Caves in Glos, the same location as *The Christmas Invasion* (167). The Ood actors wore latex masks designed by Neill Gorton, while the Beast was a CGI creation by MillTv. A walkway segment became part of the set for *Totally Doctor Who*. Space sequences were recorded on an underwater stage at Pinewood Studios.

Verdict: A richly atmospheric and frightening 'base under siege' story – at times a virtual remake of *The Robots of Death* (90). Gold's music racks up the tension and the Ood masks are chillingly original. 9/10

175. LOVE & MONSTERS (one × 45m part)

Cast: Camille Coduri (*Jackie*), Marc Warren (*Elton Pope*), Shirley Henderson (*Ursula Blake*), Peter Kay (*Victor Kennedy/Abzorbaloff*), Simon Greenall (*Skinner*), Moya Brady (*Bridget*), Kathryn Drysdale (*Bliss*), Paul Kasey (*Hoix*), Bella Emberg (*Mrs Croot*) | **Crew:** Director: Dan Zeff; Writer: Russell T Davies; Music: Murray Gold | **Broadcast:** 17 June 2006, 6.7m (DVD, 2006)

Précis: A fan's obsession with the Doctor soon turns into a nightmare . . .

Observations: The Abzorbaloff was designed by nine-year-old William Grantham for a *Blue Peter* 'Design a Monster' competition. The artist's intention was that it be the size of a double-decker bus. Comedian Peter Kay got the part by writing to Russell T Davies in praise of the revived series. The acronym LINDA had been used before in *Why Don't You . . . ?* (1973–95), a children's series produced by Davies in the 1980s. This story was shot alongside *The Impossible Planet/The Satan Pit* (174), hence the Doctor and Rose's lack of screen time. Cardiff locations included West Canal Wharf, Llandaff Fields and The Hayes.

Verdict: A slick and energetic piece of storytelling, although often inappropriately adult in tone and with a very uneasy mix of humour and horror. 6/10

176. FEAR HER (one × 45m part)

Cast: Abisola Agbaje (*Chloe Webber*), Nina Sosanya (*Trish*), Edna Doré (*Maeve*), Tim Farady (*Tom's Dad*), Abdul Salis (*Kel*), Richard Nichols (*Driver*), Huw Edwards (*Commentator*) | **Crew:** Director: Euros Lyn; Writer: Matthew Graham; Music: Murray Gold | **Broadcast:** 24 June 2006, 7.1m (DVD, 2006)

Précis: On a housing estate in 2012 London, children are vanishing into thin air . . .

Observations: A budget-saving story that replaced an abandoned one by actor/comedian Stephen Fry; location videoing centred on Page Drive, Tramorfa in Cardiff. The Olympics' opening ceremony was represented by modified footage of the 2002 Commonwealth Games in Manchester. Storyboard artist Richard Shaun Williams provided all the drawings.

Verdict: Although lifted wholesale from *Sapphire and Steel*, there are some effective moments and the story is satisfyingly structured. 5/10

177. ARMY OF GHOSTS/ DOOMSDAY
(two × 45m parts)

Cast: Camille Coduri (*Jackie*), Tracy-Ann Oberman (*Yvonne Hartman*), Raji James (*Rajesh Singh*), Freema Agyeman (*Adeola*), Hadley Fraser (*Gareth*), Oliver Mellor (*Matt*), Barbara Windsor (*Peggy Mitchell*), Derek Acorah (*Himself*), Alistair Appleton (*Himself*), Trisha Goddard (*Herself*), Shaun Dingwall (*Pete*), Andrew Hayden-Smith (*Jake*), Paul Kasey (*Cyber Leader*), Barnaby Edwards, Nicholas Pegg, Stuart Crossman, Anthony Spargo, Dan Barratt, Dave Hankinson (*Daleks*), Nicholas Briggs (*Dalek/Cybermen voices*), | **Crew:** Director: Graeme Harper; Writer: Russell T Davies; Music: Murray Gold | **Broadcast:** 1–8 July 2006, 8.2m (DVD, 2006)

Précis: Daleks and Cybermen fight a pitched battle over Torchwood HQ in Canary Wharf . . .

Observations: Torchwood's interiors were mainly studio sets, but some videoing was done at RAF St Athan in

Glamorgan and Brackla Bunkers in Bridgend. London's Brandon Estate featured again, while Rose and the Doctor's supposed last meeting took place on Southerndown Beach in the Vale of Glamorgan. A Black Dalek (a repainted prop from *Dalek*, 161) had last been seen in *Remembrance of the Daleks* (148), while the Genesis Ark, designed by Matt Savage, was a new creation. *Radio Times* publicised the story with two covers, showing Daleks or Cybermen holding a World Cup football.

Verdict: A fannish action-fest that pits two great enemies against each other to no great effect. In reintroducing various characters from *Rise of the Cybermen/The Age of Steel* (172), the story feels more like a sequel than a stand-alone adventure. Rose had become ever more clichéd and irritating throughout the season, so her departure, although emotive, comes as welcome relief. 8/10

SPECIAL

Executive Producers: Julie Gardner & Russell T Davies
Producer: Phil Collinson
Script Editor: Simon Winstone
Tenth Doctor: David Tennant
Companion: Catherine Tate (*Donna Noble*)

---

178. THE RUNAWAY BRIDE (60m)

Cast: Don Gilet (*Lance*), Howard Attfield (*Geoff*), Jacqueline King (*Sylvia*), Sarah Parish (*Empress of the Racnoss*), Trevor Georges (*Vicar*), Paul Kasey (*Robot Santa*) | **Crew:** Director: Euros Lyn; Writer: Russell T Davies; Music: Murray Gold | **Broadcast:** 25 December 2006, 9.4m (DVD, 2007)

Précis: A giant spider threatens to destroy the world . . .
Observations: The first story to be made at BBC Wales' new Upper Boat Studios in Pontypridd; London location work was conducted atop an office block in Shoe Lane and the Thames Barrier, Charlton. Cardiff locations included St Mary Street, St John the Baptist Church and corridors under the Millennium Stadium. Newport Docks' Impounding

Station was where the Empress appeared (a huge creation by Neill Gorton), while the Tardis car chase, previewed at a *Children in Need* concert on 19 November, took place mainly on Cardiff's link road. A revised *Doctor Who* logo was used for the title sequence.

Verdict: A horrible mess of a story with an incomprehensible script, a dire performance by Catherine Tate, embarrassingly feeble jokes and an impressive monster that does absolutely *nothing*. 2/10

SEASON 29

Executive Producers: Julie Gardner, Russell T Davies & Phil Collinson (185)
Producers: Phil Collinson (179–184, 186–187) & Susie Liggat (185)
Script Editors: Simon Winstone (179–181, 183, 184, 187), Lindsey Alford (182, 185) & Helen Raynor (186)
Tenth Doctor: David Tennant
Companions: Freema Agyeman (*Martha Jones*) & John Barrowman (*Captain Jack*, 187)

179. SMITH AND JONES (one × 45m part)

Cast: Anne Reid (*Florence Finnegan*), Roy Marsden (*Stoker*), Adjoa Andoh (*Francine Jones*), Gugu Mbatha-Raw (*Tish Jones*), Reggie Yates (*Leo Jones*), Trevor Laird (*Clive Jones*), Kimmi Richards (*Annalise*), Ben Righton (*Morgenstern*), Vineeta Rishi (*Julia Swales*), Paul Kasey (*Judoon Captain*), Nicholas Briggs (*Judoon voices*) | **Crew:** Director: Charles Palmer; Writer: Russell T Davies; Music: Murray Gold | **Broadcast:** 31 March 2007, 8.7m (DVD, 2007)

Précis: A hospital is transported to the Moon by intergalactic police . . .

Observations: The University of Glamorgan in Pontypridd, Singleton Hospital in Swansea and Usk Valley Business Park in Torfaen were all used as the fictitious Royal Hope Hospital. Freema Agyeman's appearance as Adeola in *Army of Ghosts/ Doomsday* (177) was explained away as being Martha Jones' cousin. A single, very heavy, Judoon head was designed by Rob Mayor, with animatronics by Gustav Hoegen. A second series of *Totally Doctor Who* began on 2 April and the story was featured on two collectable *Radio Times* covers.

Verdict: Another low-key season opener from Davies. The Judoon are marvellous creations and Agyeman shows promise, but the whole thing seems rather inconsequential. 4/10

180. THE SHAKESPEARE CODE (one × 45m part)

Cast: Dean Lennox Kelly (*William Shakespeare*), Christina Cole (*Lilith*), Amanda Lawrence (*Doomfinger*), Linda Clark (*Bloodtide*), Sam Marks (*Wiggins*), Jalaal Hartley (*Dick*), David Westhead (*Kempe*), Andrée Bernard (*Dolly Bailey*), Chris Larkin (*Lynley*), Stephen Marcus (*Jailer*) | **Crew:** Director: Charles Palmer; Writer: Gareth Roberts; Music: Murray Gold | **Broadcast:** 7 April 2007, 7.2m (DVD, 2007)

Précis: Alien witches force Shakespeare to write a sequel to *Love's Labour's Lost* . . .

Observations: Shakespeare was previously played by Hugh Walters in *The Chase* (16). To suggest Elizabethan London, location night shoots were conducted in the grounds of two historic former hospitals – Ford's Hospital in Coventry and Lord Leycester's Hospital in Warwick – as well as the reconstructed Globe Theatre on Bankside, London. CGI panoramic views of the capital were realised by MillTv.

Verdict: Beautiful-looking (and often funny) historical. Pity about Kelly's wooden performance, but Freema is excellent. 8/10

181. GRIDLOCK (one × 45m part)

Cast: Anna Hope (*Novice Hame*), Ardal O'Hanlon (*Brannigan*), Travis Oliver (*Milo*), Lenora Chrichlow (*Cheen*), Jennifer Hennessy (*Valerie*), Bridget Turner (*Alice*), Georgine Anderson (*May*), Simon Pearsall (*Whitey*), Daisy Lewis (*Javit*), Nicholas Boulton (*Businessman*), Erik Macleod (*Sally Calypso*), Judy Norman (*Ma*), Graham Padden (*Pa*), Struan Rodgers (*Face of Boe voice*) | **Crew:** Director: Richard Clark; Writer: Russell T Davies; Music: Murray Gold | **Broadcast:** 14 April 2007, 8.4m (DVD, 2007)

Précis: The populace of New Earth are trapped in an underground traffic jam . . .

Observations: The last in the loose 'Face of Boe' trilogy, in which the big-faced one finally imparts his message to the Doctor (as mentioned two years earlier in the 2005 BBC tie-in book *Monsters and Villains*). Brief location shooting took place in The Maltings (the alleyway) and the Temple of Peace and Health (as seen extensively in *The End of the World*, 158), both in Cardiff. The Macra were CGI versions of the cancrine creatures originally seen in the Troughton story *The Macra Terror* (34), while the city itself was inspired by Mega City One from the *Judge Dredd* comic strip in *2000 AD* (1977–present).

Verdict: Uplifting and elegiac, this reworking of *Paradise Towers* (145, with a hugely bigger budget) is one of the most charming tales of the Tennant era. 10/10

182. DALEKS IN MANHATTAN/ EVOLUTION OF THE DALEKS (two × 45m parts)

Cast: Miranda Raison (*Tallulah*), Ryan Carnes (*Laszlo*), Hugh Quarshie (*Solomon*), Andrew Garfield (*Frank*), Eric Loren (*Mr Diagoras/Dalek Sec*), Flik Swan (*Myrna*), Alexis Caley (*Lois*), Paul Kasey (*Hero Pig Man*), Nicholas Briggs (*Dalek voices*) | **Crew:** Director: James Strong; Writer: Helen Raynor; Music: Murray Gold | **Broadcast:** 21–28 April 2007, 6.8m (DVD, 2007)

Précis: The Daleks have taken over the Empire State Building in 1930s New York . . .

Observations: Piggybacking on the *Doctor Who Confidential* team's two-day trip to New York, director James Strong captured several 'empty plate' shots of Manhattan that were manipulated later by The Mill; this was the programme's first venture overseas since *Doctor Who* (156) in 1996. Bute Park, Cardiff, stood in for Hooverville, while the interior of the Parc & Dare Hall, Treorchy, represented the Laurenzi Theatre. The animatronic Dalek Sec/human mask was sculpted by Neill Gorton, an image of which was used for a controversial *Radio Times* cover which 'spoilered' the first episode's shock cliffhanger. 'My Angel Put the Devil in Me' was an original song by series composer Murray Gold.

Verdict: Vacuous comic-strip fare with several misfiring elements (such as the lamentable Pig Men) and a very silly-looking central villain. The first new-series Dalek dud. 4/10

183. THE LAZARUS EXPERIMENT (one × 45m part)

Cast: Adjoa Andoh (*Francine Jones*), Gugu Mbatha-Raw (*Tish Jones*), Reggie Yates (*Leo Jones*), Mark Gatiss (*Lazarus*), Thelma Barlow (*Lady Thaw*), Bertie Carvel (*Mysterious Man*), Lucy O'Connell (*Olive Woman*) | **Crew:** Director: Richard Clark; Writer: Stephen Greenhorn; Music: Murray Gold | **Broadcast:** 5 May 2007, 7.2m (DVD, 2007)

Précis: A rich businessman rejuvenates himself at the cost of his own humanity . . .

Observations: The interior of Wells Cathedral, Somerset, stood in for London's Southwark Cathedral (originally St Paul's Cathedral in Greenhorn's first draft). Cardiff's impressive Welsh National Assembly Building was the scene of Lazarus' reception. Gatiss became only the second *Doctor Who* writer to have also played a major role in the series (following Glyn Jones in *The Space Museum*, 15, and *The Sontaran Experiment*, 77).

Verdict: Enjoyable B-movie pastiche with its roots very much on show, most obviously 1953's *The Quatermass Experiment*. Terrible effects though – the monster's face doesn't look a bit like Gatiss'. 5/10

184. 42 (one × 45m part)

Cast: Michelle Collins (*Kath McDonnell*), William Ash (*Riley Vashtee*), Anthony Flanagan (*Orin Scannell*), Matthew Chambers (*Korwin McDonnell*), Gay Powell (*Dev Ashton*), Vinette Robinson (*Abi Lerner*), Rebecca Oldfield (*Erina Lessak*), Adjoa Andoh (*Francine Jones*), Elize du Tolt (*Sinister Woman*) | **Crew:** Director: Graeme Harper; Writer: Chris Chibnall; Music: Murray Gold | **Broadcast:** 19 May 2007, 7.4m (DVD, 2007)

Précis: A spaceship, its crew possessed by an alien force, is plunging into a sun . . .

Observations: The same disused paper mill in Monmouthshire, first seen in *Rose* (157), was used as the inside of the SS *Pentallian*. Although freezing in real life, extensive red lighting and baby oil applied to the actors' skin gave the impression of intense heat. The spaceship's name was changed from SS *Icarus* to avoid clashing with a similarly named ship in the movie *Sunshine*, released in April. Transmission was delayed by a week because of the Eurovision Song Contest.

Verdict: It looks great, but I still prefer *Planet of Evil* (81). 6/10

185. HUMAN NATURE/ THE FAMILY OF BLOOD (two × 45m parts)

Cast: David Tennant (*John Smith*), Jessica Hynes (*Joan Redfern*), Rebekah Staton (*Jenny*), Thomas Sangster (*Tim Latimer*), Harry Lloyd (*Baines*), Tom Palmer (*Hutchinson*), Gerald Horan (*Clark*), Lauren Wilson (*Lucy Cartwright*), Pip Torrens (*Rocastle*), Matthew White (*Phillips*), Derek Smith (*Doorman*), Peter Bourke (*Mr Chambers*), Sophie Turner (*Vicar*) | **Crew:** Director: Charles Palmer; Writer: Paul Cornell; Music: Murray Gold | **Broadcast:** 26 May–2 June 2007, 7.5m (DVD, 2007)

Précis: The Doctor becomes a human schoolteacher in 1913 England . . .

Observations: Paul Cornell adapted his 1995 New Adventures novel *Human Nature*, featuring the Seventh Doctor and Bernice Summerfield. Treberfydd House, Brecon, and Llandaff Cathedral, Cardiff, were used for Farringham School for Boys. An open-air history museum in the grounds of St Fagans Castle, Cardiff, was used as the nearby village. John Smith's parents, Sydney and Verity, were named after *Doctor Who*'s creators Sydney Newman and Verity Lambert. Smith's 'Journal of Impossible Things' featured the first on-screen reference to pre-2005 *Doctor Who*.

Verdict: Sumptuously photographed and directed, this is a brave, adult story awash with terrifying imagery and truly imaginative plot devices. 10/10

186. BLINK (one × 45m part)

Cast: Carey Mulligan (*Sally Sparrow*), Lucy Gaskell (*Kathy Nightingale*), Finlay Robertson (*Larry Nightingale*), Richard Cant (*Malcolm Wainwright*), Michael Obiora (*Billy Shipton*), Louis Mahoney (*Old Billy*), Thomas Nelstrop (*Ben Wainwright*), Ian Boldsworth (*Banto*), Ray Sawyer (*Desk Sergeant*) | **Crew:** Director: Hettie MacDonald; Writer: Steven Moffat; Music: Murray Gold | **Broadcast:** 9 June 2007, 6.6m (DVD, 2007)

Précis: In an old abandoned house, the Weeping Angels await their next victim . . .

Observations: Like *Love & Monsters* (175), this was another 'Doctor-lite' episode. Moffat based it on his short story *What I Did on My Christmas Holidays by Sally Sparrow*, which appeared in 2005's *Doctor Who* annual. Location recording was mainly conducted in places in Cardiff, Gwent and Newport. Wester Drumlins itself was an abandoned house on Field Park Road, Newport, barely altered for its TV appearance. Aga Blonska and Elen Thomas played the Weeping Angels, which were designed by Claire Folkard and created from polyfoam, polystyrene and foam latex. Carey Mulligan won a BAFTA in 2010 for her role in *An Education* (2009).

Verdict: Terrifying, funny and incredibly tense, *Blink*'s exquisitely structured script is vividly brought to the screen by Hettie MacDonald, helped enormously by Gold's best musical score to date. 10/10

187. UTOPIA/ THE SOUND OF DRUMS/ LAST OF THE TIME LORDS (two × 45m parts, one × 50m part)

Cast: Derek Jacobi (*The Master*), John Simm (*The Master/Harold Saxon*), Chipo Chung (*Chantho*), Rene Zagger (*Padra*), Neil Redman (*Lt Atillo*), Paul Marc Davis (*Chieftain*), John Bell (*Creet*), Deborah Maclaren (*Kistane*), Abigail Canton (*Wiry Woman*), Adjoa Andoh (*Francine Jones*), Gugu Mbatha-Raw (*Tish Jones*), Reggie Yates (*Leo Jones*), Trevor Laird (*Clive Jones*), Alexandra Moen (*Lucy Saxon*), Colin Stinton (*President*), Nichola McAuliffe (*Vivien Rook*), Nicholas Gecks (*Albert Dumfries*), Thomas Milligan (*Tom Ellis*), Ellie Haddington (*Prof Docherty*), Tom Golding (*Lad*), Natasha Alexander (*Woman*) | **Crew:** Directors: Graeme Harper & Colin Teague; Writer: Russell T Davies; Music: Murray Gold | **Broadcast:** 16–30 June 2007, 8m (DVD, 2007)

Précis: The Master is reborn in the far future, but causes havoc on present-day Earth . . .

Observations: Derek Jacobi also played the Master in the 2003 animated story *Scream of the Shalka* (see Spin-offs), while John Simm had recently starred as Sam Tyler in the BBC time-travel/police series *Life on Mars* (2006–07). *Utopia*'s interiors were videoed at an old glass factory in Cardiff Bay (which also stood in for industrial-looking locations in the latter two episodes), with exteriors in Argoed Quarry and Wenvoe Quarry. Nine-year-old John Bell won the role of Creet in a *Blue Peter* competition. Hensol Castle once again stood in for Downing Street (as it had done for

Aliens of London, 160), with beach scenes shot on Barry Island. Davies envisaged the wizened Doctor resembling a 'Yoda-like thing'. MP Anne Widdecombe, music manager Sharon Osbourne and pop group McFly made cameo appearances as themselves. A Doctor or Master *Radio Times* cover accompanied the final episode.

Verdict: Oh dear. As a stand-alone story, *Utopia* just about works – and is made a million times better by Jacobi's brilliant Master – but the two-part finale is an unfocused, seen-it-all-before mess. Simm is embarrassing, Tennant is replaced by an awful CGI muppet and the reliance on old Time Lord mythology is just lazy. The Master's 'surprise' return (the worst kept secret in TV history) is no substitute for a decent story. 2/10

SPECIAL

Executive Producers: Julie Gardner & Russell T Davies
Producer: Phil Collinson
Script Editor: Brian Minchin
Tenth Doctor: David Tennant
Companion: Kylie Minogue (*Astrid Peth*)

---

188. VOYAGE OF THE DAMNED (70m)

Cast: Geoffrey Palmer (*Captain Hardaker*), Russell Tovey (*Midshipman Frame*), George Costigan (*Max Capricorn*), Clive Swift (*Mr Copper*), Gray O'Brien (*Rickston Slade*), Debbie Chazen (*Foon*), Clive Rowe (*Morvin*), Jimmy Vee (*Bannakaffalatta*), Bernard Cribbins (*Wilfred Mott*), Andrew Havill (*Chief Steward*), Bruce Lawrence (*Engineer*), Paul Kasey (*The Host*), Nicholas Witchell (*Himself*) | **Crew:** Director: James Strong; Writer: Russell T Davies; Music: Murray Gold | **Broadcast:** 25 December 2007, 13.3m (DVD, 2008)

Précis: Disaster strikes an intergalactic cruise ship . . .
Observations: Australian actress and pop singer Kylie Minogue's involvement was secured at the Season 29 press launch in March 2007 and leaked to newspapers shortly after. Her character's name (which was also used in *The*

Enemy of the World, 40) is coincidentally an anagram of 'Tardis'. Geoffrey Palmer, who had appeared twice in *Doctor Who* in the 1970s, is the father of new-series director Charles Palmer. Most Titanic interiors were shot at The Coal Exchange, Cardiff Bay, and Mamhilad Park Estate, Pontypool.

Verdict: An SF retread of *The Poseidon Adventure*, this is an exciting tale that does its job well, despite the silliness of Max Capricorn and the rather ordinary performance by the 'legendary' Kylie. 7/10

SEASON 30

Executive Producers: Julie Gardner, Russell T Davies &
Phil Collinson (191–192, 194, 197)
Producers: Phil Collinson (189–190, 193, 195–196, 198) &
Susie Liggat (191–192, 194, 197)
Script Editors: Brian Minchin (190, 197), Lindsey Alford
(189, 191, 193–194, 198), Nikki Smith (192) & Helen
Raynor (195–196)
Tenth Doctor: David Tennant
Companions: Catherine Tate (*Donna Noble*), Bernard
Cribbins (*Wilfred Mott*, 189, 192, 197–198), Billie Piper
(*Rose Tyler* 189, 192, 196–198), Freema Agyeman (*Martha
Jones* 192–193, 198), John Barrowman (*Captain Jack,* 198)
& Noel Clarke (*Mickey Smith,* 198)

189. PARTNERS IN CRIME (one × 45m part)

Cast: Sarah Lancashire (*Miss Foster*), Jacqueline King (*Sylvia Noble*),
Verona Joseph (*Penny Carter*), Jessica Gunning (*Stacey Harris*), Martin
Ball (*Roger Davey*), Rachid Sabitri (*Craig Staniland*), Chandra Ruegg
(*Clare Pope*), Sue Kelvin (*Suzette Chambers*) | **Crew:** Director: James
Strong; Writer: Russell T Davies; Music: Murray Gold | **Broadcast:**
5 April 2008, 9.1m (DVD, 2008)

Précis: Weight-watchers are horrified when their fat literally walks away . . .

Observations: Bernard Cribbins' character (originally written as a one-off cameo) replaced the role of Donna's father Geoff when actor Howard Attfield became ill with cancer. Attfield recorded one scene – reshot with Cribbins – before he died in October 2007. A British Gas call centre in Cardiff was used for exterior shots of Adipose Industries. The cradle stunt – originally penned for *Smith and Jones* (179) – was performed by Gordon Seed and Jo McLaren. Billie Piper's surprise appearance was omitted from preview copies shown to the press (although photos from her night shoot had appeared in newspapers). *Radio Times* issued four collectable covers featuring guest stars from the new series.

Verdict: Rather weak comedy episode, any subtlety in the script eradicated by Gold's unsubtle score. The Adipose are, although I hate to say it, rather charming, which is perhaps more than can be said for Tate's second appearance. 6/10

190. THE FIRES OF POMPEII (one × 45m part)

Cast: Karen Gillan (*Soothsayer*), Phil Cornwall (*Stallholder*), Sasha Behar (*Spurrina*), Lorraine Burroughs (*Thalina*), Peter Capaldi (*Caecilius*), Phil Davis (*Lucius*), Tracey Childs (*Metella*), Francesca Fowler (*Evelina*), Francois Pandolfo (*Quintus*), Victoria Wicks (*High Priestess*), Gerard Bell (*Majordomo*) | **Crew:** Director: Colin Teague; Writer: James Moran; Music: Murray Gold | **Broadcast:** 12 April 2008, 9m (DVD, 2008)

Précis: Stone creatures are loose in AD 79 Pompeii . . .

Observations: Intensive overseas location shooting was done at Cinecittè Studios in Rome, Italy, using a pre-existing set of ancient Roman streets and buildings built for the BBC/HBO series *Rome* (2005–2007). Caecilius's family were based on characters in the 1970 Cambridge Latin Course. Soothsayer actress Karen Gillan would go on to play Amy Pond, companion to Eleventh Doctor Matt Smith.

Verdict: Wonderfully atmospheric historical drama, with excellent performances and stunning effects. Catherine Tate starts showing her acting skills and the story's moral dilemma is well presented. 9/10

191. PLANET OF THE OOD (one × 45m part)

Cast: Tim McInnerny (*Halpern*), Ayesha Dharker (*Solana Mercurio*), Adrian Rawlins (*Dr Ryder*), Roger Griffiths (*Kess*), Paul Clayton (*Bartle*), Paul Kasey (*Ood Sigma*), Tariq Jordan (*Rep*), Silas Carson (*Ood voice*) | **Crew:** Director: Graeme Harper; Writer: Keith Temple; Music: Murray Gold | **Broadcast:** 19 April 2008, 7.5m (DVD, 2008)

Précis: On the Ood-Sphere, the Ood are being horribly abused . . .

Observations: Location filming was conducted in an RAF hangar (interiors) and cement works (exteriors) in Barry. Halpern's transformation into an Ood was toned down to make it acceptable for the timeslot and also partly reshot to make the process clearer.

Verdict: An undeniably impressive alien world combines with the eerie and sympathetic Ood to create a memorably chilly adventure in which the Doctor plays little part. The giant brain is a bit daft though. 8/10

192. THE SONTARAN STRATAGEM/ THE POISON SKY (two × 45m parts)

Cast: Jacqueline King (*Sylvia Noble*), Ryan Sampson (*Luke Rattigan*), Rupert Holliday Evans (*Colonel Mace*), Christopher Ryan (*General Staal*), Dan Starkey (*Commander Skorr*), Eleanor Matsuura (*Jo Nakashima*), Clive Standen (*Private Harris*), Wesley Theobald (*Private Gray*), Christian Cooke (*Ross Jenkins*), Bridget Hodson (*Captain Price*), Elizabeth Ryder (*ATMOS voice*) | **Crew:** Director: Douglas Mackinnon; Writer: Helen Raynor; Music: Murray Gold | **Broadcast:** 26 April– 3 May 2008, 6.8m (DVD, 2008)

Précis: The Sontarans are planning to pollute the Earth . . .

Observations: Neill Gorton redesigned the twelve Sontaran costumes based on their first appearance in *The Time Warrior* (70); all costumes were inhabited by equally short actors to maintain the impression of a cloned race. Christopher Ryan had previously played Kiv in *The Trial of a Time Lord* (143b). Margram Country Park in Port Talport was used for the Rattigan Academy, while the Usk Valley Business Park became the ATMOS factory. A *Radio Times* cover heralded the Sontarans' return after twenty-three years.

Verdict: Better by far than Raynor's previous script (182), this is a big, brash action romp with great art design and a bonkers plot that provides great – if not hugely intelligent – entertainment. 9/10

193. THE DOCTOR'S DAUGHTER (one × 45m part)

Cast: Georgia Moffett (*Jenny*), Nigel Terry (*Cobb*), Joe Dempsie (*Cline*), Paul Kasey (*Hath Peck*), Ruari Mears (*Hath Gable*), Akin Gazi (*Carter*), Olalekan Lawal Jr (*Soldier*) | **Crew:** Director: Alice Troughton; Writer: Stephen Greenhorn; Music: Murray Gold | **Broadcast:** 10 May 2008, 7.3m (DVD, 2008)

Précis: Against his will, the Doctor creates a militaristic clone daughter . . .

Observations: Georgia Moffett is the daughter of Fifth Doctor Peter Davison (real name Peter Moffett). To represent the planet Messaline, locations included the Workmens Institute and Memorial Hall, Celynen, and the Roath Conservatory, Cardiff. Jenny's resurrection was a late suggestion by series writer (and next producer) Steven Moffatt.

Verdict: Georgia Moffett's tight T-shirt aside, this is a high-concept idea executed in a cheap-looking and formulaic way. It feels like an old *Doctor Who* annual short story, or a particularly otiose episode of *Star Trek*. The tatty Victorian theatre setting is bizarre. 5/10

194. THE UNICORN AND THE WASP
(one × 45m part)

Cast: Fenella Woolgar (*Agatha Christie*), Felicity Kendal (*Lady Eddison*), Tom Goodman-Hill (*Reverend Golightly*), Christopher Benjamin (*Colonel Hugh*), Felicity Jones (*Robina Redmond*), Adam Rayner (*Roger Curbishley*), David Quilter (*Greeves*), Daniel King (*Davenport*), Ian Barritt (*Professor Peach*), Leena Dhingra (*Miss Chandrakala*), Charlotte Eaton (*Mrs Hart*) | **Crew:** Director: Graeme Harper; Writer: Gareth Roberts; Music: Murray Gold | **Broadcast:** 17 May 2008, 8.4m (DVD, 2008)

Précis: The Doctor and Donna meet Agatha Christie and help solve a whodunnit . . .
Observations: Location videoing centred around Llansannor Court in the Vale of Glamorgan, and Tredegar House, Newport. Tennant's father, Sandy McDonald, played a footman in the garden party scene.
Verdict: A twenty-first-century *Black Orchid* (120) played almost entirely for laughs, this has a similarly light and summery feel to it and features some wonderfully arch performances. Roberts' script is consistently amusing. 8/10

195. SILENCE IN THE LIBRARY/ FOREST OF THE DEAD (two × 45m parts)

Cast: Alex Kingston (*Professor River Song*), Colin Salmon (*Dr Moon*), Eve Newton (*Girl*), Mark Dexter (*Dad*), Sarah Niles, Joshua Dallas (*Nodes*), Jessika Williams (*Anita*), Steve Pemberton (*Strackman Lux*), Talulah Riley (*Miss Evangelista*), Harry Peacock (*Proper Dave*), O-T Fagbenle (*Other Dave*), Jason Pitt (*Lee*), Eloise Rakic-Platt (*Ella*), Alex Midwood (*Joshua*), Jonathan Reuben (*Man*) | **Crew:** Director: Euros Lyn; Writer: Steven Moffatt; Music: Murray Gold | **Broadcast:** 31 May– 7 June 2008, 7.1m (DVD, 2008)

Précis: In an empty planet-sized library, the shadows are alive and hungry . . .
Observations: The main location for the library was, appropriately, Old Swansea Central Library; built in 1887,

its contents had recently been moved to a newer building. Donna's 'country retreat' was shot at Dyfrryn House and Gardens in the Vale of Glamorgan. A week's delay was caused by transmission of the 2008 Eurovision Song Contest (Russia won).

Verdict: A tick list of 'scary elements' based on the author's previous *Doctor Who* stories. It might have worked as a single episode, but this feels rather long-winded. And the walking skeletons are feeble. 5/10

196. MIDNIGHT (one × 45m part)

Cast: Lesley Sharp (*Sky Sylvestry*), Rakie Ayola (*Hostess*), David Troughton (*Professor Hobbes*), Ayesha Antoine (*Dee Dee Blasco*), Lindsey Coulson (*Val Cane*), Daniel Ryan (*Biff Cane*), Colin Morgan (*Jethro Cane*), Tony Bluto (*Driver Joe*), Duane Henry (*Mechanic Claude*) | **Crew:** Director: Alice Troughton; Writer: Russell T Davies; Music: Murray Gold | **Broadcast:** 14 June 2008, 8.1m (DVD, 2008)

Précis: An alien presence possesses a passenger on a space-age minibus . . .

Observations: Catherine Tate only appeared in two short sequences, both shot at Dylans Health and Beauty Club in The Lodge, an upmarket golf club in Newport. Due to the nature of the script, the episode was shot largely in order as well as in long, uninterrupted takes.

Verdict: A psychologically terrifying idea, brilliantly written and tautly directed. Lesley Sharp is stunning. Easily Davies' most intelligent script. 10/10

197. TURN LEFT (one × 50m part)

Cast: Jacqueline King (*Sylvia Noble*), Joseph Long (*Rocco Colasanto*), Noma Dumezweni (*Captain Magambo*), Marcia Lecky (*Mooky Kahari*), Suzann McLean (*Veena Brady*), Natalie Walker (*Alice Coltrane*), Bhasker Patel (*Jival Chowdry*), Ben Righton (*Morgenstern*), Loraine

Velez (*Chambermaid*) | **Crew:** Director: Graeme Harper; Writer: Russell T Davies; Music: Murray Gold | **Broadcast:** 21 June 2008, 8.1m (DVD, 2008)

Précis: Donna sees what life could have been like without the Doctor . . .

Observations: A house in Machen Street, Penarth, was chosen for Donna's shared house. The story used many clips from previous episodes, including *Smith and Jones* (179) and *Voyage of the Damned* (188). The 'dead' Doctor was played by Colum Sanson-Regan. A *Radio Times* cover promoted the return of Billie Piper.

Verdict: On the back of *Midnight* (196), another brilliant RTD script, very bleak in tone and played with utter conviction by the whole cast. Catherine Tate is magnificent, as is Bernard Cribbins. Everything in this dystopian alternate timeline feels horribly real, and the 'Bad Wolf' ending is a classic. Just ignore the crappy plastic Time Beetle. 10/10

198. THE STOLEN EARTH/ JOURNEY'S END
(one × 45m part, one × 65m part)

Cast: Julian Bleach (*Davros*), Elisabeth Sladen (*Sarah Jane Smith*), Gareth David-Lloyd (*Ianto*), Eve Myles (*Gwen Cooper*), Thomas Knight (*Luke Smith*), Jacqueline King (*Sylvia Noble*), Adjoa Andoh (*Francine Jones*), Camille Coduri (*Jackie Tyler*), Michael Brandon (*General Sanchez*), Andrea Harris (*Suzanne*), Lachele Carl (*Trinity Wells*), Paul Kasey (*Judoon*), Kelly Hunter (*Shadow Architect*), Amy Beth Hayes (*Albino Servant*), Nicholas Briggs (*Dalek voices*), Alexander Armstrong (*Mr Smith voice*), Penelope Wilton (*Harriet Jones*), John Leeson (*K-9 IV voice*), Valda Aviks (*German Woman*) | **Crew:** Director: Graeme Harper; Writer: Russell T Davies; Music: Murray Gold | **Broadcast:** 28 June– 5 July 2008, 9.7m (DVD, 2008)

Précis: Davros and the Daleks attempt to annihilate reality itself . . .

Observations: Julian Bleach had previously played the Ghostmaker in the *Torchwood* episode *From Out of the*

Rain (March 2008). The augmented Dalek Supreme was designed by Peter McKinstry, while Neill Gorton sculpted the Davros mask based on John Friedlander's original *Genesis of the Daleks* (78) version. A *Radio Times* cover featuring Davros accompanied the final part, together with a special eight-page feature. The story was notable for incorporating *Doctor Who*'s two spin-off TV series, *Torchwood* and *The Sarah Jane Adventures*. The Shadow Proclamation scenes originally featured a gaggle of old monsters, including Krillitane, the Gelth and Sycorax, but this was dropped for budgetary reasons. It eventually resurfaced, in amended form, in *The End of Time* (202).

Verdict: Hugely enjoyable no-holds-barred epic. It may be considerably less than the sum of its parts, but there's no denying that there are some impressive moments: the Doctor's 'death', the Tardis towing Earth, Davros' first appearance, the German Daleks and so on. Having *two* David Tennants, however, was probably a step too far. 9/10

SPECIALS

Executive Producers: Julie Gardner & Russell T Davies
Producers: Susie Liggat (199), Tracie Simpson (200, 202) &
Nikki Wilson (201)
Script Editors: Lindsey Alford (199–200) & Gary Russell
(201–202)
Tenth Doctor: David Tennant
Eleventh Doctor: Matt Smith (202)
Companions: Catherine Tate (*Donna Noble,* 202), Bernard
Cribbins (*Wilfred Mott,* 202), Billie Piper (*Rose Tyler,* 202),
Freema Agyeman (*Martha Jones,* 202), John Barrowman
(*Captain Jack,* 202) & Noel Clarke (*Mickey Smith,* 202)

199. THE NEXT DOCTOR (60m)

Cast: David Morrissey (*Jackson Lake/The Doctor*), Velile Tshabalala
(*Rosita*), Dervla Kirwan (*Miss Hartigan*), Paul Kasey (*Cyber Leader*),
Nicholas Briggs (*Cybermen voices*), Ruari Mears (*Cybershade*), Edmund
Kente (*Mr Scoones*), Michael Bertenshaw (*Mr Cole*), Jason Morell (*Vicar*),
Neil McDermott (*Jed*), Ashley Horne (*Lad*), Tom Langford (*Frederick*) |
Crew: Director: Andy Goddard; Writer: Russell T Davies; Music:
Murray Gold | **Broadcast:** 25 December 2008, 13.1m (DVD, 2009)

Précis: In Victorian London, the Doctor discovers his future incarnation . . .

Observations: Several scenes were shot outside Gloucester Cathedral and the surrounding streets. The funeral was videoed at St Woolos Cemetery, Newport. The children's workshop was actually the Torchwood Hub, heavily redressed. For the first time in the revived series, the first nine incarnations of the Doctor are referenced on screen. *Radio Times* previewed the story several weeks before transmission, accompanied by a cover showing Tennant and Morrisey.

Verdict: Two stories, clumsily merged. Morrisey's portrayal of a husband and father who has subconsciously repressed traumatic memories is infinitely more interesting than the cheaply executed Cyber invasion, with its cut-price Cybershades and silly CGI CyberKing. 6/10

200. PLANET OF THE DEAD (60m)

Cast: Michelle Ryan (*Lady Christina de Souza*), Noma Dumezweni (*Captain Magambo*), Adam James (*DI McMillan*), Glenn Doherty (*Sgt Dennison*), Victoria Alcock (*Angela Whittaker*), David Ames (*Nathan*), Ellen Thomas (*Carmen*), Reginald Tsiboe (*Lou*), Daniel Kaluuya (*Barclay*), Keith Parry (*Bus Driver*), Paul Kasey (*Sorvin*), Ruari Mears (*Praygat*), Lee Evans (*Malcolm Taylor*) | **Crew:** Director: James Strong; Writers: Russell T Davies & Gareth Roberts; Music: Murray Gold | **Broadcast:** 11 April 2009, 9.5m (DVD, 2009)

Précis: A double-decker bus drives through a wormhole and onto a desert world . . .

Observations: The production team ventured into the Dubai desert for this, the programme's most adventurous overseas shoot yet. Unfortunately, the bus was severely damaged when a container was dropped on it in the Dubai City docks; this was hurriedly written into the script. Welsh locations included Queen's Gate Tunnel, Butetown and the National Museum, Cardiff. This was the first *Doctor Who* story to be made in High Definition (HD) and was transmitted simultaneously on the BBC HD channel.

Verdict: Massively hyped adventure that promised much, but delivered very little. Michelle Ryan cannot act and the desert scenes are so unnaturally coloured that they look completely artificial. The Tritovore masks are good, but spoilt by the very human bodies. Lee Evans is not funny and the less said about the flying bus, the better. 4/10

201. THE WATERS OF MARS (60m)

Cast: Lindsay Duncan (*Adelaide Brooke*), Peter O'Brien (*Ed Gold*), Aleksandar Mikic (*Yuri Kerenski*), Gemma Chan (*Mia Bennett*), Sharon Duncan-Brewster (*Maggie Cain*), Chook Sibtain (*Tarak Ital*), Alan Ruscoe (*Andy Stone*), Cosima Shaw (*Steffi Ehrlich*), Michael Goldsmith (*Roman Groom*), Lily Bevan (*Emily*), Max Bollinger (*Mikhail*), Paul Kasey (*Ood Sigma*) | **Crew:** Director: Graeme Harper; Writers: Russell T Davies & Phil Ford; Music: Murray Gold | **Broadcast:** 15 November 2009, 10.3m (DVD, 2010)

Précis: The water on Mars is proving deadly . . .

Observations: The biodome sequences were shot at the National Botanic Garden of Wales, Carmarthenshire. Victoria Place, Newport, was used for the closing 2059 Earth scene. *Radio Times* featured a moody shot of Tennant in his spacesuit on its cover.

Verdict: Pleasingly adult storyline, with a simple but effective menace. However, the story never really develops – possessed people chase non-possessed people – and the Bowie Base CGI is distinctly underwhelming. 8/10

202. THE END OF TIME (one × 60m part, one × 75m part)

Cast: John Simm (*The Master*), Timothy Dalton (*Rassilon*), Jacqueline King (*Sylvia Noble*), June Whitfield (*Minnie Hooper*), Barry Howard (*Oliver Barnes*), Claire Bloom (*The Woman*), David Harewood (*Joshua Naismith*), Tracy Ifeachor (*Abigail Naismith*), Alexander Moen (*Lucy Saxon*), Lawry Lewin (*Rossiter*), Sinêad Keenan (*Addams*), Karl Collins

(*Shaun Temple*), Teresa Banham (*Governor*), Allister Bain (*Winston Katusi*), Sylvia Seymour (*Miss Trefusis*), Pete Lee-Wilson (*Tommo*), Dwayne Scantlebury (*Ginger*), Joe Dixon (*The Chancellor*), Julie Legrand (*The Partisan*), Brid Brennan (*The Visionary*), Krystal Archer (*Nerys*), Paul Kasey (*Ood Sigma*), Ruari Mears (*Elder Ood*), Silas Carson (*Ood Sigma voice*), Brian Cox (*Elder Ood voice*), Nicholas Briggs (*Judoon voice*), Elisabeth Sladen (*Sarah Jane Smith*), Thomas Knight (*Luke Smith*), Jessica Hynes (*Verity Newman*), Russell Tovey (*Midshipman Frame*), Dan Starkey (*Sontaran*), Camille Coduri (*Jackie*) | **Crew:** Director: Euros Lyn; Writer: Russell T Davies; Music: Murray Gold | **Broadcast:** 25 December 2009–1 January 2010, 11.9m (DVD, 2010)

Précis: Both the Master and the Time Lords return to wreak havoc on Earth . . .

Observations: Amongst the many locations used were Cardiff City Hall (the White House), Cardiff Docks (the confrontation between the Doctor and the Master) and St Mary's Church, Newport (Donna's wedding). A two-minute sequence from Part One was previewed on *Children in Need* night on 20 November. Similarly, the two-minute opening sequence from Part Two was previewed on the BBC's website. A trailer for Season 31 was broadcast after *EastEnders*, which followed the story. *Radio Times* promoted the story, with a cover, at the beginning of December.

Verdict: Curiously uninvolving tale which is overlong and lacking in any coherent threat. The Master's plan is ludicrous. The Time Lords' appearance is impressive – due mainly to Dalton's towering presence – but ultimately anticlimactic. Tennant's 'goodbyes' go on *forever* and the manner of his actual demise is unmemorable. Cribbins, as usual, steals the show. 7/10

SEASON 31

Executive Producers: Steven Moffat, Piers Wenger & Beth Willis
Producers: Tracie Simpson (203, 206, 207, 208, 210, 211), Peter Bennett (204, 205, 209, 212) & Patrick Schweitzer (208, 210, 211)
Script Editors: Lindsey Alford (203, 206, 209, 211, 212), Brian Minchin (204, 205, 207, 208, 210) & Emma Freud (210)
Eleventh Doctor: Matt Smith
Companions: Karen Gillan (*Amy Pond*) & Arthur Darvill (*Rory Williams*, 203, 207–209, 212)

---

203. THE ELEVENTH HOUR (one x 60m part)

Cast: Caitlin Blackwood (*Amelia*), Nina Wadia (*Dr Ramsden*), Marcello Magni (*Barney Collins*), Annette Crosbie (*Mrs Angelo*), Arthur Cox (*Mr Henderson*), Perry Benson (*Ice-Cream Man*), Olivia Colman (*Mother*), Eden Monteath, Merin Monteath (*Children*), Patrick Moore (*Himself*) | **Crew:** Director: Adam Smith; Writer: Steven Moffat; Music: Murray Gold | **Broadcast:** 3 April 2010, 10.1m (DVD, 2010)

Précis: The newly regenerated Doctor faces off an alien invasion in the sleepy village of Leadworth . . .

Observations: Matt Smith was officially announced to the nation on a special *Doctor Who Confidential* programme on 3 January 2009. Disliking his original piratical costume, he chose his tweed jacket and bow tie himself. Location videotaping centred on the borough of Llandaff in Cardiff (standing in for Leadworth), where BBC Wales has its headquarters. Amelia/Amy's home (seen later in *The Pandorica Opens/The Big Bang*, 212) was a Grade II listed former vicarage in Rhymney, Gwent. Caitlin Blackwood and Karen Gillan are real-life cousins, although the two had never met prior to recording. Gillan previously played a soothsayer in *The Fires of Pompeii* (190). The Tardis was redesigned inside and out by Edward Thomas, with the exterior reflecting the design seen in the two Aaru Dalek films of the 1960s. A new, bulkier sonic screwdriver also made its first appearance. MillTv created a new title sequence and a new blue logo, while Murray Gold produced a radical re-orchestration of the theme music. The *Radio Times* promoted the series with articles on Matt Smith and Karen Gillan, an (incomplete) episode guide by new producer Steven Moffat and a fold-out cover showcasing the new Tardis interior.

Verdict: A glorious introduction to the new Doctor. Dazzling, cinematic direction, a wonderful, otherworldly performance by Matt Smith – easily the best debut of any actor in the role – and a script packed full of clever jokes and iconic moments. There's not much actually going on storywise, but when it all looks this good, that's only a minor niggle. Shame the title music is so ghastly. 9/10

204. THE BEAST BELOW (one x 45m part)

Cast: Sophie Okonedo (*Liz 10*), Terrence Hardiman (*Hawthorne*), Hannah Sharp (*Mandy*), Christopher Good (*Morgan*), Catrin Richards (*Poem Girl*), Jonathan Battersby (*Winder*), Alfie Field (*Timmy*), David Ajala (*Peter*), Chris Porter (*Smiler voices/Winder*), Ian McNeice

(*Winston Churchill*) | **Crew:** Director: Andrew Gunn; Writer: Steven Moffat; Music: Murray Gold | **Broadcast:** 10 April 2010, 8.42m (DVD, 2010)

Précis: The government of Starship UK is harbouring a tragic secret . . .

Observations: The Oxford Street scenes in Starship UK were located in a disused factory on the Mamhilad Park Industrial Estate, Pontypool. The torture chamber was videoed in Neath Abbey in Swansea, later seen in *Vincent and the Doctor* (210). Sophie Okonedo had appeared in aborted internet pilot *Scream of the Shalka* (see Spin-offs) while Terrence Hardiman was famous for starring in the children's series *The Demon Headmaster* (1996–98).

Verdict: A mishmash of big, adult concepts, *The Beast Below* feels rushed and unfocused on first viewing but does repay further visits. The plotting is all over the place and the backdrop self-consciously surreal, but it certainly looks lovely. In a nutshell, it's a *Ghost Light* (153) for the twenty-first century. 6/10

205. VICTORY OF THE DALEKS (one x 45m part)

Cast: Bill Paterson (*Bracewell*), Ian McNeice (*Winston Churchill*), Nina De Cosimo (*Blanche*), Tim Wallers (*Childers*), Susannah Fielding (*Lillian*), James Albrecht (*Todd*), Colin Prockter (*Air Raid Warden*), Nicholas Pegg, Barnaby Edwards (*Daleks*), Nicholas Briggs (*Dalek voices*) | **Crew:** Director: Andrew Gunn; Writer: Mark Gatiss; Music: Murray Gold | **Broadcast:** 17 April 2010, 7.82m (DVD, 2010)

Précis: Churchill is using Daleks to fight the Nazi menace . . .

Observations: Referencing the bulkier creations of the 1960s Dalek films, six new, multicoloured Daleks were constructed by Peter McKinstry. Their eyestalks were designed to be level with Karen Gillan's eyes, making them significantly taller than the one first seen in *Dalek* (161), which corresponded to Billy Piper's eyeline. An anti-aircraft operations base at West Cross in Swansea was chosen to represent the Whitehall war rooms; roof scenes took place atop the Glamorgan Building, part of Cardiff University. The Dalek saucer scenes were shot at a former cigar factory in Grangetown, Cardiff.

Verdict: A brilliant idea disappointingly realised. The Daleks in the Cabinet War Rooms are very creepy – deliberately mimicking the 'servant' Daleks from *The Power of the Daleks* (30) – but the newly introduced versions (the sole reason this story exists) are toe-curlingly poor. The space Spitfires, although impressive, make no sense in narrative terms and the story just feels cheap and strangely unsatisfying. 4/10

206. THE TIME OF ANGELS/ FLESH AND STONE (two x 45m parts)

Cast: Alex Kingston (*River Song*), Simon Dutton (*Alistair*), Iain Glen (*Octavian*), Mark Springer (*Christian*), Troy Glasgow (*Angelo*), David Atkins (*Bob*), Darren Morfitt (*Marco*), Mark Monero (*Pedro*), George Russo (*Philip*), Mike Skinner (*Guard*) | **Crew:** Director: Adam Smith; Writer: Steven Moffat; Music: Murray Gold | **Broadcast:** 24 April–1 May 2010, 8.5m (DVD, 2010)

Précis: A spaceship containing the last Weeping Angel crashes into an ancient temple . . .

Observations: The first story to be made for this season; videoing took place in Clearwell Caves, Glos, for the Maze of the Dead sequences. An area of the nearby Forest of Dean called Puzzlewood featured as the oxygen-producing forest. The crashed Byzantium was shot on Southerndown Beach, Bridgend (Bad Wolf Bay in *Army of Ghosts/Doomsday*, 177). Mike Skinner is lead singer for one-man-band *The Streets*. A cartoon banner promoting talent show *Over the Rainbow* appeared during the cliffhanger for *The Time of Angels*, provoking over 5,000 complaints from angry viewers; the BBC later apologised for its 'inappropriate' placement.

Verdict: Not a patch on *Blink* (186), but nevertheless a very solid action romp with some marvellous special effects and a story that works well across two episodes. Alex Kingston is better than ever, and the *Ring*-style sequence with an angel emerging from a TV screen is hide-behind-the-sofa terrifying. 9/10

207. THE VAMPIRES OF VENICE (one x 50m part)

Cast: Helen McCrory (*Rosanna*), Lucian Msamati (*Guido*), Alisha Bailey (*Isabella*), Alex Price (*Francesco*), Michael Percival (*Inspector*), Simon Gregor (*Steward*), Gabriella Wilde, Hannah Steele, Elizabeth Croft, Sonila Vjeshta, Gabriela Montaraz (*Vampire Girls*) | **Crew:** Director: Jonny Campbell; Writer: Toby Whithouse; Music: Murray Gold | **Broadcast:** 8 May 2010, 7.7m (DVD, 2010)

Précis: A girls' school in sixteenth-century Venice is harbouring alien vampires . . .
Observations: The ancient town of Trogir in Croatia doubled as Venice, due to the similarity of its architecture; some shots were later done at Caerphilly Castle, Llandaff.
Verdict: A story in which the title seems to have preceded the plot; the Hammer Horror sequences are very effect- ive, the silly CGI fish monsters considerably less so. The simplistic climax features some terrible effects work, but the Croatian locations are stunning. 6/10

208. AMY'S CHOICE (one x 45m part)

Cast: Toby Jones (*Dream Lord*), Nick Hobbs (*Mr Nainby*), Joan Linder (*Mrs Hamill*), Audrey Ardington (*Mrs Pogitt*) | **Crew:** Director: Catherine Morshead; Writer: Simon Nye; Music: Murray Gold | **Broadcast:** 15 May 2010, 7.6m (DVD, 2010)

Précis: The Doctor revisits Amy and Rory five years on, only to discover Leadworth is full of homicidal geriatrics . . .
Observations: The village of Skenfrith in Monmouthshire was the main location for Upper Leadworth; some

sequences were also shot in Llantwit Major, in the Vale of Glamorgan, with a house in nearby Llanfair representing Amy and Rory's home. Simon Nye is known for his sitcom writing, in particular *Men Behaving Badly* (1992–98) while Nick Hobbs had played Aggedor in Pertwee stories *The Curse of Peladon* (61) and *The Monster of Peladon* (73).

Verdict: A delightfully written fairytale from an unexpected source. Toby Jones is chillingly funny as the low-key villain, and the three regulars are on splendid form. There's more than a touch of *The Avengers* about the dreamy village sequences and the OAP violence is handled with comic-strip panache. Only the rushed resolution disappoints. 9/10

209. THE HUNGRY EARTH/ COLD BLOOD
(one x 45m part, one x 50m part)

Cast: Neve McIntosh (*Alaya/Restac*), Meera Syal (*Nasreen Chaudhry*), Robert Pugh (*Tony Mack*), Nia Roberts (*Ambrose*), Alun Raglan (*Mo*), Samuel Davies (*Elliot*), Richard Hope (*Malohkeh*), Stephen Moore (*Eldane*) | **Crew:** Director: Ashley Way; Writer: Chris Chibnall; Music: Murray Gold | **Broadcast:** 22–29 May 2010, 7m (DVD, 2010)

Précis: A Welsh mining project detects a force drilling up from beneath . . .

Observations: The medieval hillside church of St Gwynno's, Llanwonno, in the Rhonda Valley, was used for the church in the fictitious village of Cwmtaff. Tower Colliery, a working mine near Hirwaun, and Bedwelty Pits in Tredegar, featured as the drilling site. New Silurian masks (and helmets) were designed by Millennium FX, with costumes by Lindsay Bonaccorsi. Chibnall's story – and the 'Homo Reptilia' appellation – was inspired by Malcolm Hulke's well-regarded 1974 novelisation of his first Silurian story, *Doctor Who and the Cave Monsters*.

Verdict: Wannabe Pertwee morality tale crippled by

mediocre production values, ineffectual performances and a wafer-thin 'plot'. The Silurians are hardly iconic *Who* monsters, but here, sans distinctive third eye, they hardly even register. Although the location shooting is wonderfully atmospheric, this cost-cutting non-event ultimately makes *Warriors of the Deep* (130) look like a masterpiece. 3/10

210. VINCENT AND THE DOCTOR
(one x 50m part)

Cast: Tony Curran (*Vincent van Gogh*), Bill Nighy (*Dr Black*), Nik Howden (*Maurice*), Chrissie Cotterill (*Madame Vernet*), Sarah Counsell (*Waitress*), Morgan Overton, Andrew Byrne (*Schoolchildren*) | **Crew:** Director: Johnny Campbell; Writer: Richard Curtis; Music: Murray Gold | **Broadcast:** 5 June 2010, 6.8m (DVD, 2010)

Précis: The Doctor and Amy find Vincent van Gogh battling an invisible monster . . .
Observations: To represent Auvers in France, the production team used Trogir and Vrsine in Croatia, doubling up with shooting on *The Vampires of Venice* (207). Interiors of the Musée d'Orsay took place in the National Museum of Wales. Many of the artist's most famous paintings were brought to life in the story – in particular *The Church at Auvers* (1890), *Café Terrace at Night* (1888) and *Wheatfield with Crows* (1890).
Verdict: A moving insight into the world of manic depression (the Krafayis is an obvious metaphor for the condition), this is the highlight of the season. Tony Curran gives a brave, beautiful performance as the tortured artist, and the ending is truly devastating. 10/10

211. THE LODGER (one x 45m part)

Cast: James Corden (*Craig*), Daisy Haggard (*Sophie*), Owen Donovan (*Steven*), Babatunde Aleshe (*Sean*), Jem Wall (*Michael*), Karen Seacombe

(*Sandra*), Kamera Bacchus (*Clubber*) | **Crew:** Director: Catherine Morshead; Writer: Gareth Roberts; Music: Murray Gold | **Broadcast:** 12 June 2010, 6.4m (DVD, 2010)

Précis: In present day Colchester, the Doctor pretends to be human so he can discover why people are disappearing . . .

Observations: A house on Westville Road, Cardiff, was the main location, while Victoria Park in the suburb of Canton (previously seen in *Silence in the Library/Forest of the Dead*, 195) was used for the pub football match. Matt Smith had originally wanted to be a professional footballer before a back injury forced him to change career. The story was based on Gareth Roberts' comic strip of the same name in *Doctor Who Magazine* 368 in 2006.

Verdict: *Blink* (186) may have got there first, but this is a thoroughly satisfying *Doctor Who* romcom that centres as much on the Doctor as it does on Craig and Sophie. Matt Smith absolutely nails the Doctor's eccentricity and Corden and Haggard are a likeable, and believable, couple. The space/time ship interior is a wonderful piece of design (and *so* much better than the one we were saddled with). 9/10

212. THE PANDORICA OPENS/ THE BIG BANG (one x 50m part, one x 55m part)

Cast: Tony Curran (*Vincent van Gogh*), Chrissie Cotterill (*Madame Vernet*), Bill Paterson (*Bracewell*), Ian McNeice (*Winston Churchill*), Sophie Okonedo (*Liz 10*), Alex Kingston (*River Song*), Marcus O'Donovan (*Claudio*), Clive Wood (*Commander*), Simon Fisher-Becker (*Dorium*), Joe Jacobs (*Guard*), David Fynn (*Marcellus*), Christopher Ryan (*Commander Stark*), Ruari Mears (*Cyber Leader*), Paul Kasey (*Judoon*), Howard Lee (*Dr Gachet*), Barnaby Edwards (*Dalek/Stone Dalek*), Caitlin Blackwood (*Amelia*), Susan Vidler (*Aunt Sharon*), Frances Ashman (*Christine*), William Pretsell (*Dave*), Halcro Johnston (*Augustus Pond*), Karen Westwood (*Tabetha Pond*), Nicholas Briggs (*Dalek/Cybermen voices*) | **Crew:** Director: Toby Haynes; Writer: Steven Moffat; Music: Murray Gold | **Broadcast:** 19–26 June 2010, 6.8m (DVD, 2010)

Précis: The Pandorica, containing the most feared being in the universe, is about to open . . .

Observations: Special permission was granted by English Heritage for a night shoot at Stonehenge in Wiltshire; daylight scenes were recorded just after sunrise. Stunt doubles for the Doctor, Amy and Rory raced across Gelligaer Common in Merthyr with an image of the ancient monument added in post-production. The National Museum of Wales in Cathays Park, Cardiff, was used for museum scenes; the wedding reception was shot at Miskin Manor Country Hotel in Pontyclun, Mid Glamorgan. Briefly glimpsed in the 'alien alliance' scenes were a Blowfish and Weevil from *Torchwood*, a Uvodni from *The Sarah Jane Adventures* and the Hoix from the *Doctor Who* episode *Love & Monsters* (175).

Verdict: Despite the title, this is an intellectual, rather than an explosive, season finale. *The Pandorica Opens* is great fun, very doom-laden, and builds to a brilliant climax. *The Big Bang* is almost an hour of Moffat's signature timey-wimey stuff, which – no matter how hard he tries – can't disguise the fact that it's yet another big reset button being pressed. 'The Universe has ended! Oh, erm . . . no it hasn't, sorry.' The fan-pleasing appearance of the Doctor's 'greatest' foes makes little sense: why didn't they just kill him and be done with it? All in all, a solid way of tying up narrative loose ends (the time-eating 'crack' which had featured throughout the season) but a fairly unmemorable story in its own right. 7/10

SPECIAL

Executive Producers: Steven Moffat, Piers Wenger & Beth Willis
Producer: Sanne Wohlenberg
Script Executive: Lindsey Alford
Eleventh Doctor: Matt Smith
Companions: Karen Gillan (*Amy Pond*) & Arthur Darvill (*Rory Williams*)

---

213. A CHRISTMAS CAROL (60m)

Cast: Michael Gambon (*Kazran/Elliot Sardick*), Katherine Jenkins (*Abigail Pettigrew*), Laurence Belcher (*Young Kazran*), Danny Horn (*Adult Kazran*), Leo Bill (*Pilot*), Micah Balfour (*Co-Pilot*), Pooky Quesnel (*Captain*), Steve North (*Old Benjamin*), Bailey Pepper (*Boy/ Benjamin*), Tim Plester (*Servant*), Nick Malinowski (*Eric*), Laura Rogers (*Isabella*), Meg Wynn-Owen (*Old Isabella*) | **Crew:** Director: Toby Haynes; Writer: Steven Moffat; Music: Murray Gold | **Broadcast:** 25 December 2010, 12.1m (DVD/Blu-ray, 2011)

Précis: Amy and Rory are trapped in a plunging spaceliner as the Doctor tries to melt the heart of the one man who can save them…

Observations: Exterior scenes in Sardicktown were shot inside the vast Mir Steel plant in Newport, dressed in Dickensian style by set decorator Julian Luxton, under the aegis of new production designer Michael Pickwoad. Twenty-three cryogenic units were built, mostly from polystyrene, with Pickwoad basing them on Mafia coffins. His daughter Katie painted the portraits of Kazran and Abigail. The Coal Exchange in Cardiff Bay, completed in 1886, was used for scenes in Kazran's bedroom and the adjoining rooftop. Welsh mezzo-soprano Katherine Jenkins was initially nervous about appearing, as she had never acted on television before, but writer Steven Moffat was keen that a real singer be cast. Murray Gold composed a Christmas hymn for her entitled *Silence Is All You Know* (AKA *Abigail's Song*), which she performed live on set. The ferocious shark – a childhood nightmare of Moffat's – was a mixture of CGI and animatronic prop (nicknamed 'Clive'), while the flying rickshaw utilised green-screen and traditional modelwork. *Radio Times* promoted the story across two issues. A CD of incidental music from the story, played by the National Orchestra of Wales, was released in March 2011.

Verdict: Perhaps more derivative than any *Doctor Who* Christmas special before or since – even the 'borrowed' Dickens title remains unchanged – *A Christmas Carol* nevertheless manages to put a unique science-fiction spin on an old idea. The ease with which the Doctor can pilot his Tardis does tend to trivialise the drama, and Rory and Amy's countdown to disaster is a clear case of sidelining unnecessary characters, but the central conceit is a good one. Michael Gambon excels as the curmudgeonly Scrooge – sorry, Kazran – while Katherine Jenkins radiates beauty and poise as the virginal love of his life. Matt Smith, from his grand comic entrance engulfed in soot to his thoughtful coda outside the Tardis, adds plenty of

charm to a story that is at times overburdened with senti-
ment. Production design and special effects are for the
most part excellent and the attention to detail is impressive throughout. 9/10

SEASON 32

Executive Producers: Steven Moffat, Piers Wenger & Beth Willis
Producers: Marcus Wilson (214-222, 224), Denise Paul (223)
Script Executive: Lindsey Alford
Script Editor: Caroline Henry (214-217, 219, 221, 224)
Eleventh Doctor: Matt Smith
Companions: Karen Gillan (*Amy Pond*) & Arthur Darvill (*Rory Williams*)

214. THE IMPOSSIBLE ASTRONAUT / DAY OF THE MOON (two x 45m parts)

Cast: Alex Kingston (*River Song*), Mark Sheppard (*Canton Everett Delaware III*), William Morgan Sheppard (*Old Canton Delaware*), Stuart Milligan (*President Richard Nixon*), Kerry Shale (*Dr Renfrew*), Glenn Wrage (*Gardner*), Peter Banks (*Dr Shepherd*), Chuk Iwuji (*Carl*), Mark Griffin (*Phil*), Sydney Wade (*Little Girl*), Nancy Baldwin (*Joy*), Kieran O'Connor (*Prison Guard*), Adam Napier (*Captain Simmons*), Henrietta Clemett (*Matilda*), Paul Critoph (*Charles*), Emilio Aquino (*Busboy*), Ricky Fearon (*Tramp*), Jeff Mash (*Grant*), Tommy Campbell (*Sergeant*), Frances Barber (*Madame Kovarian*), Marnix Van Den Broeke

(*Silent*) | **Crew:** Director: Toby Haynes; Writer: Steven Moffat; Music: Murray Gold | **Broadcast:** 23-30 April 2011, 8.1m (DVD/Blu-ray, 2011)

Précis: After witnessing the death of an older version of the Eleventh Doctor, Rory, Amy, River Song and a younger version inveigle their way into the Apollo program in 1969 whilst avoiding the attentions of the memory-wiping Silents...

Observations: The programme's first proper foray into stateside location work took place in Utah (Valley of the Gods and Monument Valley) and Arizona (Lake Powell and Glen Canyon Dam) for a hectic three-day shoot in November 2010. More prosaically, an industrial estate in Pontypool was used for warehouse scenes. Troy House, a derelict 17th-century convent school in Monmouth, represented the sinister Floridian children's home of Graystark Hall. Luckily, the production team found an American-style 1950s diner on Mermaid Quay, Cardiff, for scenes set early in the first episode. The Oval Office was a meticulously researched set at Upper Boat Studios, an expensive outlay offset by the Silents' spaceship, which was a re-dressed version of the one seen at the conclusion of *The Lodger* (211). The older Canton Delaware was to be played by an aged-up Mark Sheppard, an English actor who had appeared in many cult American series. But when he suggested that his father play him instead, director Toby Haynes enthusiastically took this up. The Silent costumes were made by Millennium FX and based on Edvard Munch's famous series of images entitled *The Scream of Nature* (1893-1910). A caption slide in memory of Elisabeth Sladen (who had played companion Sarah Jane Smith), was shown before *The Impossible Astronaut*; the actress had died four days earlier at the age of 65. *Radio Times* promoted the story with a cover and a guide to the first five stories of the season.

Verdict: Like 1980 season opener *The Leisure Hive* (109), this story impresses through visual spectacle alone. Director

Toby Haynes does an incredible job, assisted by director of photography Stephan Pehrsson. But does the narrative make even an iota of sense? Well, yes, an iota, but not much more. Although exciting, this two-parter is really little more than a bamboozling slideshow of disparate images. When it's all done, the eyes may be sated, but the brain's still craving. It doesn't help that it leaves many questions unanswered and features at least one scene of empty-headed cartoon violence, courtesy of rent-a-gun River Song, in which the Doctor is seemingly happy to condone alien slaughter (and all in glorious slo-mo). The Silents, however, are properly chilling new baddies. 6/10

215. THE CURSE OF THE BLACK SPOT (one x 45m part)

Cast: Hugh Bonneville (*Henry Avery*), Oscar Lloyd (*Toby Avery*), Lee Ross (*Boatswain*), Michael Begley (*Mulligan*), Tony Lucken (*DeFlorres*), Chris Jarman (*Dancer*), Carl McCrystal (*McGrath*), Lily Cole (*Sea Siren*), Frances Barber (*Madame Kovarian*) | **Crew:** Director: Jeremy Webb; Writer: Steve Thompson; Music: Murray Gold | **Broadcast:** 7 May 2011, 7.9m (DVD/Blu-ray, 2011)

Précis: The crew of a becalmed 17th-century pirate ship are terrorised by a beguiling sea spirit...

Observations: Night shooting was conducted on the *Phoenix of Dell Quay*, a former Evangelical Mission Schooner built in 1929 and moored in Charlestown Harbour, Cornwall. It had previously appeared in the ITV series *Hornblower* (1998-2003). Originally entitled *The Siren*, Thompson's story was intended for the ninth slot in the series before being moved forward to add variety to an otherwise 'dark' run of stories. Henry Avery (or Every) was a real 17th-century pirate whose hidden treasure had proved a key plot device in *Doctor Who*'s other piratical outing, *The Smugglers* (28). Fashion model Lily Cole had previously appeared in the films *St Trinian's* (2007) and *The Imaginarium of Doctor Parnassus* (2009).

Verdict: For a story that's trying hard to give the audience every swashbuckling cliché in the book, *The Curse of the Black Spot* is a curiously joyless experience. Perhaps it's the turgid direction or the choppy editing, but it's most probably down to Thompson's dull script coupled with Hugh Bonneville's sincere but uninteresting performance in the central role. The fact that the plot resolution is identical to *The Empty Child/The Doctor Dances* (164) is another reason to find the whole thing rather tiresome. 3/10

216. THE DOCTOR'S WIFE (one x 45m part)

Cast: Suranne Jones (*Idris*), Paul Kasey (*Nephew*), Adrian Schiller (*Uncle*), Elizabeth Berrington (*Auntie*), Michael Sheen (*House voice*) | **Crew:** Director: Richard Clark; Writer: Neil Gaiman; Music: Murray Gold | **Broadcast:** 14 May 2011, 8m (DVD/Blu-ray, 2011)

Précis: The Tardis' 'soul' is transported into a woman's body…

Observations: Originally planned for the previous season, Gaiman's ambitious script (initially called *Bigger on the Inside*) was deferred for budgetary reasons. Three days' night shooting was conducted at a quarry near Cardiff. The junkyard Tardis console was modelled on a drawing by 12-year-old Susannah Leah who had won a *Blue Peter* competition to design it in December 2009. Gaiman had wanted 'Nephew' to be an entirely new creation, visualised in grisly fashion by concept artist David Bonywell, but the decision was made to reuse an old Ood costume to save money. Similarly, the writer had wanted to feature a console room from the 1963-1989 series, but had to make do with the 2005-2010 version. This had been kept aside for the *Doctor Who Experience*, a BBC interactive exhibition held at Olympia Two in London.

Verdict: Many *Doctor Who*s have been scuppered by budgetary constraints, but *The Doctor's Wife* suffers more than most. It's very good as it stands, but the wide-eyed exuberance of Gaiman's concepts never quite transfers properly to the screen. The make-up on Uncle and Auntie is poor, the inclusion of an Ood unimaginative, and the cobbled-together console faintly embarrassing. The strength of this tale is in Gaiman's script, which manages to be both self-referential and populist. The title may be a silly contrivance, but the notion of a human possessed by a Tardis is strange and wonderful and gives this story a unique sense of 'otherness'. Suranne Jones' performance captures this brilliantly, and while the plot does rather collapse in on itself towards the end, *The Doctor's Wife* is a charming paean to the series' enduring magic. 8/10

217. THE REBEL FLESH / THE ALMOST PEOPLE (two x 45m parts)

Cast: Mark Bonnar (*Jimmy*), Marshall Lancaster (*Buzzer*), Sarah Smart (*Jennifer*), Raquel Cassidy (*Miranda Cleaves*), Leon Vickers (*Dicken*), Edmond Moulton (*Adam*), Frances Barber (*Madame Kovarian*) | **Crew:** Director: Julian Simpson; Writer: Matthew Graham; Music: Murray Gold | **Broadcast:** 21-28 May 2011, 7m (DVD/Blu-ray, 2011)

Précis: Duplicated factory workers are threatening real ones on a remote island during a solar storm...

Observations: Location videoing took place in arctic conditions at Cardiff Castle, Caerphilly Castle, Neath Abbey, Chepstow Castle and St Donats Castle in Glamorgan. First-time *Doctor Who* director Julian Simpson slipped on ice and injured his ankle, and one shooting day was abandoned because of health and safety concerns.

Verdict: Quite why this base-under-siege story is a two-parter is beyond me. There's barely enough plot to sustain one episode, let alone two. *Life on Mars* creator Matthew

Graham doesn't give his cast much to work with, the 'twist' is obvious from the start, and the setting doesn't really ring true. Why are these unlikeable people 'mining' acid, and why in a ruined monastery of all places? Performances are variable, and the bizarre range of dialects make deciphering the dialogue a chore. It's all so dark and gloomy – and not in a good way. 2/10

218. A GOOD MAN GOES TO WAR (one x 50m part)

Cast: Alex Kingston (*River Song*), Frances Barber (*Madame Kovarian*), Christina Chong (*Lorna Bucket*), Joshua Hayes (*Lucas*), Damian Kell (*Dominicus*), Charlie Baker (*Fat One*), Dan Johnston (*Thin One*), Danny Sapani (*Colonel Manton*), Neve McIntosh (*Madame Vastra*), Catrin Stewart (*Jenny*), Richard Trinder (*Captain Harcourt*), Annabel Cleare (*Eleanor*), Henry Wood (*Arthur*), Dan Starkey (*Strax*), Simon Fisher-Becker (*Dorium*), Hugh Bonneville (*Henry Avery*), Oscar Lloyd (*Toby Avery*), Nicholas Briggs (*Cybermen voices*) | **Crew:** Director: Peter Hoar; Writer: Steven Moffat; Music: Murray Gold | **Broadcast:** 4 June 2011, 7.5m (DVD/Blu-ray, 2011)

Précis: The Doctor acquires a gang of friends to help him rescue Amy and her baby daughter from the evil clutches of Madame Kovarian…

Observations: A large hangar at RAF St Athan in Glamorgan was used for sequences in Demons Run, alongside Uskmouth Power Station in Newport. Frances Barber was finally revealed as the villainous Madame Kovarian, having been glimpsed in several previous stories and credited as 'Eyepatch Lady' in the *Radio Times*. Neve McIntosh reprised her Silurian alter ego from *The Hungry Earth/Cold Blood* (209), Simon Fisher-Becker came back as blue-skinned Dorium Maldovar, seen briefly in *The Pandorica Opens/The Big Bang* (212), and this was Dan Starkey's third outing as a Sontaran since *The Sontaran Stratagem/The Poison Sky* (192). The Cybermen costumes were subtly altered to remove the Cybus Industries' 'C' logo from their chest pieces. The white Birth Room set was a re-dressed version of the Oval Office from the season's first story. What executive producer Steven Moffat described as an 'earth-shattering climax' led to an unprecedented twelve-week break before the continuation of the season. *Radio Times* promoted the story with a cover of Amy holding her newborn baby.

Verdict: This certainly rattles along, but the complete lack of any jeopardy for the Doctor and his chums makes for a dearth of drama. All the best stuff is over in the opening minutes. From there it's downhill to the shock revelation that River Song is Amy and Rory's daughter (sorry if I've spoilt that for you). Along the way we get butch soldiers, a butch leather-clad baddie, a butch Sontaran and a butch Silurian. The fact that it's all so terribly camp is, I suppose, this story's one saving grace. 6/10

219. LET'S KILL HITLER (one x 50m part)

Cast: Alex Kingston (*River Song*), Albert Welling (*Adolf Hitler*), Caitlin Blackwood (*Amelia Pond*), Nina Toussaint-White (*Mels*), Maya Glace-Green (*Young Mels*), Ezekiel Wigglesworth (*Young Rory*), Philip Rham (*Zimmerman*), Richard Dillane (*Carter*), Amy Cudden (*Anita*), Davood Ghadami (*Jim*), Ella Kenion (*Harriet*), Mark Killeen (*German Officer*), Paul Bentley (*Professor Candy*), Eva Alexander (*Nurse*), Tor Clark (*Teacher*) | **Crew:** Director: Richard Senior; Writer: Steven Moffat; Music: Murray Gold | **Broadcast:** 27 August 2011, 8.1m (DVD/Blu-ray, 2011)

Précis: Berlin, 1938, and the Doctor faces the wrath of a psychotic River Song and the judgement of tiny aliens…

Observations: The exteriors of Swansea's Brangwyn Hall and Guildhall were chosen to depict pre-war Berlin. Cardiff's oft-used Temple of Peace and Health stood in for the hotel restaurant where Melody/River Song bestows her regenerative powers on the Doctor. Following the summer break in transmission, Matt Smith acquired a new bottle-green overcoat. *Radio Times* promoted the second half of Season 32 with a cover (hinting at events in the final episode), an interview with Alex Kingston and a guide to the next six episodes by Steven Moffat.

Verdict: Loathe it or loathe it, *Let's Kill Hitler* is really one God-awful mess. To set a story in such a promising locale with such a promising antagonist (to be clear, I'm talking about Hitler here), and then immediately ditch both, is odd enough. But the whole tone of the story is off-kilter. It has the pace and feel of a comedy, but there's no actual comedy in it. It's like a Carry On film without any jokes. *Carry On England*, if you will. And to make Hitler into a figure of fun just seems rather offensive, and also a little dangerous. I don't mind Richard Briers having a go in *Paradise Towers* (145) but this is the real Nazi dictator here, responsible for the deaths of millions. Anyway, that's the least of this episode's problems, which boil down to a smart-arse script, a hugely irritating directing style and a storyline that has very little substance to it. A beginning, middle and end would also have been a good idea. 1/10

220. NIGHT TERRORS (one x 45m part)

Cast: Daniel Mays (*Alex*), Jamie Oram (*George*), Emma Cunniffe (*Claire*), Andy Tiernan (*Purcell*), Leila Hoffman (*Mrs Rossiter*), Sophie Cosson (*Julie*), Louise Bowen, Nathalie Cuzner, Russell Cuzner, Barbara Fadden, Ruth Webb (*Dolls*), Max Longmuir, Sonny Ashbourne Serkis (*Dolls' voices*), Fern Duncan, Frances Encell (*Nursery Rhyme voices*) | **Crew:** Director: Richard Clark; Writer: Mark Gatiss; Music: Murray Gold | **Broadcast:** 3 September 2011, 7.1m (DVD/Blu-ray, 2011)

Précis: A young boy thinks there are monsters in his bedroom – and he's right...

Observations: Waring House estate in Bristol and Pembroke House nursing home in Cardiff represented the exterior and interior, respectively, of George's council flat. To show the inside of his dolls' house, a location shoot took place at 17th-century Dyrham Park near Bath, Gloucestershire. The roughly hewn peg dolls, based on a vivid childhood fear of the author, were sculpted by Robert Allsopp. One of the young voice artistes was the son of Andy Serkis, who had played Gollum in *Lord of the Rings* (2001-3) and the title role in the 2005 *King Kong* remake. Originally planned for the fourth slot, after completion *Night Terrors* (previously called *What Are Little Boys Made Of?* and *House Call*) was shunted back later in the season and a revised ending added in early 2011.

Verdict: A generally sound, if not particularly inventive, exercise in spookiness that sees Mark Gatiss stretching his Hammer Horror muscles and giving us a straightforward, tightly written tale of monsters in suburbia. It's well done, but nothing new: *Fury From the Deep* (42), *Terror of the Autons* (55), *Fear Her* (176) and *The Lodger* (211) all covered similar ground. It's hard to know whether we're supposed to take the 'miniaturisation' of the Doctor and his friends as real or imaginary; they're clearly running around a real human-size house, not an 'enlarged' model, so the effect is ambiguous. It's also a shame that the end is so cloyingly sentimental. But along the way there are some great scary moments. 7/10

221. THE GIRL WHO WAITED (one x 45m part)

Cast: Josie Taylor (*Check-In Girl*), Imelda Staunton (*Interface voice*), Barbara Fadden, Naomi Berners, Louise Bowen, Nathalie Cuzner, Victoria Thomas, Astrid Hall (*Handbots*), Stephen Bracken-Keogh (*Handbot voices*) | **Crew:** Director: Nick Hurran; Writer: Toby Whithouse; Music: Murray Gold | **Broadcast:** 10 September 2011, 7.6m (DVD/Blu-ray, 2011)

Précis: Amy is trapped for decades in a futuristic hospital while the Doctor and Rory try to rescue her from 'helpful' robots...

Observations: For scenes set in the engine room of the Two Streams Facility, the production team returned to Uskmouth Power Station (seen in *A Good Man Goes To War*, 218), while the foyer of Cardiff's Millennium Centre (seen in *New Earth*, 168) was used as the facility's check-in area. Augmented by CGI, Dyffryn Gardens in Glamorgan also featured as one of the facility's entertainment zones. The story, originally entitled *The Visitor's Room*, is notable for having the smallest cast in any *Doctor Who* story except for *The Edge of Destruction* (3). Matt Smith's role in the original plot was reduced significantly, allowing the actor to concentrate on the Doctor-heavy story *Closing Time* (223).

Verdict: This is more like it. Toby Whithouse's disciplined and unflashy plot uses time travel as the emotional core of the story, rather than as a bolted-on gimmick. Karen Gillan is superb as the realistically older Amy (kudos to the make-up department) and there's a tangible sense of loss as Rory has to choose which 'version' he wants to keep. The three regulars are strong enough screen presences to make us forget there's no guest cast to speak of and Nick Hurran's bravura direction nails every story beat. 10/10

222. THE GOD COMPLEX (one x 50m part)

Cast: Sarah Quintrell (*Lucy Hayward*), Amara Karan (*Rita*), Dimitri Leonidas (*Howie Spragg*), Daniel Pirrie (*Joe Buchanan*), David Walliams (*Gibbis*), Caitlan Blackwood (*Amelia Pond*), Dayydd Emyr (*PE Teacher*), Spencer Wilding (*Minotaur*), Rashid Karapiet (*Rita's Father*), Roger Ennals (*Gorilla*), Ella Whilton-Stroude (*Young Lucy*), Andrew Jay (*Lucy's Husband*), Gary Dobbs (*Photographer*), Damon Jeffery (*Clown*), Louise Bowen (*Weeping Angel*) | **Crew:** Director: Nick Hurran; Writer: Toby Whithouse; Music: Murray Gold | **Broadcast:** 17 September 2011, 6.8m (DVD/Blu-ray, 2011)

Précis: At the heart of a faceless hotel lurks a creature that feeds on faith…

Observations: Alongside extensive studio sets, Seabank Hotel, Porthcawl and Manor Parc Country Hotel, Cardiff were used as the unnamed hotel in which the Tardis lands. The Minotaur was an animatronic creature built by Millennium FX and inhabited by Spencer Wilding, a 6ft 7in Welsh actor and stuntman who had previous form as a Minotaur in *Wrath of the Titans* (2011) and a television commercial for an adhesives firm. Producer Marcus Wilson and executive producer Beth Willis can be seen in photos representing the creature's previous victims.

Verdict: While arguably less original in conception than Whithouse's previous story, there's still loads to savour in this sinister slice of black humour. A top-notch cast, including a pleasantly restrained David Walliams, make the most of the writer's acerbic script. And while the visuals are clearly modelled on Stanley Kubrick's *The Shining* (1980), the doom-laden atmosphere, with its claustrophobic suggestion of menace around every flock-wallpapered corner, is entirely down to Nick Hurran and his director of photography Owen McPolin. The only thing that disappoints is the conclusion, with its ill-advised *Star Trek: The Next Generation* holodeck 'solution' trivialising what had been a thoroughly engrossing mystery. 8/10

223. CLOSING TIME (one x 45m part)

Cast: James Corden (*Craig Owens*), Daisy Haggard (*Sophie*), Seroca Davis (*Shona*), Holli Dempsey (*Kelly*), Chris Obi (*George*), Lynda Baron (*Val*), Alex Kingston (*River Song*), Frances Barber (*Madame Kovarian*), Paul Kasey, Mathew Doman, Kevin Hudson, Adam Sweet, Richard Tunesi (*Cybermen*), Nicholas Briggs (*Cybermen voices*) | **Crew:** Director: Steve Hughes; Writer: Gareth Roberts; Music: Murray Gold | **Broadcast:** 24 September 2011, 6.9m (DVD/Blu-ray, 2011)

Précis: The Doctor tries his hand as a retail assistant in order to defeat a subterranean group of rogue Cybermen...

Observations: Harking back to the first episode of the 21st-century relaunch, *Rose* (157), the House of Fraser building in Cardiff, formerly James Howell & Co Ltd, was used to represent the fictional Sanderson & Grainger department store. James Corden reprised his role from *The Lodger* (211), but Daisy Haggard was appearing in a West End play and so her role was drastically reduced. Roberts' original title was *Three Cybermen and a Baby* but this had to be changed when the number of Cybermen was increased. The Cybermats, designed by Neill Gorton's team at Millennium FX and augmented by CGI courtesy of BBC Wales, had last been seen way back in *Revenge of the Cybermen* (79). A house on Church Road, Penarth, became Craig and Sophie's new home. Lynda Baron had previously appeared as Wrack in *Enlightenment* (127) and had been heard, but not seen, as the ballad singer in *The Gunfighters* (25).

Verdict: Unfortunately, *Closing Time* adds nothing to the simple pleasures of *The Lodger*, to which it is a direct sequel. In bringing back the Cybermen (yawn) and adding a whole new level of silliness (for instance the Doctor's ability to talk 'baby', touched on in *A Good Man Goes To War*, 218), Gareth Roberts' story ends up looking decidedly pointless and padded-out. For one brief moment it appears that Craig might actually die, which suddenly ups the stakes – but, alas, we have to suffer another saccharine ending, followed by a contrived coda that jerks us back into the boring River Song story arc. Matt Smith and James Corden are excellent, individually and together, but *Closing Time* is really just filler material. Oh, and the 'psychic headbutt' is deplorable. 4/10

224. THE WEDDING OF RIVER SONG (one x 45m part)

Cast: Alex Kingston (*River Song*), Frances Barber (*Madame Kovarian*), Simon Fisher-Becker (*Dorium*), Ian McNeice (*Winston Churchill*), Richard Hope (*Dr Malokeh*), Simon Callow (*Charles Dickens*), Mark Gatiss (*Gantok*), Niall Greig Fulton (*Gideon Vandaleur*), Emma Campbell-Jones (*Dr Kent*), Richard Dillane (*Carter*), Marnix Van Den Broeke (*Silent*), Bill Turnbull (*Himself*), Meredith Vieira (*Herself*), William Morgan Sheppard (*Old Canton Delaware*) | **Crew:** Director: Jeremy Webb; Writer: Steven Moffat; Music: Murray Gold | **Broadcast:** 1 October 2011, 7.7m (DVD/Blu-ray, 2011)

Précis: With the Universe caught in a gigantic time-loop, only the Doctor's death can make things right again...

Observations: The production team revisited Mir Steel in Newport for a variety of scenes involving industrialised locations. Cardiff's City Hall and Glamorgan Building were used to represent 'Buckingham Senate', and the interior of Dyffryn House in Glamorgan became Churchill's office. Mark Gatiss, as 'live chess' player Gantok, was credited on the programme as 'Rondo Haxton', referencing facially disfigured actor Rondo Hatton (1894-1946). This was the final episode since *Rose* to be covered by *Doctor Who Confidential*, which was axed by BBC3 controller Zai Bennett. *Radio Times* promoted the season finale with a cover montage of the eyepatched cast and short interviews with Steven Moffat and Matt Smith.

Verdict: Another season finale, another wedding. I've a soft spot for this episode, despite it being (for the most part) an incoherent mess. Moffat's story may be all build-up, but there is a sense, finally, that some questions are being answered, in amongst all the red herrings. Okay, so there is too much going on, and a dearth of explanation for exactly *why* it is going on, but at least we are shot of River Song and her very silly life story. (Cross fingers.) What annoys me

most is that expensive CGI is being used on window dressing – why not save money and employ a team of good writers to make sense of Moffat's increasingly tortuous 'plots'?
6/10

SPECIAL

Executive Producers: Steven Moffat, Piers Wenger &
Caroline Skinner
Producer: Marcus Wilson
Script Executive: Caroline Henry
Eleventh Doctor: Matt Smith
Companions: Karen Gillan (*Amy Pond*) & Arthur Darvill
(*Rory Williams*)

225. THE DOCTOR, THE WIDOW AND THE WARDROBE (60m)

Cast: Claire Skinner (*Madge Arwell*), Alexander Armstrong (*Reg Arwell*), Holly Earl (*Lily Arwell*), Maurice Cole (*Cyril Arwell*), Paul Bazely (*Ven-Garr*), Bill Bailey (*Droxil*), Arabella Weir (*Billis*), Sam Stockman (*Co-Pilot*), Spencer Wilding (*Wooden King*), Paul Kasey (*Wooden Queen*) | **Crew:** Director: Farran Blackburn; Writer: Steven Moffat; Music: Murray Gold | **Broadcast:** 25 December 2011, 10.8m (DVD/Blu-ray, 2012)

Précis: The Doctor comes to the aid of a grieving widow and some sentient trees...
Observations: Based loosely on C S Lewis' Narnia stories,

The Doctor, The Widow and the Wardrobe featured Stradey Castle, Llanelli, as Uncle Digby's country estate. To represent the wintry world of the Androzani trees (a reference to *The Caves of Androzani*, 135), night shooting was carried out in Gethin Woodland Park, Merthyr Tydfil. Sequences in Reg Arwell's Lancaster Bomber were shot in a genuine aeroplane at the Lincolnshire Aviation Heritage Centre in East Kirkby. Alexander Armstrong had previously voiced the computer Mr Smith in *The Sarah Jane Adventures* and *The Stolen Earth/Journey's End* (198), while Arabella Weir had played a female version of the Doctor in an audio spin-off called *Exile*. Moffat based the names 'Ven-Garr' and 'Billis' on outgoing executive producers Piers Wenger and Beth Willis. *Radio Times* put the story on its cover of 3–9 December, with articles spread across two issues.

Verdict: The weakest Christmas special by a long way, Moffat's plodding storyline – a homage, if I'm being polite, to *The Lion, The Witch and the Wardrobe* with 1970s ecological issues thrown in for good measure – recycles every yuletide cliché in the book. Characters behave according to the exigencies of the plot, regardless of who they are. Particularly laughable is Madge Arwell. Adequately played by Claire Skinner, her remarkable ability to operate an alien harvesting machine is one of the story's many low points. Logic finally gives up the ghost (literally) with the dead husband miraculously returning to life, and the whole thing shudders to a halt. Special effects and set design are also surprisingly poor. 2/10

SEASON 33

Executive Producers: Steven Moffat & Caroline Skinner
Producer: Marcus Wilson
Script Producer: Denise Paul (226, 228, 230)
Eleventh Doctor: Matt Smith
Companions: Karen Gillan (*Amy Pond*), Arthur Darvill
(*Rory Williams*) & Jenna-Louise Coleman (*Oswin Oswald*,
226)

---

226. ASYLUM OF THE DALEKS (one x 50m part)

Cast: Anamari Marinca (*Darla Von Karlsen*), Naomi Ryan (*Cassandra*),
David Gyasi (*Harvey*), Zac Fox (*Photoshoot PA*), Barnaby Edwards,
Nicholas Pegg (*Daleks*), Nicholas Briggs (*Dalek voices*) | **Crew:** Director:
Nick Hurran; Writer: Steven Moffat; Music: Murray Gold | **Broadcast:** 1
September 2012, 8.3m (DVD/Blu-ray, 2012)

Précis: Kidnapped by the Daleks, the Doctor is forced on a
bizarre rescue mission…
Observations: Exterior sequences on the Asylum planet
were captured in the Sierra Nevada ski resort in Spain,
alongside location work for *A Town Called Mercy* (228).

Thirty Dalek props were required for studio taping, the most ever used in *Doctor Who*. Many earlier versions had to be loaned from fans and collectors, one of whom was former executive producer Russell T Davies. In a surprise move, new companion Jenna Louise-Coleman appeared, uncredited in *Radio Times*, months ahead of her 'official' appearance in *The Snowmen* (231). She had already been interviewed about the role in the 31 March–6 April issue of the magazine. A subtly altered title sequence made its debut, along with a new version of the show's logo, which would be patterned differently to reflect the content of each Season 33 story. *Radio Times* promoted the new season with a cover, a pullout poster featuring different Dalek designs and an episode guide for the first five stories.

Verdict: *Asylum of the Daleks* is a rattling good yarn, spoilt by months of pre-publicity that promised we would see every type of Dalek on screen. We didn't. And when the story specifically referenced earlier versions, we were shown instead the post-2005 ones. Technical shortcomings aside, this feels like a fresh departure for Moffat, with a strong, cohesive script allied to atmospheric direction and an interesting new dynamic for Rory and Amy. The central twist may be obvious, but it was certainly a big surprise to see Jenna Louise-Coleman months before we expected – even the newspapers kept that one quiet, God bless 'em. Fans of *Victory of the Daleks* (205), if there are any, must have been disappointed to see the hideous new Daleks sidelined. Everyone else jumped for joy. 8/10

227. DINOSAURS ON A SPACESHIP (one x 45m part)

Cast: Mark Williams (*Brian Williams*), Riann Steele (*Queen Nefertiti*), Rupert Graves (*Riddell*), Sunetra Sarker (*Indira*), David Bradley (*Solomon*), Noel Byrne, Richard Geraghty (*Robots*), David

Mitchell, Robert Webb (*Robot voices*), Richard Hope (*Bleytal*), Rudi Dharmalingam (*ISA worker*) | **Crew:** Director: Saul Metzstein; Writer: Chris Chibnall; Music: Murray Gold | **Broadcast:** 8 September 2012, 7.6m (DVD/Blu-ray, 2012)

Précis: The Doctor attempts to stop a spaceship crashing to Earth, along with its menagerie of prehistoric monsters…

Observations: Southerndown Beach in the Vale of Glamorgan, seen most recently in *The Time of Angels/Flesh and Stone* (206), became the 'engine room' of the Silurian Ark. Two actors had played major roles in the *Harry Potter* movie franchise: David Bradley as Argus Filch and Mark Williams as Arthur Weasley. Bradley would later play William Hartnell for *Doctor Who*'s fiftieth anniversary docu-drama in November 2013. Half a full-sized Triceratops was constructed by Millennium FX for the Doctor and his friends to ride, while the baby Tyrannosaurus Rex had been used previously in an exhibition; the other dinosaurs were created from CGI. The two comical robots had been used previously in a CBBC game show called *Mission 2110* (2010).

Verdict: A terrific romp, which for the most part balances humour and drama to great effect. Occasionally the comedy becomes a little too sub-*Carry On*, but Chris Chibnall displays a lightness of touch previously undemonstrated in his earlier stories. Bradley makes a fabulous, and properly unpleasant, villain, while the 'gang' of supporting actors are clearly having a ball. Only the Doctor's out-of-character nastiness at the end comes close to spoiling this hugely enjoyable tale. 9/10

228. A TOWN CALLED MERCY (one x 45m part)

Cast: Andrew Brooke (*Gunslinger*), Adrian Scarborough (*Kahler-Jex*), Ben Browther (*Isaac*), Dominic Kemp (*Kahler-Mas*), Byrd Wilkins (*Preacher*), Sean Benedict (*Dockery*), Garrick Hagon (*Abraham*), Joanne McQuinn (*Sadie*), Rob Cavazos (*Walter*) | **Crew:** Director: Saul

Metzstein; Writer: Toby Whithouse; Music: Murray Gold | **Broadcast:** 15 September 2012, 8.4m (DVD/Blu-ray, 2012)

Précis: The Doctor must rid a Wild West town of its mysterious cyborg gunslinger…

Observations: For the first *Doctor Who* Western since *The Gunfighters* (25) in 1966, extensive location shooting was conducted at Fort Bravo (previously known as Texas Hollywood) near Almería in Spain. A mock-up of a Wild West frontier town situated in Europe's only true desert, this standing set has been used for many spaghetti Westerns including *The Good, The Bad and the Ugly* (1966) and *Once Upon A Time in The West* (1968). Garrick Hagon (Abraham) had appeared previously in *The Mutants* (63).

Verdict: There's more than a hint of *Star Trek: The Next Generation* (1987-1994) in this old-fashioned morality tale set against a vaguely science-fiction backdrop. Andrew Brooke is underwhelming as the Borg… sorry, I mean the Gunslinger, and he's saddled with a silly SF voice that does him no favours. But the cinematography is gorgeous and the story is actually rather thought-provoking. 7/10

229. THE POWER OF THREE (one x 45m part)

Cast: Mark Williams (*Brian Williams*), Jemma Redgrave (*Kate Lethbridge-Stewart*), Steven Berkoff (*Shakri*), Selva Rasalingam (*Ranjit*), Alice O'Connell (*Laura*), Peter Cartwright (*Arnold Underwood*), David Beck, Daniel Beck (*Orderlies*), David Hartley (*UNIT researcher*), Sir Alan Sugar (*Himself*), Brian Cox (*Himself*) | **Crew:** Director: Douglas Mackinnon; Writer: Chris Chibnall; Music: Murray Gold | **Broadcast:** 22 September 2012, 7.7m (DVD/Blu-ray, 2012)

Précis: Earth is deluged by small black cubes, their purpose unknown…

Observations: Although supposed to be under the Tower of London (as in *The Christmas Invasion*, 167), the UNIT base sequences were shot inside Caerphilly Castle and

Neath Abbey in Swansea. Chris Chibnall's original title was
Cubed. According to producer Marcus Wilson, a hundred
cubes were made for this story, the rest being duplicated by
CGI in post-production. The character of Kate Lethbridge-
Stewart had previously appeared in two fan-produced
videos: *Downtime* (1995) by Marc Platt and *Dæmos Rising*
(2004) by David J Howe.

Verdict: A half-hearted, and seriously underfunded,
throwback to Russell T Davies' 'Earth invasion' stories,
The Power of Three resembles nothing more than odd story
ideas jumbled together in the vague hope they'll coalesce.
They don't. The idea of the Doctor moving in with a young
couple was done to perfection with *The Lodger* (211) so
why bother to repeat it? Berkoff's talents are squandered as
a generic baddie and Jemma Redgrave, normally so good,
seems rather out of her depth here. 2/10

230. THE ANGELS TAKE MANHATTAN (one x 45m part)

Cast: Alex Kingston (*River Song*), Mike McShane (*Julius Grayle*),
Rob David (*Sam Garner*), Burnell Tucker (*Old Garner*), Ozzie Yue
(*Foreman*), Bentley Kalu (*Hood*) | **Crew:** Director: Nick Hurran; Writer:
Steven Moffat; Music: Murray Gold | **Broadcast:** 29 September 2012,
7.8m (DVD/Blu-ray, 2012)

Précis: The Weeping Angels are alive and well and living in
old New York...

Observations: Although some scenes were captured in
Cardiff and Bristol, the bulk of location shooting took
place in Manhattan itself, in front of hundreds of sightseers:
Central Park, Times Square, East 43rd Street, Fifth Avenue,
Grand Central Terminal and Brooklyn Bridge Park were the
main areas chosen. The final graveyard scene was taped at
the 32-acre Llanelli District Cemetery, near Swansea. *Radio
Times* featured an interview with Matt Smith to accompany

the story, followed by a feature by Steven Moffat the week after, in which he outlined the thinking behind Rory and Amy's departure.

Verdict: *The Angels Take Manhattan* draws you in from the start. Director Nick Hurran creates an effective crime noir backdrop and Alex Kingston, freed from being a continuity-obsessed plot device, takes wing as a wickedly arch (and drop-dead sexy) femme fatale. It's not without its problems – a walking Statue of Liberty would be rather hard to ignore, and the Doctor could surely come back and visit the Ponds if he parked his Tardis outside New York. But such is the confident sweep of the storyline, complete with Moffat's de rigueur time paradoxes, that the viewer only engages his or her brain after it's finished. (Which, of course, is when it all falls to pieces.) Amy's final moment is suitably emotional and makes a fitting bookend to the events of *The Eleventh Doctor* (203). 8/10

SPECIAL

Executive Producers: Steven Moffat & Caroline Skinner
Producer: Marcus Wilson
Script Producer: Denise Paul
Eleventh Doctor: Matt Smith
Companion: Jenna-Louise Coleman (*Clara Oswin Oswald*)

231. THE SNOWMEN (60m)

Cast: Richard E Grant (*Dr Walter Simeon*), Tom Ward (*Captain Latimer*), Neve McIntosh (*Madame Vastra*), Catrin Stewart (*Jenny*), Dan Starkey (*Strax*), Joseph Darcey-Alden (*Digby*), Ellie Darcey-Alden (*Francesca*), Liz White (*Alice*), Jim Conway (*Uncle Josh*), Cameron Strefford (*Young Walter*), Annabelle Dowler (*Walter's Mother*), Ben Addis (*Bob Chilcott*), Daniel Hyde (*Lead Workman*), Sophie Miller-Sheen (*Girl*), Ian McKellen (*Great Intelligence voice*), Juliet Cadzow (*Ice Governess voice*) | **Crew:** Director: Saul Metzstein; Writer: Steven Moffat; Music: Murray Gold | **Broadcast:** 25 December 2012, 9.9m (DVD/Blu-ray, 2013)

Précis: Telepathic snow is preying on the inhabitants of Victorian London…

Observations: A brand new title sequence, suggesting

various elements of past versions and incorporating the Doctor's face for the first time since *Survival* (155), was designed by the Peter Anderson Studio. Murray Gold composed a new arrangement of the theme music to go with it; this again suggested elements of previous arrangements. Accompanying this was a brand new Tardis interior designed by Michael Pickwoad, smaller and more mechanical in appearance, as executive producer Steven Moffat felt that the previous one had become too 'whimsical'. The redesign was also a practical decision as *Doctor Who* had moved from its old Upper Boat studios to the BBC Drama Village in Roath Lock, Cardiff and transporting the console room would have been too expensive. For the first time in the programme's history, the camera tracked from the exterior Police Box shell to the studio interior, an effect that had only been seen once before, in BBC documentary *Thirty Years in the Tardis* (1993). Conversely, a tracking shot showing the Doctor and companions moving from the Tardis interior to the outside had been achieved as early as 1964 in *The Sensorites* (7). The Doctor's costume received a radical overhaul, reflecting the Victorian feel of the story. Richard E Grant had played the Doctor twice before, in *Doctor Who and the Curse of Fatal Death* (Spin-Offs, 16) and *Scream of the Shalka* (Spin-Offs, 19). The Great Intelligence was an old foe from *The Abominable Snowmen* (38) and *The Web of Fear* (41). The 8–14 December edition of *Radio Times* heralded the story with a cover and a set report, followed by a feature written by Steven Moffat in its Christmas issue. A three-minute prelude by Moffat, entitled *The Great Detective*, was shown on 16 November as part of the BBC's annual Children in Need telethon.

Verdict: This is a joyful return to form for the *Doctor Who* yuletide special. Not only does the whole thing look and feel magical, Moffat has cleverly balanced humour and scares in a story that feels at once familiar and unexpected. Playing it straight, Richard E Grant is a glorious baddie (with a sympathetic side) and Jenna-Louise Coleman is instantly appealing as a feisty, and mysterious, new companion. (A companion we will have to get used to dying in each story, I fear.) Vastra, Jenny and Strax make a delightful trio of amateur sleuths, and Matt Smith's appearance as an incompetent Sherlock Holmes is hilarious. The inclusion of the Great Intelligence adds a real sense of gravitas – alongside McKellen's pitch-perfect vocal tones – to a story already brimming with class. 10/10

AFTERWORD

WHAT MAKES A GOOD *DOCTOR WHO* STORY?

Being a *Doctor Who* fan is – and I'm guessing here – a bit like supporting a minor league football team. You might slag off the members, the manager, the tactics, spend hours reminiscing with other supporters on how much better they were in the past; but if an outsider, a 'not-we' (cue self-indulgent *Kinda* [118] reference), enters the room, then you suddenly become your team's staunchest defender. Welling United can do no wrong.

It's the same with *Doctor Who*. Privately – or not so privately in these times of Internet forums and the like – we fans have the capacity to rip to shreds the programme we profess to love. But to someone who doesn't watch the show (and apparently such people do exist), we invariably consider it our duty to evangelise to them in a way that would make a Jehovah's Witness blush.

This odd mixture of love and hate makes it hard to answer the central question: what makes a good *Doctor Who* story? I'm a fan. I love them all. Yet as this book demonstrates, I also think some of them are rubbish. Is that unconditional love? I guess so. Sometimes I'm in the mood for *The Caves of Androzani* (135), sometimes *The Mutants* (63). *The Mutants* is often very poor, but it's got fabulous monsters in and some of the effects work is excellent. *Caves* has a very poor monster, but features the series' most spine-tingling performances. To many fans, the latter is the epitome of a 'good' *Doctor Who* story. But why?

Twenty-first century *Who* emphasises individual writers in a way that no other era ever did. This is thanks to Russell T Davies, a noted television scriptwriter and the new-look series' first executive producer. Read his magnificent *The Writer's Tale* and you'll get some idea of the man's clout. Combined with gung-ho BBC producer Julie Gardner, this was a (non-sexual) marriage made in heaven. They both knew that, without good writing, it would just be *Randall and Hopkirk (Deceased)* all over again (the awful Reeves and Mortimer revival, not the sublime original). Or, God forbid, another *Bugs*. The writers may have all been *Doctor Who* fans, but they knew how to tell a good story and, with Davies' fingerprints on every page, the series had never appeared so consistently well crafted.

Doctor Who isn't about special effects. *An Unearthly Child* (1) had some amazing ones for its time but, in telling a beautifully paced small-scale story with characters with whom one could instantly empathise, it provided the perfect template for all future adventures. Reality mattered. This was not airy-fairy fantasy or nuts-and-bolts hard SF. This was a human story set in a credible alternate world. Based on an idea by CE Webber, Anthony Coburn's script is thoughtful and concise. Waris Hussein's direction assured – fluid but not fussy. In fact, I would suggest that there is not a single flaw in the first episode as transmitted. Design, music, sound effects, acting – it's the best introductory episode of any series ever made. Compare it with *The Big Bang* (212) and you'll see that little of importance has changed over the past fifty years. It's still all about the people.

Robert Holmes is often named as the series' finest writer. He had some duds, it's true, but most of his stories are universally acknowledged as classics: *Carnival of Monsters* (66), *The Ark in Space* (76, ghosting for John Lucarotti), *The Talons of Weng-Chiang* (91). Three stories, three disparate styles, each pulsating with wit, style and scares. But for sheer consistency of form, fellow scribe Terrance Dicks surely deserves some kind of medal. *The Five Doctors* (129) is only as good as it is – yes folks, it could have been worse – because trusty Mr Dicks made it that way (after Holmes famously gave up on it). *Robot* (75), *The Brain of Morbius* (84) and *Horror of Fang Rock* (92) are all lovingly written pastiches that just *work*. Quite why he has not been brought onto the new series is beyond me. Imagine *The Hungry Earth/Cold Blood* (209) as scripted by Terry. He might actually have made us care a toss.

Second to the writers are the script editors (in the early days, 'story editors', but it's the same thing). These largely overlooked individuals steer the writers towards vaguely sensible narrative choices, tighten their verbose dialogue, highlight discrepancies and, for instance, ensure two identical stories don't pop up in the same series. (If Andrew Cartmel hadn't fallen asleep on the job, *Remembrance of the Daleks* [148] and *Silver Nemesis* [150] should never have happened so close together.) Although Davies has publicly boasted of his input in other writers' tales, for my money, the acme of the script editor's art occurred during Jon Pertwee's tenure. From Season 8 onwards, the combination of producer Barry Letts, script editor Terrance Dicks and writers like Robert Holmes, Robert Sloman and – arguably the series' most intelligent scribe – the late, great Malcolm Hulke forged *Doctor Who* gold, time and time again. These middle-aged, besuited, pipe-smoking BBC employees had an amazingly focused idea of just how the programme should look and feel.

It used to be fashionable to knock the conservatism of the Pertwee era. Ignore *The Mind of Evil* (56), *The Green Death* (69), *Invasion of the Dinosaurs* (71) and *Planet of the Spiders* (74) and you might have a point. But these are iconic stories, and they're as politically left of centre as was *The Happiness Patrol* (149) over a decade later (the one with *Over the Rainbow* judge Sheila Hancock doing her best Maggie Thatcher impression). Apart from *The Beast Below* (204), the 2000s series has rarely touched politics, preferring instead to highlight spiritual and religious themes: *The Impossible Planet/The Satan Pit* (174), *Gridlock* (181), *Human Nature/The Family of Blood* (185). Christian imagery features heavily in *Father's Day* (163), *Blink* (186) and *Voyage of the Damned* (188). There are priest soldiers in *The Time of Angels/Flesh and Stone* (206) but I don't think they count.

So – writers, script editors, producers. All key to a story's success, provided they all work together. The reason why the quality of early to mid-1980s *Who* was so variable is simply because Eric Saward (scriptwriter) and John Nathan-Turner (producer) didn't have that unity of vision. If you believe Saward (JNT being sadly no longer with us), they couldn't agree on *anything*. Hardly a surprise then that *Time-Flight* (122) followed *Earthshock* (121). There have been some dips in present-day *Doctor Who*, but nothing to compare with the Himalayan peaks and troughs of the early JNT era. Once Andrew Cartmel arrived, things stabilised and the future looked promising. Ah well, shows how wrong you can be.

Perhaps surprisingly, the Doctor and his assistant are not so important when it comes to judging what makes a good *Doctor Who* story. Some Doctors are more popular than others (Tom Baker, David Tennant), some assistants likewise (Sarah Jane Smith, Jo, Rose) – but the actor is slave to the script. An actor, after all, is being paid to interpret the writer's words excitingly (or at least interestingly). That's his or her job. They're professionals. But they'll only look any good if the script's okay. Patrick Troughton, wasted in *The Dominators* (44); Tom Baker, bored to tears in *The Armageddon Factor* (103); Colin Baker, relishing *The Twin Dilemma* (136).

Direction on *Doctor Who* is sometimes singled out as a key factor in a story's popularity. But ideally it should be invisible. If you notice it, it's wrong. That's not to say you can't have groovy camerawork (*The Claws of Axos*, 57), but it's got to help tell the story. Graeme Harper is the only pre-1989 director to work on the new series, and his style – so revolutionary in *Caves of Androzani* back in 1984 – now seems rather passé when compared with the work of lean, young twenty-first-century apprentices like Joe Ahearne (*Dalek*, 161), Euros Lyn (*Tooth and Claw*, 169), Dan Zeff (*Love & Monsters*, 175) and Hettie MacDonald (*Blink*, 186). Many TV programmes have been scuppered by artsy-fartsy directing – usually to disguise a crappy script – so cross fingers *Doctor Who* doesn't go any further down that route. As much as I'm enjoying Steven Moffat's reimagined *Sherlock*, the visual jiggery-pokery can be a bit hard to get past. But if you really want to know what 'death by direction' is like, try watching *Eleventh Hour* (sound familiar?), a 2006 ITV series starring James Corden-hating thespian Patrick Stewart. If *Doctor Who* starts looking like that, we're doomed.

Okay, so I haven't really answered the question: what makes a good *Doctor Who* story? That's because they're all good, in their own way, if seen through the eyes of fan-love. It's easy to drool over *The Caves of Androzani*, harder to rave about *The Sensorites* (7). *Amy's Choice* (208) is the flipside of *Boom Town* (165), but it is possible to love both, with a bit of effort. My own personal mission in life is to love *Ghost Light* (153), and I am getting there. Slowly.

There are a million people I haven't mentioned: Delia Derbyshire, Ken Dodd, Raymond Cusick, John Normington, Matt Smith, Michael Wisher, Bernard Lodge, Tony Beckley, Bernard Cribbins, Dudley Simpson, Terry Nation, Georgia Moffett, John Friedlander, Tony Curran, Simon Rouse, Alan Wareing, Hugh Lund ... without any one of these fine folk, *Doctor Who* just wouldn't be the same.

Which means I wouldn't be the same either.

Mark Campbell

AUDIO

Unless stated, all stories are from Big Finish, listed in release order for each Doctor. For reasons of space, the following have been excluded: Companion Chronicles, Lost Stories, subscriber-only releases, anthologies, spin-off series (eg. *Jago & Litefoot*) and webcasts.

Tom Baker

Hornet's Nest: The Stuff of Nightmares Paul Magrs, BBC, 2009 (9/10)
Hornet's Nest: The Dead Shoes Paul Magrs, BBC, 2009 (5/10)
Hornet's Nest: The Circus of Doom Paul Magrs, BBC, 2009 (4/10)
Hornet's Nest: A Sting in the Tale Paul Magrs, BBC, 2009 (7/10)
Hornet's Nest: Hive of Horror Paul Magrs, BBC, 2009 (8/10)
Demon Quest: The Relics of Time Paul Magrs, BBC, 2010
Demon Quest: The Demons of Paris Paul Magrs, BBC, 2010
Demon Quest: A Shard of Ice Paul Magrs, BBC, 2010
Demon Quest: Starfall Paul Magrs, BBC, 2010
Demon Quest: Sepulchre Paul Magrs, BBC, 2010
Serpent Crest: Tsar Wars Paul Magrs, BBC, 2011
Serpent Crest: The Broken Crown Paul Magrs, BBC, 2011
Serpent Crest: Aladdin Time Paul Magrs, BBC, 2011
Serpent Crest: The Hexford Invasion Paul Magrs, BBC, 2011

Serpent Crest: Survivors in Space Paul Magrs, BBC, 2011
Destination: Nerva Nicholas Briggs, 2012 (4/10)
The Renaissance Man Justin Richards, 2012 (5/10)
The Wrath of the Iceni John Dorney, 2012 (3/10)
Energy of the Daleks Nicholas Briggs, 2012 (9/10)
Trail of the White Worm Alan Barnes, 2012 (8/10)
The Oseidon Adventure Alan Barnes, 2012 (7/10)
The Auntie Matter Jonathan Morris, 2013 (8/10)
The Sands of Life Nicholas Briggs, 2013
War Against the Laan Nicholas Briggs, 2013
The Justice of Jalxar John Dorney, 2013
Phantoms of the Deep Jonathan Morris, 2013
The Dalek Contract Nicholas Briggs, 2013
The Final Phase Nicholas Briggs, 2013

Peter Davison

Phantasmagoria Mark Gatiss, 1999 (8/10)
Land of the Dead Stephen Cole, 2000 (5/10)
Red Dawn Justin Richards, 2000 (4/10)
Winter for the Adept Andrew Cartmel, 2000 (6/10)
The Mutant Phase Nicholas Briggs, 2000 (7/10)
Loups-Garoux Marc Platt, 2001 (8/10)
The Eye of the Scorpion Iain McLaughlin, 2001 (7/10)
Primeval Lance Parkin, 2001 (5/10)
Excelis Dawns Paul Magrs, 2002 (3/10)
Spare Parts Marc Platt, 2002 (9/10)
The Church and the Crown Cavan Scott & Mark Wright, 2002 (8/10)
Nekromanteia Austen Atkinson, 2003 (3/10)
Creatures of Beauty Nicholas Briggs, 2003 (8/10)
Omega Nev Fountain, 2003 (7/10)
The Axis of Insanity Simon Furman, 2004 (8/10)
The Roof of the World Adrian Rigelsford, 2004 (4/10)
The Game Darin Henry, 2005 (7/10)
Three's a Crowd Colin Brake, 2005 (5/10)
The Council of Nicaea Caroline Symcox, 2005 (7/10)
Singularity James Swallow, 2005 (8/10)
The Kingmaker Nev Fountain, 2006 (3/10)
The Gathering Joseph Lidster, 2006 (6/10)
Circular Time Paul Cornell & Mike Maddox, 2007 (4/10)
Renaissance of the Daleks Christopher H Bidmead, 2007 (7/10)
Exotron Paul Sutton, 2007 (6/10)

Son of the Dragon Steve Lyons, 2007 (8/10)
The Mind's Eye Colin Brake, 2007 (4/10)
The Bride of Peladon Barnaby Edwards, 2008 (7/10)
The Haunting of Thomas Brewster Jonathan Morris, 2008 (8/10)
The Boy That Time Forgot Paul Magrs, 2008 (9/10)
Time Reef Marc Platt, 2008 (4/10)
The Judgement of Isskar Simon Guerrier, 2009 (5/10)
The Destroyer of Delights Jonathan Clements, 2009 (4/10)
The Chaos Pool Peter Anghelides, 2009 (8/10)
Castle of Fear Alan Barnes, 2009 (9/10)
The Eternal Summer Jonathan Morris, 2009 (8/10)
Plague of the Daleks Mark Morris, 2009 (9/10)
Cobwebs Jonathan Morris, 2010 (8/10)
The Whispering Forest Stephen Cole, 2010 (5/10)
The Cradle of the Snake Marc Platt, 2010 (8/10)
The Demons of Red Lodge and Other Stories various, 2010 (6/10)
Heroes of Sontar Alan Barnes, 2011 (8/10)
Kiss of Death Stephen Cole, 2011 (5/10)
Rat Trap Tony Lee, 2011 (6/10)
The Emerald Tiger Barnaby Edwards, 2012 (9/10)
The Jupiter Conjunction Eddie Robson, 2012 (7/10)
The Butcher of Brisbane Marc Platt, 2012 (4/10)
The Burning Prince John Dorney, 2012 (5/10)
1001 Nights various, 2012 (7/10)

Colin Baker

Whispers of Terror Justin Richards, 1999 (7/10)
The Marian Conspiracy Jacqueline Rayner, 2000 (4/10)
The Spectre of Lanyon Moor Nicholas Pegg, 2000 (8/10)
The Apocalypse Element Stephen Cole, 2000 (5/10)
The Holy Terror Robert Shearman, 2000 (7/10)
Bloodtide Jonathan Morris, 2001 (9/10)
Project: Twilight Cavan Scott & Mark Wright, 2001 (6/10)
The One Doctor Gareth Roberts & Clayton Hickman, 2001 (10/10)
Excelis Rising David A McIntee, 2002 (5/10)
. . . ish Philip Pascoe, 2002 (8/10)
The Sandman Simon A Forward, 2002 (5/10)
Jubilee Rob Shearman, 2003 (7/10)
Doctor Who and the Pirates Jacqueline Rayner, 2003 (9/10)
Project: Lazarus Cavan Scott & Mark Wright, 2003 (5/10)

Davros Lance Parkin, 2003 (10/10)
The Wormery Paul Magrs & Steve Cole, 2003 (6/10)
Arrangements for War Paul Sutton, 2004 (2/10)
Medicinal Purposes Robert Ross, 2004 (7/10)
The Juggernauts Scott Alan Woodard, 2005 (8/10)
Her Final Flight Julian Shortman, 2005 (3/10)
Catch-1782 Alison Lawson, 2005 (4/10)
Thicker than Water Paul Sutton, 2005 (2/10)
Pier Pressure Robert Ross, 2006 (3/10)
Nowhere Place Nicholas Briggs, 2006 (8/10)
The Reaping Joseph Lidster, 2006 (4/10)
Year of the Pig Matthew Sweet, 2006 (4/10)
ID Eddie Robson, 2007 (3/10)
The Wishing Beast Paul Magrs, 2007 (7/10)
100 various, 2007 (5/10)
The Condemned Eddie Robson, 2008 (9/10)
Assassin in the Limelight Robert Ross, 2008 (4/10)
The Doomwood Curse Jacqueline Rayner, 2008 (6/10)
Brotherhood of the Daleks Alan Barnes, 2008 (8/10)
The Raincloud Man Eddie Robson, 2008 (4/10)
Patient Zero Nicholas Briggs, 2009 (5/10)
Paper Cuts Marc Platt, 2009 (3/10)
Blue Forgotten Planet Nicholas Briggs, 2009 (7/10)
City of Spires Simon Rowley, 2010 (8/10)
The Wreck of the Titan Barnaby Edwards, 2010 (7/10)
Legend of the Cybermen Mike Maddox, 2010 (9/10)
The Crimes of Thomas Brewster Jonathan Morris, 2011 (7/10)
The Feast of Axos Mike Maddox, 2011 (5/10)
Industrial Evolution Eddie Robson, 2011 (6/10)
Recorded Time and Other Stories various, 2011 (4/10)
The Curse of Davros Jonathan Morris, 2012 (6/10)
The Fourth Wall John Dorney, 2012 (7/10)
Wirrn Isle William Gallagher, 2012 (9/10)
The Acheron Pulse Rick Briggs, 2012 (8/10)
The Wrong Doctors Matt Fitton, 2013 (7/10)
Spaceport Fear William Gallagher, 2013 (5/10)

Sylvester McCoy

The Fearmonger Jonathan Blum, 2000 (4/10)
The Genocide Machine Mike Tucker, 2000 (8/10)
The Fires of Vulcan Steve Lyons, 2000 (3/10)

The Shadow of the Scourge Paul Cornell, 2000 (7/10)

Dust Breeding Mike Tucker, 2001 (8/10)

Colditz Steve Lyons, 2001 (2/10)

Excelis Decays Craig Hinton, 2002 (4/10)

The Rapture Joseph Lidster, 2002 (6/10)

Bang-Bang-a-Boom! Gareth Roberts & Clayton Hickman, 2002 (8/10)

The Dark Flame Trevor Baxendale, 2003 (7/10)

Flip-Flop Jonathan Morris, 2003 (9/10)

Master Joseph Lidster, 2003 (9/10)

The Harvest Dan Abnett, 2004 (8/10)

Dreamtime Simon A Forward, 2005 (3/10)

Unregenerate! David A McIntee, 2005 (7/10)

Live 34 James Parsons & Andrew Stirling-Brown, 2005 (8/10)

Night Thoughts Ed Young, 2006 (4/10)

The Settling Simon Guerrier, 2006 (7/10)

Red Stewart Sheargold, 2006 (7/10)

No Man's Land Martin Day, 2006 (3/10)

Nocturne Dan Abnett, 2007 (8/10)

Valhalla Marc Platt, 2007 (5/10)

Frozen Time Nicholas Briggs, 2007 (4/10)

The Dark Husband David Quantick, 2008 (8/10)

The Death Collectors Stewart Sheargold, 2008 (5/10)

Kingdom of Silver James Swallow, 2008 (7/10)

Forty-Five various, 2008 (6/10)

The Magic Mousetrap Matthew Sweet, 2009 (7/10)

Enemy of the Daleks David Bishop, 2009 (8/10)

The Angel of Scutari Paul Sutton, 2009 (3/10)

Project: Destiny Cavan Scott & Mark Wright, 2010 (4/10)

A Death in the Family Steven Hall, 2010 (9/10)

Lurkers at Sunlight's Edge Marty Ross, 2010 (8/10)

Robophobia Nicholas Briggs, 2011 (10/10)

The Doomsday Quatrain Emma Beeby & Gordon Rennie, 2011 (6/10)

House of Blue Fire Mark Morris, 2011 (9/10)

Protect and Survive Jonathan Morris, 2012 (10/10)

Black and White Matt Fitton, 2012 (7/10)

Gods and Monsters Mike Maddox & Alan Barnes, 2012 (9/10)

Love and War Paul Cornell, 2012 (9/10)

The Shadow Heart Jonathan Morris, 2012 (7/10)

Paul McGann

Storm Warning Alan Barnes, 2001 (8/10)
Sword of Orion Nicholas Briggs, 2001 (7/10)
The Stones of Venice Paul Magrs, 2001 (5/10)
Minuet in Hell Alan W Lear & Gary Russell, 2001 (8/10)
Invaders from Mars Mark Gatiss, 2002 (9/10)
The Chimes of Midnight Robert Shearman, 2002 (10/10)
Seasons of Fear Paul Cornell & Caroline Symcox, 2002 (8/10)
Embrace the Darkness Nicholas Briggs, 2002 (7/10)
The Time of the Daleks Justin Richards, 2002 (9/10)
Neverland Alan Barnes, 2002 (8/10)
Zagreus Alan Barnes & Gary Russell, 2003 (3/10)
Scherzo Rob Shearman, 2003 (4/10)
The Creed of the Kromon Philip Martin, 2004 (2/10)
The Natural History of Fear Jim Mortimore, 2004 (8/10)
The Twilight Kingdom Will Shindler, 2004 (7/10)
Faith Stealer Graham Duff, 2004 (4/10)
The Last Gary Hopkins, 2004 (9/10)
Caerdroia Lloyd Rose, 2004 (5/10)
The Next Life Alan Barnes & Gary Russell, 2004 (8/10)
Terror Firma Joseph Lidster, 2005 (8/10)
Scaredy Cat Will Shindler, 2005 (7/10)
Other Lives Gary Hopkins, 2005 (6/10)
Time Works Steve Lyons, 2006 (6/10)
Something Inside Trevor Baxendale, 2006 (4/10)
Memory Lane Eddie Robson, 2006 (8/10)
Blood of the Daleks Steve Lyons, 2007 (8/10)
Horror of Glam Rock Paul Magrs, 2007 (9/10)
Immortal Beloved Jonathan Clements, 2007 (4/10)
Phobos Eddie Robson, 2007 (3/10)
No More Lies Paul Sutton, 2007 (9/10)
Human Resources Eddie Robson, 2007 (8/10)
Absolution Scott Alan Woodard, 2007 (7/10)
The Girl Who Never Was Alan Barnes, 2007 (7/10)
Dead London Pat Mills, 2008 (8/10)
Max Warp Jonathan Morris, 2008 (7/10)
Brave New Town Jonathan Clements, 2008 (9/10)
The Skull of Sobek Marc Platt, 2008 (5/10)
Grand Theft Cosmos Eddie Robson, 2008 (6/10)
The Zygon Who Fell to Earth Paul Magrs, 2008 (8/10)
Sisters of the Flame Nicholas Briggs, 2008 (5/10)

The Vengeance of Morbius Nicholas Briggs, 2008 (9/10)
Orbis Alan Barnes & Nicholas Briggs, 2009 (7/10)
Hothouse Jonathan Morris, 2009 (4/10)
The Beast of Orlok Barnaby Edwards, 2009 (6/10)
Wirrn Dawn Nicholas Briggs, 2009 (7/10)
The Company of Friends various, 2009 (5/10)
The Scapegoat Pat Mills, 2009 (8/10)
The Cannibalists Jonathan Morris, 2009 (6/10)
The Eight Truths Eddie Robson, 2009 (5/10)
Worldwide Web Eddie Robson, 2009 (7/10)
Death in Blackpool Alan Barnes, 2009 (8/10)
Situation Vacant Eddie Robson, 2010 (4/10)
Nevermore Alan Barnes, 2010 (7/10)
The Book of Kells Barnaby Edwards, 2010 (4/10)
Deimos Jonathan Morris, 2010 (8/10)
The Resurrection of Mars Jonathan Morris, 2010 (9/10)
Relative Dimensions Marc Platt, 2010 (9/10)
Prisoner of the Sun Eddie Robson, 2011 (6/10)
Lucie Miller Nicholas Briggs, 2011 (8/10)
To the Death Nicholas Briggs, 2011 (9/10)
The Silver Turk Marc Platt, 2011 (7/10)
The Witch from the Well Rick Briggs, 2011 (6/10)
Army of Death Jason Arnopp, 2011 (5/10)
Dark Eyes: The Great War Nicholas Briggs, 2012 (9/10)
Dark Eyes: Fugitives Nicholas Briggs, 2012 (7/10)
Dark Eyes: Tangled Web Nicholas Briggs, 2012 (8/10)
Dark Eyes: X and the Daleks Nicholas Briggs, 2012 (9/10)

BOOKS

Titles listed in publication order.

William Hartnell

Venusian Lullaby Paul Leonard, Virgin, 1994 (6/10)
The Sorcerer's Apprentice Christopher Bulis, Virgin, 1995 (8/10)
The Empire of Glass Andy Lane, Virgin, 1995 (6/10)
The Man in the Velvet Mask Daniel O'Mahony, Virgin, 1996 (7/10)
The Plotters Gareth Roberts, Virgin, 1996 (8/10)
The Witch Hunters Steve Lyons, BBC, 1998 (7/10)
Salvation Steve Lyons, BBC, 1999 (6/10)
City at World's End Christopher Bulis, BBC, 1999 (8/10)
Bunker Soldiers Martin Day, BBC, 2001 (7/10)
Byzantium! Keith Topping, BBC, 2001 (8/10)
Ten Little Aliens Stephen Cole, BBC, 2002 (9/10)
The Eleventh Tiger David A McIntee, BBC, 2004 (7/10)
The Time Travellers Simon Guerrier, BBC, 2005 (8/10)

Patrick Troughton

The Menagerie Martin Day, Virgin, 1995 (3/10)
Invasion of the Cat-People Gary Russell, Virgin, 1995 (6/10)
Twilight of the Gods Christopher Bulis, Virgin, 1996 (4/10)

The Dark Path David A McIntee, Virgin, 1997 (6/10)
The Murder Game Steve Lyons, BBC, 1997 (5/10)
The Roundheads Mark Gatiss, BBC, 1997 (8/10)
Dreams of Empire Justin Richards, BBC, 1998 (7/10)
The Final Sanction Steve Lyons, BBC, 1999 (6/10)
Heart of Tardis Dave Stone, BBC, 2000 (5/10)
Dying in the Sun Jon de Burgh Miller, BBC, 2001 (5/10)
Combat Rock Mick Lewis, BBC, 2002 (8/10)
The Colony of Lies Colin Brake, BBC, 2003 (3/10)
The Indestructible Man Simon Messingham, BBC, 2004 (8/10)
World Game Terrance Dicks, BBC, 2005 (7/10)
The Wheel of Ice Stephen Baxter, BBC, 2012 (10/10)

Jon Pertwee

The Paradise of Death Barry Letts, Target, 1994 (3/10)
The Ghosts of N-Space Barry Letts, Virgin, 1995 (1/10)
Dancing the Code Paul Leonard, Virgin, 1995 (8/10)
The Eye of the Giant Christopher Bulis, Virgin, 1996 (7/10)
The Scales of Injustice Gary Russell, Virgin, 1996 (8/10)
Speed of Flight Paul Leonard, Virgin, 1996 (6/10)
The Devil Goblins from Neptune Keith Topping & Martin Day, BBC, 1997 (8/10)
The Face of the Enemy David A McIntee, BBC, 1998 (6/10)
Catastrophea Terrance Dicks, BBC, 1998 (5/10)
The Wages of Sin David A McIntee, BBC, 1999 (6/10)
Interference 2: The Hour of the Geek Lawrence Miles, BBC, 1999 (7/10)
Last of the Gaderene Mark Gatiss, BBC, 2000 (9/10)
Verdigris Paul Magrs, BBC, 2000 (8/10)
Rags Mick Lewis, BBC, 2001 (9/10)
Amorality Tale David Bishop, BBC, 2002 (4/10)
The Suns of Caresh Paul Saint, BBC, 2002 (7/10)
Deadly Reunion Terrance Dicks & Barry Letts, BBC, 2003 (5/10)
Island of Death Barry Letts, BBC, 2005 (5/10)

Tom Baker

Evolution John Peel, Virgin, 1994 (2/10)
The Romance of Crime Gareth Roberts, Virgin, 1995 (10/10)
System Shock Justin Richards, Virgin, 1995 (7/10)
Managra Stephen Marley, Virgin, 1995 (4/10)

The English Way of Death Gareth Roberts, Virgin, 1996 (7/10)
The Shadow of Weng-Chiang David A McIntee, Virgin, 1996 (4/10)
A Device of Death Christopher Bulis, Virgin, 1997 (5/10)
The Well-Mannered War Gareth Roberts, Virgin, 1997 (9/10)
Eye of Heaven Jim Mortimore, BBC, 1998 (7/10)
Last Man Running Chris Boucher, BBC, 1998 (7/10)
Millennium Shock Justin Richards, BBC, 1999 (8/10)
Corpse Marker Chris Boucher, BBC, 1999 (4/10)
Tomb of Valdemar Simon Messingham, BBC, 2000 (8/10)
Festival of Death Jonathan Morris, BBC, 2000 (6/10)
Asylum Peter Darvill-Evans, BBC, 2001 (3/10)
Psi-ence Fiction Chris Boucher, BBC, 2001 (5/10)
Drift Simon A Forward, BBC, 2002 (8/10)
Wolfsbane Jacqueline Rayner, BBC, 2003 (9/10)
Match of the Day Chris Boucher, BBC, 2005 (5/10)

Peter Davison

Goth Opera Paul Cornell, Virgin, 1994 (8/10)
The Crystal Bucephalus Craig Hinton, Virgin, 1994 (1/10)
Lords of the Storm David A McIntee, Virgin, 1995 (5/10)
The Sands of Time Justin Richards, Virgin, 1996 (7/10)
Cold Fusion Lance Parkin, Virgin, 1996 (5/10)
The Ultimate Treasure Christopher Bulis, BBC, 1997 (2/10)
Zeta Major Simon Messingham, BBC, 1998 (7/10)
Deep Blue Mark Morris, BBC, 1999 (9/10)
Divided Loyalties Gary Russell, BBC, 1999 (7/10)
Imperial Moon Christopher Bulis, BBC, 2000 (9/10)
The King of Terror Keith Topping, BBC, 2000 (4/10)
Superior Beings Nick Walters, BBC, 2001 (7/10)
Warmonger Terrance Dicks, BBC, 2002 (5/10)
Fear of the Dark Trevor Baxendale, BBC, 2003 (8/10)
Empire of Death David Bishop, BBC, 2004 (4/10)

Colin Baker

State of Change Christopher Bulis, Virgin, 1994 (6/10)
Time of Your Life Steve Lyons, Virgin, 1995 (7/10)
Millennial Rites Craig Hinton, Virgin, 1995 (3/10)
Killing Ground Steve Lyons, Virgin, 1996 (6/10)
Burning Heart Dave Stone, Virgin, 1997 (4/10)

Business Unusual Gary Russell, Virgin, 1997 (7/10)
Mission: Impractical David A McIntee, BBC, 1998 (3/10)
Players Terrance Dicks, BBC, 1999 (7/10)
Grave Matter Justin Richards, BBC, 2000 (8/10)
The Quantum Archangel Craig Hinton, BBC, 2001 (2/10)
The Shadow in the Glass Justin Richards & Stephen Cole, BBC, 2001 (7/10)
Instruments of Darkness Gary Russell, BBC, 2001 (1/10)
Palace of the Red Sun Christopher Bulis, BBC, 2002 (4/10)
Blue Box Kate Orman, BBC, 2003 (7/10)
Synthespians Craig Hinton, BBC, 2004 (6/10)
Spiral Scratch Gary Russell, BBC, 2005 (6/10)

Sylvester McCoy

Timewyrm: Genesys John Peel, Virgin, 1991 (4/10)
Timewyrm: Exodus Terrance Dicks, Virgin, 1991 (6/10)
Timewyrm: Apocalypse Nigel Robinson, Virgin, 1991 (3/10)
Timewyrm: Revelation Paul Cornell, Virgin, 1991 (7/10)
Cat's Cradle: Time's Crucible Marc Platt, Virgin, 1992 (2/10)
Cat's Cradle: Warhead Andrew Cartmel, Virgin, 1992 (8/10)
Cat's Cradle: Witch Mark Andrew Hunt, Virgin, 1992 (5/10)
Nightshade Mark Gatiss, Virgin, 1992 (10/10)
Love and War Paul Cornell, Virgin, 1992 (7/10)
Transit Ben Aaronovitch, Virgin, 1992 (1/10)
The Highest Science Gareth Roberts, Virgin, 1993 (9/10)
The Pit Neil Penswick, Virgin, 1993 (2/10)
Deceit Peter Darvill-Evans, Virgin, 1993 (6/10)
Lucifer Rising Andy Lane & Jim Mortimore, Virgin, 1993 (4/10)
White Darkness David A McIntee, Virgin, 1993 (5/10)
Shadowmind Christopher Bulis, Virgin, 1993 (8/10)
Birthright Nigel Robinson, Virgin, 1993 (6/10)
Iceberg David Banks, Virgin, 1993 (8/10)
Blood Heat Jim Mortimore, Virgin, 1993 (8/10)
The Dimension Riders Daniel Blythe, Virgin, 1993 (4/10)
The Left-Handed Hummingbird Kate Orman, Virgin, 1993 (7/10)
Conundrum Steve Lyons, Virgin, 1994 (5/10)
No Future Paul Cornell, Virgin, 1994 (7/10)
Tragedy Day Gareth Roberts, Virgin, 1994 (6/10)
Legacy Gary Russell, Virgin, 1994 (5/10)
Theatre of War Justin Richards, Virgin, 1994 (6/10)
All-Consuming Fire Andy Lane, Virgin, 1994 (9/10)

Blood Harvest Terrance Dicks, Virgin, 1994 (8/10)
Strange England Simon Messingham, Virgin, 1994 (4/10)
First Frontier David A McIntee, Virgin, 1994 (3/10)
St Anthony's Fire Mark Gatiss, Virgin, 1994 (6/10)
Falls the Shadow Daniel O'Mahony, Virgin, 1994 (7/10)
Parasite Jim Mortimore, Virgin, 1994 (3/10)
Warlock Andrew Cartmel, Virgin, 1995 (8/10)
Set Piece Kate Orman, Virgin, 1995 (5/10)
Infinite Requiem Daniel Blythe, Virgin, 1995 (6/10)
Sanctuary David A McIntee, Virgin, 1995 (3/10)
Human Nature Paul Cornell, Virgin, 1995 (9/10)
Original Sin Andy Lane, Virgin, 1995 (9/10)
Sky Pirates! Dave Stone, Virgin, 1995 (4/10)
Zamper Gareth Roberts, Virgin, 1995 (7/10)
Toy Soldiers Paul Leonard, Virgin, 1995 (8/10)
Head Games Steve Lyons, Virgin, 1995 (4/10)
The Also People Ben Aaronovitch, Virgin, 1995 (3/10)
Shakedown Terrance Dicks, Virgin, 1995 (8/10)
Just War Lance Parkin, Virgin, 1996 (9/10)
Warchild Andrew Cartmel, Virgin, 1996 (7/10)
Sleepy Kate Orman, Virgin, 1996 (6/10)
Death and Diplomacy Dave Stone, Virgin, 1996 (5/10)
Happy Endings Paul Cornell, Virgin, 1996 (4/10)
GodEngine Craig Hinton, Virgin, 1996 (2/10)
Christmas on a Rational Planet Lawrence Miles, Virgin, 1996 (7/10)
Return of the Living Dad Kate Orman, Virgin, 1996 (6/10)
The Death of Art Simon Bucher-Jones, Virgin, 1996 (7/10)
Damaged Goods Russell T Davies, Virgin, 1996 (9/10)
Bad Therapy Matthew Jones, Virgin, 1996 (8/10)
Eternity Weeps Jim Mortimore, Virgin, 1997 (4/10)
The Room With No Doors Kate Orman, Virgin, 1997 (3/10)
Lungbarrow Marc Platt, Virgin, 1997 (8/10)
So Vile a Sin Ben Aaronovitch & Kate Orman, Virgin, 1997 (7/10)
Illegal Alien Mike Tucker & Robert Perry, BBC, 1997 (8/10)
The Hollow Men Martin Day & Keith Topping, BBC, 1998 (7/10)
Matrix Robert Perry & Mike Tucker, BBC, 1998 (8/10)
Storm Harvest Robert Perry & Mike Tucker, BBC, 1999 (6/10)
Prime Time Mike Tucker, BBC, 2000 (7/10)
Independence Day Peter Darvill-Evans, BBC, 2000 (5/10)
Bullet Time David A McIntee, BBC, 2001 (3/10)
Relative Dementias Mark Michalowski, BBC, 2002 (9/10)
Heritage Dale Smith, BBC, 2002 (4/10)

Loving the Alien Mike Tucker & Robert Perry, BBC, 2003 (8/10)
The Algebra of Ice Lloyd Rose, BBC, 2004 (9/10)
Atom Bomb Blues Andrew Cartmel, BBC, 2005 (8/10)

Paul McGann

The Dying Days Lance Parkin, Virgin, 1997 (8/10)
The Eight Doctors Terrance Dicks, BBC, 1997 (4/10)
Vampire Science Jonathan Blume & Kate Orman, BBC, 1997 (7/10)
The Bodysnatchers Mark Morris, BBC, 1997 (6/10)
Genocide Paul Leonard, BBC, 1997 (7/10)
War of the Daleks John Peel, BBC, 1997 (3/10)
Alien Bodies Lawrence Miles, BBC, 1997 (8/10)
Kursaal Peter Anghelides, BBC, 1998 (5/10)
Option Lock Justin Richards, BBC, 1998 (8/10)
Longest Day Michael Collier, BBC, 1998 (2/10)
Legacy of the Daleks John Peel, BBC, 1998 (4/10)
Dreamstone Moon Paul Leonard, BBC, 1998 (6/10)
Seeing I Jonathan Blume & Kate Orman, BBC, 1998 (7/10)
Placebo Effect Gary Russell, BBC, 1998 (4/10)
Vanderdeken's Children Christopher Bulis, BBC, 1998 (7/10)
The Scarlet Empress Paul Magrs, BBC, 1998 (5/10)
The Janus Conjunction Trevor Baxendale, BBC, 1998 (8/10)
Beltempest Jim Mortimore, BBC, 1998 (6/10)
The Face-Eater Simon Messingham, BBC, 1999 (7/10)
The Taint Michael Collier, BBC, 1999 (4/10)
Demontage Justin Richards, BBC, 1999 (6/10)
Revolution Man Paul Leonard, BBC, 1999 (8/10)
Dominion Nick Walters, BBC, 1999 (7/10)
Unnatural History Jonathan Blume & Kate Orman, BBC, 1999 (8/10)
Autumn Mist David A McIntee, BBC, 1999 (4/10)
Interference 1: Shock Tactic Lawrence Miles, BBC, 1999 (9/10)
The Blue Angel Paul Magrs & Jeremy Hoad, BBC, 1999 (4/10)
The Taking of Planet 5 Simon Bucher-Jones & Mark Clapham, BBC, 1999 (6/10)
Frontier Worlds Peter Anghelides, BBC, 1999 (7/10)
Parallel 59 Natalie Dallaire & Stephen Cole, BBC, 2000 (5/10)
The Shadows of Avalon Paul Cornell, BBC, 2000 (6/10)
The Fall of Yquatine Nick Walters, BBC, 2000 (3/10)
Coldheart Trevor Baxendale, BBC, 2000 (7/10)
The Space Age Steve Lyons, BBC, 2000 (7/10)
The Banquo Legacy Andy Lane & Justin Richards, BBC, 2000 (2/10)

The Ancestor Cell Peter Anghelides & Stephen Cole, BBC, 2000 (4/10)
The Burning Justin Richards, BBC, 2000 (9/10)
Casualties of War Steve Emmerson, 2000 (9/10)
The Turing Test Paul Leonard, BBC, 2000 (7/10)
Endgame Terrance Dicks, BBC, 2000 (5/10)
Father Time Lance Parkin, BBC, 2001 (8/10)
Escape Velocity Colin Brake, BBC, 2001 (7/10)
Earthworld Jacqueline Rayner, BBC, 2001 (6/10)
Vanishing Point Stephen Cole, BBC, 2001 (5/10)
Eater of Wasps Trevor Baxendale, BBC, 2001 (9/10)
The Year of Intelligent Tigers Kate Orman, BBC, 2001 (10/10)
The Slow Empire Dave Stone, BBC, 2001 (3/10)
Dark Progeny Steve Emmerson, BBC, 2001 (5/10)
The City of the Dead Lloyd Rose, BBC, 2001 (8/10)
Grimm Reality Simon Bucher-Jones & Kelly Hale, BBC, 2001 (1/10)
The Adventuress of Henrietta Street Lawrence Miles, BBC, 2001 (8/10)
Mad Dogs and Englishmen Paul Magrs, BBC, 2002 (10/10)
Hope Mark Clapham, BBC, 2002 (6/10)
Anachrophobia Jonathan Morris, BBC, 2002 (7/10)
Trading Futures Lance Parkin, BBC, 2002 (5/10)
The Book of the Still Paul Ebbs, BBC, 2002 (7/10)
The Crooked World Steve Lyons, BBC, 2002 (8/10)
History 101 Mags L Halliday, BBC, 2002 (7/10)
Camera Obscura Lloyd Rose, BBC, 2002 (6/10)
Time Zero Justin Richards, BBC, 2002 (8/10)
The Infinity Race Simon Messingham, BBC, 2002 (6/10)
The Domino Effect David Bishop, BBC, 2003 (6/10)
Reckless Engineering Nick Walters, BBC, 2003 (9/10)
The Last Resort Paul Leonard, BBC, 2003 (8/10)
Timeless Stephen Cole, BBC, 2003 (9/10)
Emotional Chemistry Simon A Forward, BBC, 2003 (3/10)
Sometime Never . . . Justin Richards, BBC, 2004 (6/10)
Halflife Mark Michalowski, BBC, 2004 (9/10)
The Tomorrow Windows Jonathan Morris, BBC, 2004 (9/10)
The Sleep of Reason Martin Day, BBC, 2004 (7/10)
The Deadstone Memorial Trevor Baxendale, BBC, 2004 (8/10)
To the Slaughter Stephen Cole, BBC, 2005 (9/10)
The Gallifrey Chronicles Lance Parkin, BBC, 2005 (9/10)
Fear Itself Nick Wallace, BBC, 2005 (8/10)

Christopher Eccleston

The Clockwise Man Justin Richards, BBC, 2005 (7/10)
The Monsters Inside Stephen Cole, BBC, 2005 (4/10)
Winner Takes All Jacqueline Rayner, BBC, 2005 (7/10)
The Deviant Strain Justin Richards, BBC, 2005 (6/10)
Only Human Gareth Roberts, BBC, 2005 (9/10)
The Stealers of Dreams Steve Lyons, BBC, 2005 (8/10)

David Tennant

The Stone Rose Jacqueline Rayner, BBC, 2006 (7/10)
The Feast of the Drowned Stephen Cole, BBC, 2006 (8/10)
The Resurrection Casket Justin Richards, BBC, 2006 (8/10)
I Am a Dalek Gareth Roberts, BBC, 2006 (2/10)
The Nightmare of Black Island Mike Tucker, BBC, 2006 (6/10)
The Art of Destruction Stephen Cole, BBC, 2006 (3/10)
The Price of Paradise Colin Brake, BBC, 2006 (5/10)
Made of Steel Terrance Dicks, BBC, 2007 (6/10)
Sting of the Zygons Stephen Cole, BBC, 2007 (3/10)
The Last Dodo Jacqueline Rayner, BBC, 2007 (4/10)
Wooden Heart Martin Day, BBC, 2007 (7/10)
Forever Autumn Mark Morris, BBC, 2007 (8/10)
Sick Building Paul Magrs, BBC, 2007 (7/10)
Wetworld Mark Michalowski, BBC, 2007 (7/10)
Wishing Well Trevor Baxendale, BBC, 2007 (9/10)
The Pirate Loop Simon Guerrier, BBC, 2007 (5/10)
Peacemaker James Swallow, BBC, 2007 (6/10)
Martha in the Mirror Justin Richards, BBC, 2008 (5/10)
Snowglobe 7 Mike Tucker, BBC, 2008 (6/10)
The Many Hands Dale Smith, BBC, 2008 (4/10)
Ghosts of India Mark Morris, BBC, 2008 (7/10)
The Doctor Trap Simon Messingham, BBC, 2008 (3/10)
Shining Darkness Mark Michalowski, BBC, 2008 (4/10)
The Story of Martha Dan Abnett et al, BBC, 2008 (7/10)
Beautiful Chaos Gary Russell, BBC, 2008 (4/10)
The Eyeless Lance Parkin, BBC, 2008 (6/10)
Judgement of the Judoon Colin Brake, BBC, 2009 (5/10)
The Slitheen Excursion Simon Guerrier, BBC, 2009 (4/10)
Prisoner of the Daleks Trevor Baxendale, BBC, 2009 (10/10)
The Taking of Chelsea 426 David Llewellyn, BBC, 2009 (8/10)

Autonomy Daniel Blythe, BBC, 2009 (4/10)
The Krillitane Storm Christopher Cooper, BBC, 2009 (7/10)

Miscellaneous

Turlough and the Earthlink Dilemma Tony Attwood, Target, 1986 (1/10)
Harry Sullivan's War Ian Marter, Target, 1986 (8/10)
The Nightmare Fair Graham Williams, Target, 1989 (6/10)
The Ultimate Evil Wally K Daly, Target, 1989 (5/10)
Mission to Magnus Philip Martin, Target, 1990 (3/10)
Downtime Marc Platt, Virgin, 1996 (7/10)
Who Killed Kennedy James Stevens & David Bishop, Virgin, 1996 (7/10)
The Infinity Doctors Lance Parkin, BBC, 1998 (9/10)

MISSING EPISODES

The videotapes of *Doctor Who* during the 1960s were copied onto 16mm film for overseas sales, while the original tapes were then reused for other productions. Many of these filmed copies were then destroyed on an irregular basis up until the mid-1970s. What remains today are the film copies kept by the BBC, together with others recovered from a variety of sources, most notably overseas television stations. Whilst every Pertwee episode now resides in the BBC archive, it is the first two Doctors' episodes that have suffered the most.

William Hartnell

(44 episodes missing)
Marco Polo 1–7
The Reign of Terror 4–5
The Crusade 2, 4
Galaxy 4 1–2, 4
Mission to the Unknown
The Myth Makers 1–4
The Daleks' Master Plan 1, 3–4, 6–9, 11–12
The Massacre of St Bartholomew's Eve 1–4
The Celestial Toymaker 1–3

The Savages 1–4
The Smugglers 1–4
The Tenth Planet 4

Patrick Troughton

(62 episodes missing)
The Power of the Daleks 1–6
The Highlanders 1–4
The Underwater Menace 1, 4
The Moonbase 1, 3
The Macra Terror 1–4
The Faceless Ones 2, 4–6
The Evil of the Daleks 1, 3–7
The Abominable Snowmen 1, 3–6
The Ice Warriors 2–3
The Enemy of the World 1–2, 4–6
The Web of Fear 2–6
Fury From the Deep 1–6
The Wheel in Space 1–2, 4–5
The Invasion 1, 4
The Space Pirates 1, 3–6
The Underwater Menace 1, 4
The Moonbase 1, 3
The Invasion 1, 4

SPIN-OFFS

Excludes comic strips, short stories, sketches and documentaries.

1. DR. WHO AND THE DALEKS

Cast: Peter Cushing (*Doctor*), Roy Castle (*Ian*), Jennie Linden (*Barbara*), Roberta Tovey (*Susan*), Barrie Ingham (*Alydon*), Geoffrey Toone (*Temmosus*), Michael Coles (*Ganatus*), John Brown (*Antodus*), Yvonne Antrobus (*Dyoni*), Mark Petersen (*Elyon*), David Graham, Peter Hawkins (*Dalek voices*) | **Crew:** Director: Gordon Flemying; Writer: Milton Subotsky; Producers: Milton Subotsky & Max J Rosenberg | **Film:** Aaru, UK premiere 25 June 1965 (DVD, 2006; CD, 2009)

Précis: The Tardis occupants encounter the Daleks and Thals on Skaro . . .
Observations: Widescreen version of the BBC serial.
Verdict: Colourfully made, but a bit slow. 7/10

2. THE CURSE OF THE DALEKS

Cast: Nicholas Hawtrey (*Redway*), Colin Miller (*Sline*), John Line (*Ladiver*), John Moore (*Vanderlyn*), Nicholas Bennett (*Dexion*), Suzanne Mockler (*Ijayna*) | **Crew:** Director: Gillian Howell; Writers:

David Whitaker & Terry Nation; Producer: John Gale & Ernest Hecht |
Theatre: Wyndham's Theatre, London, premiere 21 December 1965
(CD, 2008)

Précis: A prison ship lands on Skaro and one of the prisoners tries to control the Daleks . . .
Observations: The Doctor does not feature in the story.
Verdict: A whodunnit in space, this simple tale proved popular with a Dalek-hungry audience. 7/10

3. DALEKS' INVASION EARTH 2150 AD

Cast: Peter Cushing (*Doctor*), Bernard Cribbins (*Tom Campbell*),
Roberta Tovey (*Susan*), Jill Curzon (*Louise*), Ray Brooks (*David*),
Philip Madoc (*Brockley*), Andrew Keir (*Wyler*), Roger Avon (*Wells*),
Eddie Powell (*Thompson*), Godfrey Quigley (*Dortmun*), Sheila Steafel
(*Young Woman*), Eileen Way (*Old Woman*), Kenneth Watson
(*Craddock*), Peter Hawkins, David Graham (*Dalek voices*) | **Crew:**
Director: Gordon Flemying; Writer: Milton Subotsky; Producers:
Milton Subotsky & Max J Rosenberg | **Film:** Aaru, UK premiere 22 July
1966 (DVD, 2006; CD, 2009)

Précis: The Daleks invade Earth in the year 2150 (as the title
suggests) . . .
Observations: Widescreen version of the BBC serial.
Verdict: Wonderfully entertaining after all these years. 10/10

4. DOCTOR WHO AND THE DALEKS IN SEVEN KEYS TO DOOMSDAY

Cast: Trevor Martin (*Doctor*), Wendy Padbury (*Jenny*), James Mathews
(*Jimmy*), Simon Jones (*Master of Karn*) | **Crew:** Director: Mick Hughes;
Writer: Terrance Dicks; Producer: Trevor Mitchell | **Theatre:** Adelphi
Theatre, London, premiere 16 December 1974 (CD, 2008)

Précis: The Doctor assembles a crystal which is stolen by
the Daleks . . .

Observations: Plot elements would later feature in *The Brain of Morbius* (84).
Verdict: By all accounts, a stunning production. 8/10

5. DOCTOR WHO AND THE PESCATONS

Cast: Tom Baker (*Doctor*), Elisabeth Sladen (*Sarah Jane Smith*), Bill Mitchell (*Zor*) | **Crew:** Directors: Harvey Usill & Don Norman; Writer: Victor Pemberton; Producer: Don Norman | **LP:** Argo Records, July 1976 (N, 1991; CD, 2005)

Précis: The Doctor and Sarah stop the shark-like Pescaton leader Zor from invading Earth . . .
Observations: Scripted by former script editor/writer Victor Pemberton.
Verdict: Surprisingly spooky. 7/10

6. EXPLORATION EARTH: THE TIME MACHINE

Cast: Tom Baker (*Doctor*), Elisabeth Sladen (*Sarah Jane Smith*), John Westbrook (*Megron*) | **Crew:** Writer: Bernard Venables; Producer: Mike Howarth | **Radio:** Radio 4, 4 October 1976 (CD, 2001)

Précis: The Doctor and Sarah defend the newly formed Earth from the deadly Megron . . .
Observations: Transmitted as part of a schools' educational series.
Verdict: Worthy, but dull. 2/10

7. SHADA

Cast: Tom Baker (*Doctor*), Lalla Ward (*Romana II*), John Leeson (K-9 II voice), Denis Carey (*Chronotis*), Victoria Burgoyne (*Clare*), Daniel Hill (*Chris*), Christopher Neame (*Skagra*), Gerald Campion (*Porter*), James Coombes (*Krarg voices*), Derek Pollitt (*Caldera*) | **Crew:** Director: Pennant Roberts; Writer: Douglas Adams | **Television:** BBC1, 1980, uncompleted & untransmitted (CD, 2003)

Précis: In Cambridge, an alien plans to release an evil Time Lord from his prison planet . . .

Observations: Conceived as the six-part Season 17 finale, but despite extensive location filming in Cambridge, studio recording was never completed because of a BBC strike. The preserved material was later released on video in 1992 with narration by Tom Baker. Portions of the film material were included in *The Five Doctors* (129). A rewritten version with a new cast was released on CD.

Verdict: Lovely filmwork and some nice performances, but it's probably not the 'lost epic' everyone wants it to be. 6/10

8. K-9 AND COMPANY: A GIRL'S BEST FRIEND

Cast: Elisabeth Sladen (*Sarah Jane Smith*), John Leeson (*K-9 III voice*), Bill Fraser (*Pollock*), Ian Sears (*Brendan*), Colin Jeavons (*George Tracey*), Mary Wimbush (*Aunt Lavinia*), Linda Polan (*Juno Baker*), Gilliam Martell (*Lilly Gregson*), John Quarmby (*Henry Tobias*), Neville Barber (*Howard Baker*) | **Crew:** Director: John Black; Writer: Terence Dudley; Producer: John Nathan-Turner | **Television:** BBC1, 28 December 1981 (N, 1987; DVD, 2008)

Précis: Sarah and K-9 Mk III foil the machinations of a local witches' coven . . .

Observation: The pilot for a series that never happened.

Verdict: A charming adventure story with a pleasantly naturalistic flavour. 8/10

9. A FIX WITH SONTARANS

Cast: Colin Baker (*Doctor*), Gareth Jenkins (*Himself*), Janet Fielding (*Tegan*), Clinton Greyn (*Nathan*), Jimmy Saville OBE (*Himself*) | **Crew:** Director: Marcus Mortimer; Writer: Eric Saward; Producer: Roger Ordish | **Television:** BBC1, 23 February 1985 (DVD, 2003 [*The Two Doctors*])

Précis: Gareth helps the Doctor to defeat two Sontarans in the Tardis . . .

Observations: Nine-minute insert shown as part of *Jim'll Fix It*.

Verdict: Likeable nonsense. 6/10

10. SLIPBACK

Cast: Colin Baker (*Doctor*), Nicola Bryant (*Peri*), Jane Carr (*Computer voice*), Jon Glover (*Grant*), Nick Revell (*Bates*), Valentine Dyall (*Slarn*), Ron Pember (*Seedle*) | **Crew:** Director/Producer: Paul Spencer; Writer: Eric Saward | **Radio:** Radio 4, 25 July–8 August 1985 (N, 1986; CD, 2001)

Précis: The Doctor tries to stop a schizophrenic computer from destroying the universe . . .

Observations: Transmitted during the Saturday morning children's show, *Pirate Radio Four*.

Verdict: Dislikeable nonsense. 2/10

11. DOCTOR WHO: THE ULTIMATE ADVENTURE

Cast: Jon Pertwee/Colin Baker/David Banks (*Doctor*), Rebecca Thornhill (*Crystal*), Graeme Smith/David Bingham (*Jason*), David Banks/Chris Beaumont (*Karl*) | **Crew:** Director: Carole Todd; Writer: Terrance Dicks; Producer: Mark Furness | **Theatre:** Wimbledon Theatre, London, premiere 23 March 1989 (CD, 2008)

Précis: The Daleks and Cybermen team up to invade Earth . . .

Observations: Toured the UK for five months, with Colin Baker (and David Banks for two performances) taking over from Pertwee.

Verdict: Thrilling entertainment for all the family, spoilt by unnecessary songs. 9/10

12. SEARCH OUT SPACE

Cast: Sylvester McCoy (*Doctor*), Sophie Aldred (*Ace*), John Leeson (*K-9 voice*), Stephen Johnson (*Cedric*) | **Crew:** Director: Berry-Anne Billingsley; Producer: Lambros Atteshlis | **Television:** BBC2, 21 November 1990 (DVD, 2007 [*Survival*])

Précis: The Doctor, Ace, K-9 and Cedric find out about space . . .
Observations: Shown as part of the BBC Schools series, *Search Out Science*.
Verdict: The regulars are in character, but it's all rather mystifying. 5/10

13. THE PARADISE OF DEATH

Cast: Jon Pertwee (*Doctor*), Elisabeth Sladen (*Sarah Jane Smith*), Nicholas Courtney (*Brigadier*), Peter Miles (*Tremayne*), Harold Innocent (*Freeth*), Richard Pearce (*Jeremy*), Maurice Denham (*President*), Trevor Martin (*Various*) | **Crew:** Writer: Barry Letts; Producer: Phil Clarke | **Radio:** Radio 5, 27 August–24 September 1993 (N, 1994; CD, 2000)

Précis: Aliens from Parakon offer Earth a miracle plant called Rapine . . .
Observations: During the Radio 2 repeat, episode four was transmitted twice in error.
Verdict: Good in places, but it doesn't seem much like a Third Doctor story and Pertwee himself sounds ancient. 4/10

14. DIMENSIONS IN TIME

Cast: Jon Pertwee, Tom Baker, Peter Davison, Colin Baker, Sylvester McCoy (*Doctor*), Kate O'Mara (*Rani*), Sophie Aldred (*Ace*), Bonnie Langford (*Mel*), Carole Ann Ford (*Susan*), Elisabeth Sladen (*Sarah Jane Smith*), Nicola Bryant (*Peri*), Sarah Sutton (*Nyssa*), Caroline John (*Liz Shaw*), Richard Franklin (*Yates*), Nicholas Courtney (*Brigadier*), Lalla Ward (*Romana II*), Deborah Watling (*Victoria*), Louise Jameson (*Leela*), John Leeson (*K-9 voice*) | **Crew:** Director: Stuart McDonald; Writers:

John Nathan-Turner & David Roden; Producer: John Nathan-Turner |
Television: BBC1, 26–27 November 1993

Précis: The Rani captures the Doctor and his companions
in a time loop in fictional Walford . . .
Observations: Shown as part of the BBC charity telethon
Children in Need.
Verdict: A desperately misguided attempt to make a
'serious' *Doctor Who* story for charity, but the 3D effect is
occasionally impressive. 4/10

15. THE GHOSTS OF N-SPACE

Cast: Jon Pertwee (*Doctor*), Elisabeth Sladen (*Sarah Jane Smith*), Nicholas
Courtney (*Brigadier*), Richard Pearce (*Jeremy*), Stephen Thorne (*Max*),
Sandra Dickinson (*Maggie*), Harry Towb (*Various*) | **Crew:** Writer: Barry
Letts; Producer: Phil Clarke | **Radio:** Radio 2, 20 January–24 February
1996 (N, 1995; CD, 2000)

Précis: In Italy, the Doctor stops ghosts from invading the
Earth . . .
Observations: Recorded in November 1994, it took over
12 months to make it on air.
Verdict: Drivel. 1/10

16. DOCTOR WHO AND THE CURSE OF FATAL DEATH

Cast: Rowan Atkinson, Richard E Grant, Jim Broadbent, Hugh Grant,
Joanna Lumley (*Doctor*), Julia Sawalha (*Emma*), Jonathan Pryce (*The
Master*), Roy Skelton, Dave Chapman (*Dalek voices*) | **Crew:** Director:
John Henderson; Writer: Steven Moffatt; Producer: Sue Vertue | **Television:**
BBC1, 12 March 1999

Précis: The Master joins the Daleks in trying to kill the
Doctor . . .
Observations: Shown as part of the BBC Comic Relief Red
Nose Day.

Verdict: Spot-on pastiche, with wonderful performances from all the cast. 10/10

17. DEATH COMES TO TIME

Cast: Sylvester McCoy (*Doctor*), Sophie Aldred (*Ace*), John Culshaw (*Guard/Senator Hawk*), Jacqueline Pearce (*Admiral Mettna*), Kevin Eldon (*Antimony*), Leonard Fenton (*Casmus*), Stephen Fry (*Minister of Chance*), John Sessions (*General Tannis*) | **Crew:** Writer: Colin Meek; Producer: Dan Freedman | **Internet:** BBCi, 13 July 2001–3 May 2002 (CD, 2002)

Précis: In the middle of an intergalactic war, the Doctor has to rescue Ace . . .
Verdict: Patchy self-styled epic with many silly moments. 4/10

18. REAL TIME

Cast: Colin Baker (*Doctor*), Maggie Stables (*Evelyn*), Yee Jee Tso (*Goddard*), Christopher Scott (*Isherwood*), Jane Goddard (*Savage*), Nicholas Briggs (*Osborn/Cyber Leader*), Stewart Lee (*Carey*), Richard Herring (*Renchard*) | **Crew:** Writer: Gary Russell; Producers: Gary Russell & Jason Haigh-Ellery | **Internet:** BBCi, 2 August–6 September 2002 (CD, 2002)

Précis: An Earth expedition discovers the seemingly dormant lair of the Cybermen . . .
Verdict: A fairly straightforward Cyber romp, much better than the previous webcast attempt. 8/10

19. SCREAM OF THE SHALKA

Cast: Richard E Grant (*Doctor*), Derek Jacobi (*The Master*), Sophie Okonedo (*Alison Cheney*), Jim Norton (*Thomas Kennett*), Diana Quick (*Prime*) | **Crew:** Director: Wilson Milam; Writer: Paul Cornell; Producer: Muirinn Lane Kelly | **Internet:** BBCi, 13 November–18 December 2003 (N, 2004)

Précis: A Lancashire town is under siege from mysterious forces . . .

Verdict: Good old-fashioned entertainment, albeit with a rather unlikeable Doctor. 7/10

20. ATTACK OF THE GRASKE

Cast: David Tennant (*Doctor*), Lisa Palfrey (*Mum*), Nicholas Beveney (*Dad*), Mollie Kabia (*Girl*), James Harris (*Boy*), Robin Meredith (*Granddad*), Gwenyth Petty (*Grandma*), Jimmy Vee (*Graske*) | **Crew:** Director: Ashley Way; Writer: Gareth Roberts; Producers: Sophie Fante, Jo Pearce & Andrew Whitehouse | **Internet:** BBCi, 25 December 2005

Précis: The Doctor requests the viewers' help to defeat the diminutive Graske . . .

Verdict: Clever interactive adventure with a hilarious performance by Tennant. 9/10

21. TORCHWOOD

Cast: John Barrowman (*Captain Jack Harkness*), Eve Myles (*Gwen Cooper*), Burn Gorman (*Owen Harper*), Naoki Mori (*Toshiko Sato*), Gareth David-Lloyd (*Ianto Jones*) | **Crew:** Directors: Brian Kelly, Colin Teague, James Strong, Alice Troughton, Ashley Way, Andy Goddard, Jonathan Fox Bassett, Mark Everest & Euros Lyn, Bharat Nalluri, Billy Gierhart, Guy Ferland, Gwyneth Horder-Payton; Writers: Russell T Davies, Chris Chibnall, Helen Raynor, PJ Hammond, Toby Whithouse, Paul Tomalin & Dan McCulloch, Jacquetta May, Catherine Tregenna, Noel Clarke, James Moran, JC Wilsher, Matt Jones, Joseph Lidster, Phil Ford & John Fay, Jane Espenson, Doris Egan, Jim Gray, John Shiban, Ryan Scott; Producers: Richard Stokes, Sophie Fante, Chris Chibnall, Peter Bennett, Kelly A Manners & Brian Minchin | **Television:** Series 1: BBC3, 22 October 2006–1 January 2007 (DVD, 2007); 2: BBC2, 16 January–4 April 2008 (DVD, 2008); Season 3: BBC1, 6–10 July 2009 (DVD, 2009); Season 4: BBC1, 14 July–15 September 2011 (DVD/Blu-ray, 2011)

Précis: A covert investigation team deals with phenomena emerging from the Cardiff rift . . .

Observations: *Torchwood*, an anagram of *Doctor Who*, was the codename for early episodes of Season 27. It was first heard in *Bad Wolf* (166) and the organisation featured heavily in *The Christmas Invasion* (167) and *Army of Ghosts/Doomsday* (177). Two thirteen-part series were followed by one five-part story, *Children of Earth*, shown on consecutive evenings on BBC1. A final ten-part American-funded series, subtitled *Miracle Day*, aired two years later.

Verdict: Starting as a wildly variable series of movie plagiarisms with many silly moments and a collection of deeply dislikeable characters, it does get better. Dispensing with the gimmickry, *Children of Earth* is easily the best, while the less said about the frustratingly poor US series the better. 6/10

22. THE SARAH JANE ADVENTURES

Cast: Elisabeth Sladen (*Sarah Jane Smith*), Yasmin Paige (*Maria*), Thomas Knight (*Luke*), Anjili Mohindra (*Rani*), Daniel Anthony (*Clyde Langer*), Alexander Armstrong (*Mr Smith voice*), John Leeson (*K-9 VI voice*), Sinead Michael (*Sky*) | **Crew:** Directors: Colin Teague, Alice Troughton, Charles Martin, Graeme Harper, Joss Agnew, Michael Kerrigan, Ashley Way; Writers: Russell T Davies, Gareth Roberts, Phil Ford, Phil Gladwin, Joseph Lidster & Rupert Laight; Ashley Way; Clayton Hickman Producers: Susie Liggat, Matthew Bouch, Nikki Wilson, Phil Ford & Brian Minchin | **Television:** Pilot: BBC1, 1 January 2007 (DVD, 2007); Season 1: BBC1, 24 September–19 November 2007 (DVD, 2008); Season 2: BBC1, 29 September–8 December 2008 (DVD, 2009); Season 3: BBC1, 15 October–20 November 2009 (DVD, 2010); Season 4: BBC1, 11 October–16 November 2010 (DVD/Blu-ray, 2011); Season 5: BBC1, 3–18 October 2011 (DVD/Blu-ray, 2012)

Précis: Sarah and her young friends investigate strange goings-on . . .

Observations: Spin-off from *School Reunion* (170). David Tennant appeared as the Doctor in the Season 3 story *The Wedding of Sarah Jane Smith*. A 60-minute pilot preceded series four, a truncated fifth following Elizabeth Sladen's sudden death in April 2011 at the age of 65.

Verdict: Bright, cheerfully made children's series with the occasional scary moment. 9/10

23. THE INFINITE QUEST

Cast: David Tennant (*Doctor*), Freema Agyeman (*Martha Jones*), Anthony Head (*Baltazar*), Toby Longworth (*Caw/Squawk*), Liza Tarbuck (*Captain Kaliko*), Tom Farrelly (*Swabb*), Lizzie Hopley (*Mantasphid Queen*), Paul Clayton (*Mergrass*), Stephen Greif (*Gurney*) | **Crew:** Director: Gary Russell; Writer: Alan Barnes; Producers: James Goss & Ros Attille | **Television:** BBC1, 2 April–30 June 2007 (DVD, 2007)

Précis: The Doctor must stop the evil Baltazar finding a mythical spaceship . . .

Observations: Twelve animated episodes stripped across *Totally Doctor Who* and then shown as an omnibus on 30 June 2007.

Verdict: Sterling attempt at a cartoon *Doctor Who* epic; kids will probably love it. 7/10

24. TIME CRASH

Cast: Peter Davison, David Tennant (*Doctor*) | **Crew:** Director: Graeme Harper; Writer: Steven Moffat; Producer: Phil Collinson | **Television:** BBC1, 16 November 2007 (DVD, 2008)

Précis: Doctor Five bumps into Doctor Ten in the Tardis . . .

Observations: Skit written for *Children in Need*, which also explained the Tardis' impact with the Titanic in *Voyage of the Damned* (188).

Verdict: One big in-joke, but rather charmingly done. 8/10

25. K-9

Cast: John Leeson (K-9 voice), Philippa Coulthard (*Jorjie Turner*), Keegan Joyce (*Starkey*), Daniel Webber (*Darius Pike*), Robert Moloney (*Professor Gryffen*), Robyn Moore (*Jane Turner*), Connor Van Vuuren (*Inspector Drake*), Jaraed Robinson (*Inspector Thorne*) | **Crew:** Directors: David Caesar, Mark DeFriest, David Napier, Daniel Nettheim, Karl Zwicky, James Bogle & Dale Bradley; Writers: Bob Baker, Paul Tams, Shane Krause, Shayne Armstrong, Jim Noble, Tim Pye, Ian McFadyen, Deborah Parons, Evertt DeRoche, Graeme Farmer, Lindsay James, Dave Warner, Chris Roach, Jason Bourque, John O'Brien & Anthony Morris; Producers: Penny Wall, Richard Stewart & Simon Barnes | **Television:** Series 1: Disney XD, 31 October 2009–20 November 2010 (DVD, 2011)

Précis: A modified K-9 helps teenagers fight monsters in future London . . .

Observations: A twenty-six part Australian/British co-production, Bob Baker and Paul Tams' comedy/adventure series was first mooted back in 1997. In the first episode, the K-9 familiar to viewers of *Doctor Who* is seen to regenerate into a drastically modified version, partly rendered by CGI, that is able to fly around.

Verdict: The sort of thing that the makers of the Sarah Jane Adventures strove hard to avoid, this is childish kids' entertainment for an undiscerning audience. 3/10

26. DREAMLAND

Cast: David Tennant (*Doctor*), Georgia Moffett (*Cassie*), Tim Howar (*Jimmy*), Lisa Bowerman (*Saruba Velak*), David Warner (*Lord Azlok*), Stuart Milligan (*Colonel Stark*), Clarke Peters (*Night Eagle*), Nicholas Rowe (*Rivesh Mantilax*), Peter Guinness (*Mr Dread*) | **Crew:** Director: Gary Russell; Writer: Phil Ford; Producers; Ed Cross & Mat Fidell | **Television:** BBC Red Button, 21–26 December 2009 (DVD, 2010)

Précis: The Doctor investigates an alien ship in Roswell in 1958 . . .

Observations: An omnibus version was broadcast on 5 December 2009. Georgia Moffett played the title character in *The Doctor's Daughter* (193).

Verdict: Excellent animation for inanimate objects, but the flesh-and-blood characters look appalling. Pretty clichéd story too. 4/10

27. DOCTOR WHO LIVE: THE MONSTERS ARE COMING!

Cast: Nigel Planer (*Vorgenson*), Nicholas Briggs (*Winston Churchill*) | **Crew:** Director: Will Brenton; Writers: Gareth Roberts & Will Brenton; Producer: Craig Stanley | **Stadium Tour:** 8 October–7 November 2010

Précis: An intergalactic monster show gets out of control...

Observations: Matt Smith appeared in pre-filmed sequences in this two-hour stage show that featured a 16-piece band playing live music, conducted by Ben Foster, with appearances by various monsters. It began at Wembley Arena in London, before touring the UK and finishing up at Belfast's Odyssey Arena.

Verdict: A glorified concert of *Doctor Who* music, akin to the Proms events, but on a much grander scale. 8/10

28. SPACE / TIME

Cast: Matt Smith (*Doctor*), Karen Gillan (*Amy*), Arthur Darvill (*Rory*) | **Crew:** Director: Richard Senior; Writer: Steven Moffat; Producer: Annabella Hurst-Brown | **Television:** BBC1, 18 March 2011 (DVD/ Blu-ray, 2011)

Précis: The Tardis materialises inside itself and Amy meets herself...

Observations: This two-part comedy sketch (the first entitled *Space*, the second *Time*) lasted approximately six minutes in total and was transmitted as part of the BBC's Red Nose Day telethon.

Verdict: A little adult in tone, but entertaining enough for what it is. 7/10

29. THE CRASH OF THE ELYSIUM

Crew: Director: Felix Barrett; Writer: Tom MacRae (from an idea by Steven Moffat) | **Theatre:** MediaCity UK, Manchester, 1–17 July 2011

Précis: The Doctor asks for help in investigating the disappearance of a Victorian steamship...

Observations: This was a one-hour piece of 'immersive theatre' developed by interactive performance company Punchdrunk, initially aimed at children between 6 and 12, although adults were later allowed to participate. Matt Smith appeared in pre-filmed segments, although for one show he made a surprise appearance in person. The production was later remounted at the New Wolsey Theatre, Ipswich in July 2012.

Verdict: An amazing interactive experience for children of all ages. 10/10

30. DEATH IS THE ONLY ANSWER

Cast: Matt Smith (*Doctor*), Nickolas Grace (*Einstein*), Paul Kasey (*Ood*) | **Crew:** Director: Jeremy Webb; Writers: various; Producer: Marcus Wilson | **Television:** BBC3, 1 October 2011

Précis: The Doctor bumps into Albert Einstein...

Observations: A four-minute story written by pupils from Oakley Junior School in Basingstoke, winners of a script-to-screen competition run by, and shown on, *Doctor Who Confidential*.

Verdict: Matt Smith is clearly enjoying himself, and it's fun to see him up against another 'mad genius'. 6/10

31. GOOD AS GOLD

Cast: Matt Smith (*Doctor*), Karen Gillan (*Amy*), Elliot Barnes-Worrell (*Torch Bearer*), Sarah Louise Madison (*Weeping Angel*) | **Crew:** Director: Saul Metzstein; Writers: various; Producer: Marcus Wilson | **Television:** CBBC, 24 May 2012

Précis: A terrified Olympic athlete claims he's being chased by a Weeping Angel...

Observations: This three-minute story was written by pupils of Ashdene Primary School in Wilmslow for a second script-to-screen competition, this time organised by, and shown on, *Blue Peter*.

Verdict: Silly, but fun. 7/10

REFERENCE MATERIALS

BOOKS

The following is a selection of recommended *Doctor Who* non-fiction titles:

The Making of Doctor Who Malcolm Hulke & Terrance Dicks, Piccolo, 1972

The Doctor Who Monster Book Terrance Dicks, Target, 1975

A Day With a TV Producer Graham Rickard, Wayland, 1980

Doctor Who – The Making of a Television Series Alan Road, André Deutsch, 1982

Doctor Who – A Celebration Peter Haining, WH Allen, 1983

Doctor Who – The Unfolding Text John Tulloch & Manuel Alvarado, Macmillan Press, 1983

Doctor Who – The Early Years Jeremy Bentham, WH Allen, 1986

Doctor Who – The Programme Guide Jean-Marc Lofficier, Virgin, 1989

Doctor Who – The Terrestrial Index Jean Marc-Lofficier, Virgin, 1991

Doctor Who – The Sixties Howe, Stammers & Walker, Virgin, 1992

Doctor Who – The Universal Databank Jean-Marc Lofficier, Virgin, 1992

Doctor Who – The Seventies Howe, Stammers & Walker, Virgin, 1994

Doctor Who – The Discontinuity Guide Paul Cornell, Martin Day & Keith Topping, Virgin, 1995

Ace! The Inside Story of the End of an Era Sophie Aldred & Mike Tucker, Virgin, 1996

Doctor Who – The Eighties Howe, Stammers & Walker, Virgin, 1996

Who's There? The Life and Career of William Hartnell Jessica Carney, Virgin, 1996

Who on Earth is Tom Baker? Tom Baker, HarperCollins, 1997

I, Who 1–3 Lars Pearson, Mad Norwegian Press, 1999–2003

The Doctor's Affect Steve Cambden, FX Fanzines, 1999

Doctor Who – Regeneration Philip Segal with Gary Russell, Harper-Collins, 2000

Doctor Who on Location Richard Bignell, Reynolds & Hearn, 2001

Doctor Who – The Scripts: Tom Baker 1974/5 Justin Richards & Andrew Pixley, BBC, 2001

The Doctor's Effects Steve Cambden, FX Fanzines, 2001

Dimensions in Time and Space Mark Campbell, SciFiCollector.co.uk, 2003

The Television Companion David J Howe & Stephen James Walker, Telos, 2003

About Time 1–6 Lawrence Miles & Tat Wood, Mad Norwegian Press, 2004–07

BFI TV Classics: Doctor Who Kim Newman, BFI, 2005

Doctor Who – The Shooting Scripts Russell T Davies et al, BBC, 2005

The Handbook David J Howe, Stephen James Walker & Mark Stammers, Telos, 2005

Script Doctor Andrew Cartmel, Reynolds & Hearn, 2005

Back To The Vortex J Shaun Lyon, Telos, 2005

Second Flight J Shaun Lyon, Telos, 2006

Doctor Who – The Inside Story Gary Russell, BBC, 2006

Third Dimension Stephen James Walker, Telos, 2007

The Target Book David J Howe, Telos, 2007

Monsters Within Stephen James Walker, Telos, 2008

Who & Me Barry Letts, Fantom Films, 2009

Doctor Who – The Tardis Handbook Steve Tribe, BBC, 2010

The Writer's Tale: The Final Chapter Russell T Davies & Benjamin Cook, BBC, 2010

Doctor Who – The Visual Dictionary various, Dorling Kindersley, 2010

End of Ten Stephen James Walker, Telos, 2010

Doctor Who – The Encyclopedia Gary Russell, BBC, 2011

Doctor Who – The Dalek Handbook Steve Tribe & James Goss, BBC, 2011

Elizabeth Sladen: The Autobiography Elizabeth Sladen, Aurum, 2011

The Man Who Invented the Daleks Alwyn W Turner, Aurum, 2011

Cracks in Time Stephen James Walker, Telos, 2012

The Comic Strip Companion: 1964-1979 Paul Scoones, Telos, 2012
Doctor Who – A History of the Universe in 100 Objects James Goss & Steve Tribe, BBC, 2012
The Doctor's Monsters Graham Sleight, I B Tauris, 2012
Wiped! Doctor Who's Missing Episodes (2nd Ed) Richard Molesworth, Telos, 2013

INTERNET

Big Finish Information on the company's expanding range of CDs
www.bigfinish.com

A Brief History of Time (Travel) Neat overview of every story
www.shannonsullivan.com

The DiscContinuity Guide Minutia on *Doctor Who* audio stories
www.tetrap.com/drwho/disccon

The Discontinuity Guide Minutia on everything else
www.whoniverse.net/discontinuity

Doctor Who Appreciation Society The UK's oldest fan organisation
www.dwasonline.co.uk

Doctor Who BBC Site Trailers, video diaries, news and games
www.bbc.co.uk/doctorwho

Doctor Who Experience The BBC's permanent exhibition in Cardiff
www.doctorwhoexperience.com

Doctor Who News Premier news site and Gallifrey Base forum
www.doctorwhonews.net

Doctor Who Online Premier news site
www.drwho-online.co.uk

Doctor Who Reference Guide In-depth story synopses
www.drwhoguide.com

The Doctor Who Site Excellent resource for merchandise
www.thedoctorwhosite.co.uk

Eyespider Chronological listing of stories in all media
www.eyespider.freeserve.co.uk

Galaxy 4 Sheffield-based *Doctor Who* stockist
www.galaxy4.co.uk

Junkyard BBC artist Max Ellis' own website
www.junkyard.co.uk

On Target In-depth detail on every Target novelisation
www.personal.leeds.ac.uk/~ecl6nb/OnTarget

Restoration Team Information on classic DVD releases
www.restoration-team.co.uk

SciFiCollector Central London *Doctor Who* stockist
www.scificollector.co.uk

Tardis Data Core Exhaustive *Doctor Who* wiki
www.tardis.wikia.com

10th Planet Events Convention organiser and retailer
www.tenthplanetevents.co.uk

The Who Shop International East Ham *Doctor Who* shop
www.thewhoshop.com

This Planet Earth Full-size memorabilia for sale
www.thisplanetearth.co.uk

TV Tropes Narrative clichés in *Doctor Who*
www.tvtropes.org/pmwiki/pmwiki.php/Recap/Doctolynda

Whoniverse Diverse guide to all things *Who*
www.whoniverse.net

Who One Ltd Essex *Doctor Who* retailer, formerly Burton's
www.whoone.co.uk

Contact the author: If you would like to correspond with Mark Campbell and give him some feedback on this guide, please email mark.campbell10@virgin.net

INDEX